GOD'S SAVING GRACE

GOD'S SAVING GRACE

A Pauline Theology

Frank J. Matera

WILLIAM B. EERDMANS PUBLISHING COMPANY

GRAND RAPIDS, MICHIGAN / CAMBRIDGE, U.K.

Published 2012 by

Wm. B. Eerdmans Publishing Co.

2140 Oak Industrial Drive N.E., Grand Rapids, Michigan 49505 /

P.O. Box 163, Cambridge CB3 9PU U.K.

www.eerdmans.com

Printed in the United States of America

18 17 16 15 14 13   7 6 5 4 3 2

Library of Congress Cataloging-in-Publication Data

Matera, Frank J.

   God's saving grace: a Pauline theology / Frank J. Matera.

   p.   cm.

   Includes bibliographical references (p.   ) and indexes.

   ISBN 978-0-8028-6747-6 (pbk.: alk. paper)

   1. Grace (Theology) — Biblical teaching.

   2. Bible. N.T. Epistles of Paul — Theology.

   3. Bible. N.T. Epistles of Paul — Criticism, interpretation, etc.

   I. Title.

BS2655.G65M38   2012

227'.06 — dc23

                                          2012014983

Unless otherwise noted, the Scripture quotations in this publication are from the New Revised Standard Version Bible, copyright © 1989 by the Division of Christian Education of the National Council of Churches of Christ in the U.S.A., and used by permission.

Dedicated to

my students,

my colleagues,

and my friends

at the Catholic University of America

1988-2012

Contents

Preface

For the past several years I have focused my attention on topics of biblical theology in order to bridge the gap between exegesis and theology. Such a gap, of course, ought not to exist. And once it did not. Throughout the patristic period and most of the medieval period, theology was the study of the Sacred Page. To comment on Scripture was to do theology, and to do theology was to comment on the Sacred Page. But this is no longer the case; indeed, it has not been the case for a very long time. Exegesis and theology have been compartmentalized, each discipline becoming more and more specialized. Although such specialization has its benefits, it results in the anomalous situation that theologians no longer feel competent to do exegesis, and exegetes no longer view themselves as theologians.

Biblical theology provides a way to overcome this impasse. On the one hand it forces exegetes to think theologically once more. On the other it provides theologians with an entrée to the text that can be fruitful for their own discipline. Given the importance of the Pauline writings for theology, I have written this brief work to provide biblical students and theologians with a summary of the main theological themes in the Pauline letters: Christology, soteriology, ethics, ecclesiology, eschatology, and most importantly "theology," by which I mean the study of the mystery that is God. If this small book encourages some to engage the theological dimension of the text, it will have served its purpose.

I express my gratitude to my colleagues Christopher Begg and John Paul Heil, who generously read and commented on portions of this manuscript, and I gratefully dedicate this work to the many students, colleagues, and friends who have encouraged and supported me during my years at the Catholic University of America.

September 14, 2011	FRANK J. MATERA
The Feast of the Exaltation	*The Andrews-Kelly-Ryan Professor*
of the Holy Cross	*of Biblical Studies*
	The Catholic University of America
	Washington DC

Abbreviations

AB	Anchor Bible
AnBib	Analecta biblica
BDAG	W. Bauer, F. W. Danker, W. F. Arndt, and F. W. Gingrich. *Greek-English Lexicon of the New Testament and Other Early Christian Literature.* 3rd ed. Chicago: University of Chicago Press, 1999.
Bib	*Biblica*
CBQ	*Catholic Biblical Quarterly*
EBib	*Études bibliques*
EDNT	*Exegetical Dictionary of the New Testament,* ed. H. Balz and G. Schneider. 3 vols. English translation, Grand Rapids: Eerdmans, 1990-93.
EstBib	*Estudios bíblicos*
GNS	Good News Studies
HTKNT	Herders theologischer Kommentar zum Neuen Testament
ICC	International Critical Commentary
JBL	*Journal of Biblical Literature*
JSNT	*Journal for the Study of the New Testament*
JSNTSup	*Journal for the Study of the New Testament* Supplement Series
LXX	Septuagint
MdB	*Le Monde de la Bible*
NAB	New American Bible
NET	New English Translation
NovTSup	*Novum Testamentum* Supplements
NRSV	New Revised Standard Version

NT	New Testament
NTL	New Testament Library
NTS	*New Testament Studies*
NTT	New Testament Theology
SBT	Studies in Biblical Theology
SNTSMS	Society for New Testament Studies Monograph Series
SP	Sacra Pagina
TB	Theologische Bücherei. Neudrücke und Berichte aus dem 20. Jahrhundert
TDNT	*Theological Dictionary of the New Testament,* ed. G. Kittel and G. Friedrich, tr. G. W. Bromiley. 10 vols. Grand Rapids: Eerdmans, 1964-76.
WUNT	Wissenschaftliche Untersuchungen zum Neuen Testament

1. A Pauline Theology of God's Saving Grace

Introduction

The Pauline letters have had an immense impact on the growth and development of Christian theology. While the Fourth Evangelist is the great theologian of the incarnation, the Apostle Paul is the great theologian of grace and redemption. Writing occasional letters rather than theological treatises, it is Paul who focuses our attention on the saving event of Christ's death and resurrection.[1] It is Paul who lays bare the human predicament apart from Christ. It is Paul who provides us with the most important metaphors for understanding what happened on the cross. It is Paul who portrays the church as a sanctified sphere, the body of Christ. It is Paul who instructs believers, who are no longer under the law, to live a morally good life in Christ through the power of God's Spirit. It is Paul who provides believers with an eschatological vision that embraces the destiny of creation as well as of humanity. In a word, it is Paul who laid the foundation for what theology calls theological anthropology, Christology, soteriology, ecclesiology, ethics, pneumatology, and eschatology.

Despite this theological achievement, Paul was not writing as a theologian, nor did he attempt to construct a coherent theological system. A pastor, a missionary, an apostle to Gentiles, his primary purpose was to preach the gospel to as many people as possible before the Lord's return so that he

---

1. By "occasional letters" I mean letters that were *occasioned* by specific situations in the communities to which Paul was writing. For example, 1 Corinthians appears to have been "occasioned" by oral reports that Paul received about the community, as well as by a letter that the community sent to him (1 Cor 1:11; 7:1).

might save as many as possible for Christ. In the midst of his missionary work, however, this extraordinary individual wrote a number of letters in which he tended to the pastoral needs of small, struggling congregations of Christ-believers in the Greco-Roman world. Responding to the needs of these believers in light of the gospel he preached, the Apostle provided them with a way to live in the world according to the gospel. More specifically, he taught them how to live in light of the saving death and resurrection of Jesus Christ. A good part of the edifice of contemporary Christian theology, then, rests on the foundation of the thirteen letters attributed to Paul, all of which are pastoral in tone and intent.

Given the important role that the Pauline letters have played in the growth and development of Christian theology, it is not surprising that New Testament scholars have sought to clarify and synthesize the central themes of Paul's writings. This project, however, is not without its pitfalls; nor does it lack critics. Accordingly, while there are many good reasons to undertake such a project, there are objections to it. In the remainder of this chapter, I will explore the nature and challenges of writing a Pauline theology before outlining the character and methodology of my Pauline theology.

The Nature and Challenges of Writing a Pauline Theology

Anyone who embarks on the task of writing a Pauline theology must ask, What am I doing? Am I writing a work that summarizes the theology of the Apostle Paul? Or, am I writing a work that summarizes the theology of the Pauline letters? Although closely related to each other, these two projects are distinct. For the sake of clarity, I will call the first project *A Theology of Paul* and the second *A Pauline Theology*.

A theology of Paul seeks to clarify and synthesize the theology of the historical figure Paul. Consequently, it is a historical as well as theological task. Those who undertake it must deal with a number of historical questions. For example, is Paul the author of all the letters that the New Testament attributes to him?[2] If the answer to this question is negative, then one

2. Contemporary NT scholarship distinguishes between those letters whose Pauline authorship is not disputed (Romans, 1 and 2 Corinthians, Galatians, Philippians, 1 Thessalonians, and Philemon) and those whose Pauline authorship is disputed (Ephesians, Colossians, 2 Thessalonians, 1 and 2 Timothy, and Titus). In an attempt to use nontendentious language, I refer to the first group as "the non-disputed Pauline letters" and to the second group as "the disputed Pauline letters."

must inquire about the nature and character of the letters that others have written in Paul's name. Do they contribute to an understanding of Paul's theology, or do they deviate from it? Likewise, since Paul plays such an important role in the Acts of the Apostles, one must inquire about the historical reliability of the data regarding Paul in Acts.[3] Finally, one must decide if a theology of Paul should proceed letter by letter, taking into account the chronological order in which the letters were written, or provide a synthesis of the letters whose Pauline authorship is not disputed.[4] Writing a theology of Paul, then, requires careful historical work as well as theological insight.

The second project, a Pauline theology, seeks to clarify and synthesize the theology embedded in the thirteen canonical Pauline letters. Consequently, in addition to being a historical and theological task, it is also a canonical and literary task.[5] Those who undertake it must address a number of questions. If certain letters were written in Paul's name rather than by Paul, what is the relationship between the letters whose Pauline authorship is not disputed and those whose authorship is disputed? Since a Pauline

3. This data includes the theological content of the speeches and sermons that Paul delivers in the Acts of the Apostles, as well as biographical details that Luke provides about Paul's life such as his education in Jerusalem under Gamaliel (Acts 22:3) and his Roman citizenship (16:37; 22:25).

4. The Pauline Theology Seminar of the Society of Biblical Literature (1986-95) approached the task of Paul's theology by systematically working its way through the non-disputed letters. Four volumes were eventually published under the title *Pauline Theology:* vol. 1, *Thessalonians, Philippians, Galatians, Philemon,* ed. Jouette M. Bassler (Minneapolis: Fortress, 1991); vol. 2, *1 and 2 Corinthians,* ed. David M. Hay (Minneapolis: Fortress, 1993); vol. 3, *Romans,* ed. David M. Hay and E. Elizabeth Johnson (Minneapolis: Fortress, 1995); and vol. 4, *Looking Back, Pressing On,* ed. E. Elizabeth Johnson and David M. Hay (Atlanta: Scholars, 1997). James D. G. Dunn edited a series of volumes in the series New Testament Theology, published by Cambridge University Press and dealing with the theology of the individual writings of the New Testament. The volumes on the Pauline letters are Karl P. Donfried, *The Theology of the Shorter Pauline Letters* (1993); James D. G. Dunn, *The Theology of Paul's Letter to the Galatians* (1993); Victor Paul Furnish, *The Theology of the First Letter to the Corinthians* (1999); Klaus Haacker, *The Theology of Paul's Letter to the Romans* (2003); Andrew Lincoln and A. J. M. Wedderburn, *The Theology of the Later Pauline Letters* (1993); Jerome Murphy-O'Connor, *The Theology of Second Corinthians* (1991); and Frances Young, *The Theology of the Pastoral Epistles* (1994).

5. Brevard Childs (*The Church's Guide for Reading Paul: The Canonical Shaping of the Pauline Corpus* [Grand Rapids: Eerdmans, 2008]) disagrees with the approach of the SBL Pauline Seminar and has proposed a program for reading the Pauline letters in their canonical context.

theology deals with the thirteen canonical letters, should the Acts of the Apostles play a role in such a theology? What is the relationship between history and theology in Pauline theology? Is a Pauline theology unrelated to history, or does historical investigation continue to play a role in such a theology? Finally, should a Pauline theology proceed according to the canonical order of the letters in the New Testament, or should it provide a synthesis of the theological themes of the letters?

Most contemporary authors provide their readers with a theology of Paul.[6] Accordingly, they tend to focus on the letters whose authorship is not disputed; they pay careful attention to the historical circumstances that gave rise to these letters and to the chronological order in which they were composed. Moreover, rather than proceed letter by letter, in most instances they provide a synthesis of Paul's theology.[7] The strength of this project is its careful attention to history. By emphasizing the historical circumstances in which Paul composed his letters, theologies of Paul offer their readers an account of the historical circumstances in which he wrote and developed his theology. The weakness of this approach, however, is that it may neglect those letters whose Pauline authorship is disputed. Consequently, whereas the voices of Romans, Galatians, the Corinthian correspondence, Philippians, and 1 Thessalonians sound forth clearly, the voices of Ephesians, Colossians, 2 Thessalonians, and the Pastorals are often muted. In some instances, they may even be viewed as a betrayal of Paul's theology.[8]

In contrast to a theology of Paul, a Pauline theology focuses on the theological vision of the thirteen letters that the New Testament attributes to Paul. Rather than undertake a historical investigation of the theology of Paul, this approach directs its attention to the thirteen canonical letters attributed to the Apostle, even though Paul may not have authored all of them.[9] While such a project must take into consideration historical ques-

6. Two recent examples of this approach are the works of James D. G. Dunn, *The Theology of Paul the Apostle* (Grand Rapids: Eerdmans, 1998), and Udo Schnelle, *Apostle Paul: His Life and Theology* (Grand Rapids: Baker, 2003).

7. Schnelle *(Apostle Paul)* employs both approaches. He considers the non-disputed Pauline letters individually before concluding with a synthesis of Paul's theology.

8. This appears to be less true today than in the past when letters such as Colossians, Ephesians, and the Pastorals were sometimes viewed as examples of "early catholicism" and so a falling away from Paul's authentic teaching. While many Pauline scholars continue to question the Pauline authorship of Ephesians, Colossians, 2 Thessalonians, and the Pastorals, most acknowledge the theological richness of these letters.

9. Thomas Schreiner (*Paul: Apostle of God's Glory in Christ: A Pauline Theology* [Downers Grove: InterVarsity, 2001]) adopts this approach, as do I in *New Testament Theol-*

tions, it must also pay attention to canonical and literary issues as well. The strength of this project, then, is the attention it gives to all of the letters. Rather than view some as more important than others, it listens to all the voices in the Pauline corpus. The weakness of this approach, however, is that it may gloss over or neglect differences among the letters for the sake of its synthesis. For example, it may overlook the different ways in which justification is presented in Romans and Galatians on the one hand and Ephesians and the Pastorals on the other. Or it may neglect the differences in the eschatology of 1 Thessalonians and 1 Corinthians on the one hand and 2 Thessalonians, Colossians, and Ephesians on the other. Finally, this approach is liable to the following objection: if certain letters attributed to Paul were not written by him, how can their theological vision be integrated into the theological vision of the letters that the Apostle wrote? If a synthesis of the disputed correspondence is artificial, it would appear that a synthesis of the Pauline corpus is even more so.

The strength of each approach, however, is also its weakness. For example, whereas the strength of writing a theology of Paul is the attention it gives to history, this approach must contend with the shifting sands of historical research.[10] Likewise, whereas the strength of writing a Pauline theology is the attention it gives to the letters as literary products, this approach can result in a non-historical reading of the text. How then should we proceed? How have I approached my Pauline Theology?

The Character and Method of This Pauline Theology

My own work is a Pauline theology that deals with the theology that underlies and comes to expression in the thirteen letters the New Testament attributes to Paul (the Pauline Corpus). This work, then, is an attempt not to reconstruct the theology of the historical Paul but to summarize the

---

ogy: *Exploring Diversity and Unity* (Louisville: Westminster John Knox, 2007). However, whereas Schreiner attempts a synthesis of Pauline theology, I worked through the Pauline Corpus letter by letter. Having approached Pauline theology letter by letter, my goal in this work is to show the coherence of the theology in the Pauline Corpus.

10. Victor Paul Furnish ("On Putting Paul in His Place," *JBL* 113 [1994]: 3-17, here 9) makes this perceptive remark about historical research: "Pauline scholarship has not been exempt from that immutable law of all historical inquiry that, the more one learns, the more one discovers how much there is yet to learn, and how tentative all historical results must remain."

theology of the canonical letters that bear his name. This statement, however, should not be construed to mean that there is no relationship between Paul's theology and the theology of the letters that bear his name. The theology in the canonical letters attributed to him is indebted to him, even in the case of those letters that were not written by him. There is, however, an important distinction between Paul's own theology and the theology of the Pauline letters. Whereas the theology of the Pauline letters is the theology embedded in the letters, Paul's own theology encompasses *more* than the theology in his letters. For example, in addition to the Pauline letters we possess, Paul wrote letters we do not possess.[11] Furthermore, he regularly preached and taught the gospel. Thus there is a great deal about the theology and thought of the historical Paul we do not and cannot know. Our knowledge of Paul's theology, then, is limited in a way that our knowledge of the theology in the Pauline letters is not. In saying this, I am not implying that we can write a definitive Pauline theology. Inasmuch as the Pauline Corpus is a literary product, it can always be interpreted anew. Such a project, however, has the advantage of focusing our attention on a specific body of writings rather than speculating about what we do not know or possess.[12]

But what do we mean by "theology" when we speak of the theology of Paul or the theology of the Pauline letters? If Paul did not write theological treatises and was not a theologian, how can we speak of his theology or of a Pauline theology? As I have already acknowledged, Paul was not a theologian in our sense of the term. Rather than speculate about the nature of God and Christ in theological treatises, he wrote about God and Christ in letters occasioned by the needs of those to whom he wrote.

Nevertheless, even though Paul did not write theological treatises, the letters he composed are informed by the gospel that he received when God revealed his Son to him and called him to be the Apostle to the nations. In light of this gospel, he speaks about Christ. In light of this gospel, he speaks

11. Paul's statement in 1 Cor 5:9 indicates that he sent a letter to the Corinthians prior to 1 Corinthians that we do not possess. Likewise, his statements in 2 Corinthians about a harsh letter that he wrote in much anguish (2:4, 9; 7:8, 12) indicate that he composed a letter between the writing of 1 and 2 Corinthians that we do not possess. Finally, in Col 4:16 he refers to a letter from Laodicea that he wants the Colossians to read.

12. A theology of Paul the Apostle would have to deal with the complicated partition theories about the origin of 2 Corinthians and Philippians, whereas a Pauline theology deals with the canonical form of the Pauline letters, even if they were composed from earlier fragments.

about God's work of salvation. In light of this gospel, he speaks about the human condition. In light of this gospel, he speaks about the church and the morally good life. In light of this gospel, he speaks about the hope that believers have for final salvation. Stated simply, *what Paul writes about the gospel is his theology; it is his understanding of God, Christ, the Spirit, humankind, and the world.*

The theology of the Pauline letters, then, is not found in carefully crafted theological ideas and concepts but in the way that Paul interprets what has happened, what is happening, and what will happen in light of the gospel of God that was revealed to him. Because Pauline theology is inseparable from the gospel that Paul preaches, it is embedded in the concrete and diverse ways that he proclaims the gospel.[13] A few examples will clarify what I mean. When Paul says that the righteousness of God is being revealed in the gospel (Rom 1:16-17), he is affirming how God is presently acting in the world. When Paul writes that the power of God is revealed in the weakness and folly of the cross (1 Cor 1:21-25), he is making a paradoxical statement about God's wisdom and power. When Paul calls Christ the image of God (2 Cor 4:4), he is affirming that Christ is the way we know God. When Paul insists that human beings are justified on the basis of faith apart from doing the works of the Mosaic Law (Gal 2:16), he is making a soteriological statement about what it means to stand in a right relationship to God. When Paul calls the church the body of Christ (Eph 1:22-23; Col 1:24), he is making an important ecclesiological statement about the nature and being of the church. Or when he says that those who have died in Christ will rise at the parousia (1 Thess 4:16), he is affirming that God's victory in Christ is more powerful than death.

The difference between contemporary theology and Pauline theology is that whereas the former presents a systematic, philosophical reflection on the topics mentioned above, Paul presents a concrete pastoral reflection on these issues. He is not so much interested in developing the notion of God's righteousness for the sake of exploring the notion of God's being as he is concerned to show the faithfulness and reliability of God. Likewise, he is not so much interested in telling believers that Christ is the image of God as he is in teaching them that they are being transformed into the image of

---

13. J. Christiaan Beker (*Paul the Apostle: The Triumph of God's Word in Life and Thought* [Philadelphia: Fortress, 1980], 35) makes this point when he discusses the contingency and coherence of Paul's letters. Although the letters are contingent, they receive their coherence from the gospel that Paul preaches. Beker writes, "They [the letters] should be interpreted as gospel for particular situations, 'enfleshing' the gospel into human particularity."

Christ, who is the image of God. Pauline theology, then, is embedded in the pastoral responses that Paul gives when he encourages, rebukes, and counsels the communities to which he writes *in light of the gospel he has received.*

If this is the nature of Pauline theology, how can we weave the theological threads of the Pauline letters into a coherent tapestry? More importantly, should we? Is not the very act of writing a Pauline theology a betrayal of the Apostle's pastoral approach? Would it not be better to focus on aspects of Pauline theology rather than attempt to synthesize it? These are legitimate questions, and they suggest that since Paul's theology is found in the responses he gives to the pastoral problems he encountered, it may be more prudent to concern ourselves with a thorough exegesis of particular texts and set aside any hope of seeking coherence in this material. After all, good exegesis is good theology, and some of the most insightful theology is found in commentaries.[14] Commentaries provide exegetes with an opportunity to examine the religious meaning of a particular text in greater detail within its literary and historical context. But as is often the case, the strength of a particular approach is also its weakness. Accordingly, while a good commentary provides profound insight into the theology of a particular letter, it is not intended to integrate that letter into the whole of the Pauline Corpus.

One of the values of a Pauline theology, then, is its potential for revealing the coherence within the Pauline Corpus so that readers will be able to see relationships among the letters they might otherwise overlook. For example, anyone who reads through Romans and Galatians is immediately struck by the manner in which these letters focus on Paul's teaching about justification on the basis of faith. But how does this teaching cohere with what Colossians and Ephesians say about reconciliation or with what the Pastorals write about salvation? What is the relationship between justification on the one hand and transformation and sanctification on the other? In other words, although a particular letter may help us understand aspects of the Pauline gospel, no single letter (with the possible exception of Romans) provides us with a comprehensive understanding of the Pauline gospel.[15] At the risk of claiming too much, I propose that the goal of Pau-

14. The commentary of Brendan Byrne (*Romans* [SP 6; Collegeville: Liturgical, 1996]) provides a good example of exegesis that exhibits profound theological insight. Although the commentary of Karl Barth (*The Epistle to the Romans* [London: Oxford University Press, 1933]) is of a different kind, it is a good example of theological exegesis: exegesis that is concerned with the theological meaning of the text rather than with the world behind the text.

15. This statement about Romans is problematic since contemporary exegesis tends to

line theology is to provide a coherent presentation of the theology in the Pauline letters. By a coherent presentation, I do not mean a synthesis that harmonizes difference but a presentation that explains — as best as one can — how the different Pauline letters are related to and cohere with each other.[16]

But can we achieve such coherence? How can we bring together statements from diverse letters, some of which Paul may not have written? Here, I make two points. First, those who seek to uncover the coherence within the Pauline letters must remember that they are not dealing with theological statements and theses but with the diverse ways in which Paul applies the gospel to the needs of those to whom he writes. For example, several texts in the Pauline Corpus are important for understanding Pauline soteriology, but these texts are found in different letters written in response to diverse occasions. Accordingly, if we are to explain the coherence of this material, we must keep in mind the life-situations that occasioned it. An example will clarify what I mean. Paul has a great deal to say about the parousia, but what he writes is closely related to the questions to which he is responding. In 1 Thessalonians the question is what will happen at the parousia to those who have already died. In 2 Thessalonians the question is whether the parousia has already occurred. And in 1 Corinthians the question is whether there will be a bodily resurrection at the parousia. Since each situation determines how Paul responds, it is clear that his individual statements and descriptions about the parousia cannot be treated as if they were theological theses. While each of them deals with the Lord's return, none of them provides a complete teaching about the parousia, and other letters present the teaching about the parousia differently. Every attempt at coherence ought to acknowledge and respect these tensions, drawing together those things that can be brought together and acknowledging tensions and differences when they exist.[17]

Second, every Pauline theology requires a framework to organize the material of the letters into a meaningful whole. The framework that a par-

---

view Romans as an occasional letter. However, even if Romans is an occasional writing, it does provide its readers with the fullest expression of the Pauline gospel that we have.

16. The distinction that I am making between coherence and harmonization was suggested to me by Udo Schnelle (*Apostle Paul,* 517) who speaks of bringing together a series of statements "conceptually without harmonization."

17. For example, a statement about the coherence of what the Pauline corpus says about the parousia might affirm that, despite the different ways in which the parousia is portrayed, the Pauline letters testify that God will manifest his final and definitive victory in Christ.

ticular work employs distinguishes it from other Pauline theologies, giving each its distinctive character. Although all frameworks are artificial, some are more helpful than others. A framework that grows out of the material, for example, is of more value than one imposed on it, and a framework that encompasses as much of the material as possible is of more interest than one that highlights only some of the material.[18]

The framework I have chosen for my Pauline theology is guided by two principles. The first is the theme of God's saving grace, which Paul experienced at his call and conversion.[19] That grace was the unmerited favor God extended to Paul in the Damascus road christophany, when Paul received his gospel and apostleship. Although Paul experienced this grace in a particularly dramatic fashion, all Christ-believers are the beneficiaries of this grace inasmuch as they have been called into the eschatological community of the church. It is this experience of grace that enabled Paul to understand what happened in his own life and is presently happening in the life of the church. From start to finish, all is grace: the manifestation of God's unmerited favor in Christ. It is not too much to say, then, that *the Pauline gospel is a gospel of grace:* the unmerited favor that the elect experience when they are called, justified, and reconciled to God.

The second principle I have employed to develop my framework arises from three implicit narratives that underlie Pauline theology. The first is the narrative of Paul's own life. It begins with the experience of God's saving grace in Christ that was revealed to Paul at the moment of his call and conversion. It was in light of that experience that Paul developed the second narrative, the narrative of what God had done in Christ. On the basis of the narratives of what happened in his own life and on the basis of the narrative of what God had done in Christ, Paul proclaimed God's saving grace to others, thereby forming communities of believers with their own

18. There has been a lively discussion in Pauline studies about "the center" of Pauline theology. The following essays are especially helpful: Paul J. Achtemeier, "The Continuing Quest for Coherence in St. Paul: An Experiment in Thought," in *Theology and Ethics in Paul and His Interpreters: Essays in Honor of Victor Paul Furnish,* ed. Eugene H. Lovering, Jr., and Jerry L. Sumney (Nashville: Abingdon: 1996), 114-32; J. C. Beker, "Paul's Theology: Consistent or Inconsistent?" 34 *NTS* (1988): 364-77; Joseph Plevnik, "The Center of Pauline Theology," *CBQ* 51 (1989): 461-78; Stanley E. Porter, "Is There a Center to Paul's Theology? An Introduction to the Study of Paul and His Theology," in *Paul and His Theology* (Pauline Theology 3; Leiden: Brill, 2006), 1-19.

19. This point is also made by Dunn (*The Theology of Paul the Apostle,* 179), who writes: "The theology of Paul was neither born nor sustained by or as a purely cerebral exercise. It was his own experience of grace which lay at its heart."

narrative that can be summarized in this way: having been rescued from a past defined by sin and rebellion against God, believers presently live their lives within the eschatological people of God as they wait for the return of their Lord, when they will be conformed to his resurrection. Thus, we can speak of three narratives: the narrative of God's saving grace in Paul's life, the narrative of God's saving grace in Christ, and the narrative of God's saving grace in the lives of those in Christ. I have developed these narratives in the following way.

Since Paul's call/conversion was the moment when he experienced God's saving grace in Christ for the first time, I have entitled chapter 2 "Paul's Experience of God's Saving Grace." In this chapter, I contend that Paul's Damascus Road experience is "the generative center" of his theology.[20] It was at that moment that God revealed his Son to Paul and commissioned him to be the Apostle to the Gentiles; it was at that moment that Paul received his gospel and apostleship. While Paul grew in his understanding of his gospel and apostleship, it was this experience that determined the nature and content of his gospel. This gospel, which is God's own gospel, is the good news of what God has done in Christ.

Since Christ is the content of the gospel Paul proclaims, I have entitled chapter 3 "Christ the Embodiment of God's Saving Grace." In this chapter, I discuss the major ways in which Paul identifies the one whom he preaches: Son of God, Christ, and Lord. Since the Pauline letters presuppose that the one who exists with God is the one who preexisted with God before coming into the world, I then take up the question of preexistence in relation to three christological hymns. Finally, I consider Christ as a corporate figure with and in whom believers live.

Since Pauline Christology implies a soteriology, I have entitled chapter 4 "The Saving Grace of Jesus Christ." Here I begin with a consideration of unredeemed humanity. Apart from Christ, humanity is alienated from God, under the power of sin and death, subjected to the power of this sinful age, under the discipline of the Mosaic Law. Next, I consider the new situation in which humanity finds itself. In Christ, humanity has been justified and reconciled to God. It is redeemed, freed, and forgiven. Sanctified and a new creation in Christ, it is being transformed day by day as it waits

---

20. The term "generative center" is the term that Achtemeier ("The Continuing Quest for Coherence in St. Paul") introduces and employs throughout his essay. Whereas Achtemeier uses this term in reference to the resurrection, I employ it in reference to Paul's call, when God revealed his risen Son to him.

for its final salvation and glorification that will occur at the general resurrection of the dead. The purpose of this chapter, then, is to explain why God sent his Son into the world and highlight the benefits that Christ brings to humanity.

Since God's saving work in Christ called into existence a new people, I have entitled chapter 5 "Living in the Community of God's Saving Grace." In this chapter I deal with the church as the eschatological people of God and the body of Christ. After considering the church I deal with ministry and ministers within the church. The chapter concludes with a discussion of Israel and the church that explains the relationship between Israel and the eschatological People of God that has been called into existence from among the Gentiles as well as the Jews.

Since those who belong to the eschatological people of God are called to live lives that correspond to their new life in Christ, I have entitled chapter 6 "Living according to God's Saving Grace." In this chapter, I deal with Pauline ethics from five perspectives: soteriology, the Spirit, the sacraments, the love commandment, and eschatology. The chapter begins by noting that what God has done for those in Christ (the indicative of salvation) is the ground for the moral life (the moral imperative). Those who have experienced this saving grace are called to live in the newness of life that the Spirit brings. Since they have died to sin through their baptism into Christ, they are no longer under the power of sin. Accordingly, they can live a morally good life that finds its fulfillment in the love commandment, as they wait for the final appearance of their Lord.

Since the justified and reconciled wait for the fullness of salvation, I have entitled chapter 7 "Waiting for the Final Appearance of God's Saving Grace." This chapter begins with a discussion of the eschatological existence of those who belong to Christ. Inasmuch as they have received the gift of the Spirit, the future has invaded their present existence, making it an eschatological existence. This eschatological existence is the ground for their hope. Because of this hope, they are waiting for the parousia, the resurrection of the dead, God's final victory in Christ, their heavenly inheritance, and the final appearance of Christ.

Finally, since theology is ultimately about God, I have entitled chapter 8 "The God Revealed through the Saving Grace of Jesus Christ." This chapter begins by pointing to the continuity and newness in the way that Paul understands God. On the one hand, he continues to understand God in terms of Israel's Scriptures, thereby affirming the continuity between old and new and highlighting the faithfulness of God. On the other hand,

Paul's encounter with the risen Lord brings something new to his understanding of God. This chapter presents the Pauline understanding of God in terms of election, weakness and suffering, judgment and acquittal, the faithfulness of God, God who shares his name with Christ, God revealed in Christ and in the economy of salvation, and the Savior God.

"Paul" and "the Pauline Letters"

As you read this book, you will notice that sometimes I speak of the "Pauline letters" and other times of "Paul." This may cause some confusion since I have said that I am writing a Pauline theology rather than a theology of the historical person Paul. Two points need to be made here. First, although this is a Pauline theology, it is not devoid of or adverse to historical research. The theology embedded in the letters is indebted to a historical individual. Consequently, one cannot speak of Pauline theology without speaking of Paul. Second, although Paul may not be the author of certain letters (Ephesians, Colossians, 2 Thessalonians, 1 and 2 Timothy, and Titus), all of these letters claim him as their author. Accordingly, I refer to "Paul" when discussing them. In doing so, I am not making a judgment about their authorship but simply identifying the author of these letters in the way that the letters themselves do. Although this may not be historically accurate in some cases, it avoids the use of circumlocutions that divide the Pauline corpus into two parts: letters that Paul wrote and letters that he did not.

My own judgment about the authorship of the Pauline letters is as follows. With nearly all scholars, I agree there are seven letters whose Pauline authorship is beyond dispute: Romans, 1 and 2 Corinthians, Galatians, Philippians, 1 Thessalonians, and Philemon. This leaves six letters whose authorship is disputed. Of these six, I am inclined to think that there is evidence that Paul was the author of 2 Thessalonians and Colossians. I am not quite as confident, however, that he is the author of Ephesians and the Pastorals. However, if I were to learn that he was, I would not be surprised. For, while the style and theology of these letters diverge from the style and theology of the non-disputed letters, these letters are essentially faithful to the thought and theology of the one whose name they bear. Thus, if they were not written by Paul, they were composed by followers who knew and cherished his thought and so updated and applied it to new circumstances.

Finally, there are some occasions when I make use of material from the

Acts of the Apostles. Again, this may seem inconsistent with a Pauline theology, which focuses on the theology embedded in the Pauline letters. There are times, however, when this material helps us to get a perspective on the letters that we might otherwise overlook. Accordingly, I have made use of this material for this purpose, fully aware that technically it does not belong to a Pauline theology.

Although this is a brief Pauline theology, I hope that it will provide readers with an overview of the contours and structure of Pauline theology. Those who work through this volume will want to move on to more advanced works that present them with a fuller discussion of Pauline theology.

For Further Reading

Bassler, Jouette M., ed. *Pauline Theology,* vol. 1: *Thessalonians, Philippians, Galatians, Philemon.* Minneapolis: Fortress, 1991.

Becker, Jürgen. *Paul: Apostle to the Gentiles.* Louisville: Westminster/John Knox, 1993.

Beker, J. Christiaan. *Paul the Apostle: The Triumph of God's Word in Life and Thought.* Philadelphia: Fortress, 1980.

Cerfaux, Lucien. *Christ in the Theology of St. Paul.* New York: Herder and Herder, 1959.

———. *The Christian in the Theology of St. Paul.* New York: Herder and Herder, 1967.

———. *The Church in the Theology of St. Paul.* New York: Herder and Herder, 1959.

Childs, Brevard S. *The Church's Guide for Reading Paul: The Canonical Shaping of the Pauline Corpus.* Grand Rapids: Eerdmans, 2008.

Dunn, James D. G. *The Theology of Paul the Apostle.* Grand Rapids: Eerdmans, 1998.

Fitzmyer, Joseph A. *Paul and His Theology: A Brief Sketch.* 2nd ed. Englewood Cliffs: Prentice Hall, 1989.

Hay, David M., ed. *Pauline Theology,* vol. 2: *1 and 2 Corinthians.* Minneapolis: Fortress, 1993.

Hay, David M., and E. Elizabeth Johnson, eds. *Pauline Theology,* vol. 3: *Romans.* Minneapolis: Fortress, 1995.

Johnson, E. Elizabeth, and David M. Hay. *Pauline Theology,* vol. 4: *Looking Back, Pressing On.* Atlanta: Scholars, 1997.

Porter, Stanley E. *Paul and His Theology.* Pauline Studies 3. Leiden: Brill, 2006.

Pratt, Fernand. *The Theology of Saint Paul.* 2 vols. Trans. John L. Stoddard from the 11th French edition. Westminster: Newman, 1958.

Ridderbos, Herman. *Paul: An Outline of His Theology.* Grand Rapids: Eerdmans, 1975.

Schnelle, Udo. *Apostle Paul: His Life and Theology.* Grand Rapids: Baker, 2003.

Schreiner, Thomas R. *Paul: Apostle of God's Glory in Christ: A Pauline Theology.* Downers Grove: InterVarsity, 2001.

Whiteley, D. E. H. *The Theology of St. Paul.* Philadelphia: Fortress, 1966.

In addition to the works listed above, works on New Testament theology, ethics, and Christology contain substantial sections on Paul's theology.

2. Paul's Experience of God's Saving Grace

Introduction

The Pauline gospel proclaims God's saving grace in Jesus Christ for all humanity, Gentile and Jew alike. For Paul, the mystery of this saving grace is grounded in the death and resurrection of Christ. Although the Apostle grew in his understanding of this mystery throughout his ministry and developed new ways of expressing it, his gospel of God's saving grace was rooted in a profound experience of God's grace in his own life that we traditionally name Paul's call and conversion. At that moment, Paul the persecutor experienced a Christophany in which he encountered the risen Lord, who commissioned him to preach the gospel among the Gentiles. Paul's gospel of grace, then, begins with a personal experience of God's saving grace. Without that experience, Paul could not have proclaimed the gospel he did. Given the importance of Paul's experience of God's saving grace, my Pauline theology begins with a consideration of that extraordinary event that transformed Paul's life.[1]

Exactly what happened at the moment of Paul's call and conversion is a matter of conjecture. While most would agree that he underwent a life-changing experience, there has been a lively scholarly debate about the precise nature of that experience and its impact on the content of the gospel he preached in the years that followed. At one end of the spectrum,

---

1. The collection of essays edited by Richard N. Longenecker (*The Road from Damascus: The Impact of Paul's Conversion on His Life, Thought, and Ministry* [Grand Rapids: Eerdmans, 1997]) provides a helpful introduction to the issues surrounding Paul's call and conversion.

there are scholars who argue that the essential content of Paul's gospel (most notably his Christology and soteriology) was already present in that experience.[2] Consequently, even though Paul may have reformulated his theological insights in the period following his call, there is no need to suppose that other events altered the essential contours of the gospel he preached. For these scholars, the content of the gospel (who Christ is and what God accomplished in him) was disclosed in the Damascus road Christophany. At the other end of the spectrum, there are scholars who acknowledge the centrality of this Christophany but contend that the content and shape of Paul's gospel developed as he encountered and responded to the pastoral challenges and conflicts of his ministry.[3] Accord-

2. This position is supported by Seyoon Kim, *The Origin of Paul's Gospel* (2nd ed.; Tübingen: Mohr Siebeck, 1984); Martin Hengel, "The Stance of the Apostle Paul toward the Law in the Unknown Years between Damascus and Antioch," in *Justification and Variegated Nomism* 2: *The Paradoxes of Paul*, ed. D. A. Carson, Peter T. O'Brien, and Mark A. Seifrid (Grand Rapids: Baker Academic, 2004), 75-103; and Peter Stuhlmacher, "'The End of the Law': On the Origin and Beginning of Pauline Theology," in *Reconciliation, Law, and Righteousness: Essays in Biblical Theology* (Philadelphia: Fortress, 1986), 134-54. For example, Kim (*The Origin of Paul's Gospel*, 103) writes: "it is more sensible to suppose that Paul had clearly formulated the main lines of his theology very soon after the Damascus revelation than to posit a rather slow development in Paul's interpretation of it." Hengel ("The Stance of the Apostle Paul," 85) concludes: "In my judgment it is impossible to demonstrate a *fundamental* change in the center of the Pauline message from the time of his conversion or from the beginning of his missionary activity as an apostle." Stuhlmacher ("The End of the Law," 140) contends: "Through the Damascus-epiphany Paul came to know Jesus Christ as the end of the law, and the justification of the ungodly without works of the law solely by faith happened to the apostle himself at the same time as and of a piece with this coming to know Christ."

3. James D. G. Dunn has defended this position in a number of essays: "'A Light to the Gentiles' or 'The End of the Law'? The Significance of the Damascus Road Christophany for Paul," in *Jesus and the Law: Studies in Mark and Galatians* (Louisville: Westminster, 1990), 89-107; "Paul and Justification by Faith," in *The Road from Damascus*, 85-101; "Paul's Conversion — A Light to Twentieth Century Disputes," in *The New Perspective on Paul* (rev. ed., Grand Rapids: Eerdmans, 2005), here 89-107. Dunn argues that the primary purpose of the Damascus Christophany was to send Paul to the Gentiles. The more elaborate Christology and soteriology of Paul's letters were worked out over a period of time in light of Paul's ministry and in light of the Christophany. Heikki Räisänen ("Paul's Conversion and the Development of His View of the Law," *NTS* 33 [1987]: 404-19, here 415) represents a similar view when he writes: "This suggests that the radical developments in Paul's complex view of the law are in one way or another due to his missionary experience and the conflicts he became involved in because of this mission." Udo Schnelle (*Apostle Paul: His Life and Theology* [Grand Rapids: Baker Academic, 2003], 100) suggests a mediating position when he writes: "The *subject matter* of justification and law had always been present with Paul since his conversion, but not the *doctrine* of justification and the law as found in Galatians and Romans."

ing to this view, it was in controversies such as those reflected in his letter to the Galatians that the Apostle forged his teaching on justification by faith.

Despite the immense amount of scholarly energy that has been invested in the question of Paul's call, there are two reasons why the precise historical nature of his Damascus road experience remains elusive. First, since the literary evidence we possess is limited and varied, Paul's experience can be interpreted in conflicting ways. Second, since his encounter with the risen Christ was a transcendent experience, it can never be adequately expressed in words, even if Paul had described it in greater detail. Attempting to reconstruct exactly what happened at that moment is like trying to describe the transcendent dimension of love and beauty. Although poets, artists, and musicians have sought to do so, their words, art, and music always prove inadequate. In saying this, I am not advocating that we cease all historical investigation into what happened to Paul, but I am suggesting that we acknowledge the limits of such investigations, which rarely, if ever, result in consensus among scholars. The transcendent meaning of Paul's Damascus road Christophany will always escape us, as does the transcendent mystery of Jesus' resurrection.[4]

Rather than try to reconstruct what happened to Paul on the Damascus road, a more fruitful approach may be to examine the literary evidence of the Pauline letters and the Acts of the Apostles in order to understand how they use the account of Paul's call/conversion to preach, teach, and persuade those who already believe in the gospel. Doing so will help us to see more clearly the intimate relationship that the Pauline letters and the Acts of the Apostles establish between the Damascus road experience on the one hand and the content of Paul's preaching on the other.[5] It may also help us to understand how the Pauline gospel of

4. Alan F. Segal (*Paul the Convert: The Apostolate and Apostasy of Saul the Pharisee* [New Haven: Yale University Press, 1990], 70) writes: "We shall never know Paul's experience. But we can see how Paul reconstructs it. In retrospect, Paul construes his first Christian experience as (ecstatic) conversion."

5. What I am attempting to do in this chapter is a literary project rather than a historical investigation. I am asking what kind of relationship the Pauline letters and the Acts of the Apostles establish between Paul's call on the one hand and his gospel and apostleship on the other. I am aware that Paul's preaching as presented in Acts does not always correspond with his preaching as reflected in his letters. Moreover, apart from 14:4, 14, Acts never calls Paul an apostle, and, apart from 20:24, it does not summarize the message Paul preaches as "the gospel." It does, however, establish a relationship between Paul's call on the one hand and his preaching and ministry on the other.

God's saving grace is rooted in Paul's personal experience of God's saving grace.

Paul's Call and Conversion According to the Letters

Although Paul's call was the defining moment of his life, he does not describe that event in the detailed manner that Luke does in the Acts of the Apostles. His most explicit statement (Gal 1:15-17) occurs in the midst of an extended autobiographical section (1:13–2:21) in which he recounts certain events of his past in order to persuade the Galatians of "the truth of the gospel" that he preached to them (2:5, 14). Given the occasional nature of Paul's letters, which were composed in response to specific questions and problems that arose in the congregations to which he wrote, it is not surprising that he does not provide us with an extended description of this seminal event. Paul did not write to inform his converts of the events of his past life but to remind them of the gospel he preached and to exhort them to embody that gospel in their lives. When he does refer to his call, it is in support of his gospel and apostleship.[6]

Although the most familiar accounts of Paul's call and conversion are Luke's narrative in the Acts of the Apostle and Paul's autobiographical statement in Galatians, the letters contain other references to this experience.[7] I have categorized them in the following way: references in letter openings (Rom 1:1, 5; 1 Cor 1:1; 2 Cor 1:1; Gal 1:1; Eph 1:1; Col 1:1; 1 Tim 1:1; 2 Tim 1:1); references to the grace, mercy, stewardship, or message given or entrusted to Paul (Rom 12:3; 15:15; 1 Cor 3:10; 7:25; 15:10; Gal 2:9; Eph 3:2, 7, 8; Col 1:25; 1 Thess 2:4); references in defense of Paul's gospel and apostleship (1 Cor 9:1; 15:8-10; Gal 1:15-17); references to Paul's ministry (2 Cor 3:4–4:6; Eph 3:1-13; Col 1:23-29); and references to the change that occurred in Paul's life (1 Cor 9:16-17; Phil 3:4-11; 2 Cor 5:16; 1 Tim 1:12-17).[8]

---

6. One can reasonably assume that Paul told his converts about his call and conversion when he first preached the gospel to them. Having informed them of this event, he could then allude to it in his letters without describing it in detail.

7. Kim (*The Origin of Paul's Gospel*, 3-31) and Carey C. Newman (*Paul's Glory-Christology: Tradition and Rhetoric* [NovTSup 69; Leiden: Brill, 1992], 165-66) provide extensive lists of texts that explicitly or implicitly refer to Paul's Damascus road experience.

8. I have included texts from the disputed as well as from the non-disputed correspondence here, for even if certain letters were not written by Paul, they witness to how later tradition interpreted and viewed his call.

The Letter Openings

Profoundly aware that God called him to be an apostle for the sake of the gospel, Paul frequently alludes to his call in the opening greetings of his letters.[9] For example in 1 Cor 1:1 he writes, "Paul, called to be an apostle of Christ Jesus by the will of God," thereby grounding his apostleship in the call he received at the Damascus road Christophany. By emphasizing that this call occurred "through the will of God," Paul highlights its divine origin. Although the opening greeting of 2 Cor 1:1 does not explicitly refer to Paul's call in the way that 1 Corinthians does, it employs the phrase "by the will of God" to establish Paul's right to be called an apostle of Christ Jesus: "Paul, an apostle of Christ Jesus by the will of God." Given the importance that Paul's apostleship plays in 2 Corinthians, it should be apparent that this phrase has Paul's call in view. At the beginning of both letters to the Corinthians, then, Paul grounds his right to be called an apostle in the commission he received at the Damascus road Christophany.

The opening greetings of Romans and Galatians are more elaborate and explicit (Rom 1:1-7; Gal 1:1-4). Romans begins with "Paul, a servant of Jesus Christ, called to be an apostle, set apart for the gospel of God" (Rom 1:1). Here Paul emphasizes that he is a called apostle set apart for the sake of the gospel of God, by which he means the good news of what God has brought about in the death and resurrection of his Son. The use of the participle *aphōrismenos* ("set apart") is notable since Paul employs it also in Gal 1:15 when he describes his call. He goes on to write in Rom 1:5 that he received this grace, which is his apostleship *(charin apostolēn)*, through Jesus Christ for the purpose of bringing about "the obedience of faith" among the Gentiles.

Paul emphatically insists on the divine origin of his apostleship in Gal 1:1 when he writes: "Paul an apostle — sent neither by human commission nor from human authorities, but through Jesus Christ and God the Father." Here he qualifies the origin of his apostleship in three ways: it did not come from human beings or through human beings; rather, it came through Jesus Christ and God the Father, who raised Jesus from the dead. In 1:12 Paul insists on the origin of his gospel in a similar way. He did not receive his gospel from human beings, nor was he taught it; he received it from "a revelation of Jesus Christ" *(apokalypseōs Iēsou Christou)*. In the let-

---

9. Jürgen Becker *(Paul: Apostle to the Gentiles* [Louisville: Westminster John Knox, 1993], 70-71) develops this point.

ter openings of Romans and Galatians, then, Paul draws an intimate relationship between his call and his right to be called an apostle. He emphatically affirms that his gospel and apostleship are rooted in the Damascus road Christophany.

The opening verses of Colossians and Ephesians repeat the language of 2 Cor 1:1, "Paul, an apostle of Christ Jesus by the will of God." Although the phrase "by the will of God" does not explicitly refer to Paul's call, the manner in which Paul describes his ministry as revealing the hidden mystery that was made known to him (Eph 3:1-13; Col 1:23-29) suggests that he has his call in view when he writes "by the will of God." Similar allusions to Paul's call are found in the letter openings of 1 and 2 Timothy. In 1 Tim 1:1 Paul identifies himself as an apostle of Christ Jesus according to the "command" *(epitagēn)* of the Savior God and Christ Jesus. This is an appropriate expression since Paul is handing on to Timothy what was first entrusted to him. In 2 Tim 1:1 we find the same kind of language we encountered in 2 Cor 1:1; Eph 1:1; and Col 1:1: Paul is an apostle of Christ Jesus through "the will of God." Since his apostolic authority plays an important role in 1 and 2 Timothy, and since Paul reminds Timothy of the glorious gospel with which he has been entrusted (1 Tim 1:11) and of his conversion (vv. 12-17), it is likely that he has his call in view when he affirms that he is an apostle through "the will of God."

To summarize, the letter openings of all the Pauline letters except Philippians, 1 and 2 Thessalonians, and Titus explicitly refer to Paul's call. In doing so, they remind those who hear or read them that the one who writes derives his gospel and office as an apostle of Jesus Christ from his call in accordance with God's will.[10]

The Grace Given to Paul

In addition to beginning many of his letters by referring to his call, Paul alludes to his call when he mentions the grace of God given to him. Although this expression can have a broad semantic range,[11] there are several

---

10. Becker (*Paul*, 71) writes: "If indeed Paul intentionally placed this context [calling, apostleship, gospel for the Gentiles, and resurrection of Jesus Christ] at the beginning of the letters, this has fundamental significance for the letters — that is for Pauline theology. . . . The connection — called as apostle, gospel for the nations, church of Jesus Christ — is at the same time a structural principle and material foundation of his theology."

11. It could refer to either Paul's call to be an apostle to the Gentiles or his call to be a

instances when it appears that Paul has in view the grace or favor bestowed on him when God called and entrusted him with the gospel and apostleship at his call. For example, in 1 Thess 2:4 Paul speaks of having been "approved by God to be entrusted *(dedokimasmetha)* with the message of the gospel." Although there is no explicit reference to his call here, it is apparent that Paul is alluding to his call. At that moment, God entrusted him with the gospel about his Son. Although Paul does not otherwise refer to this call in 1 Thessalonians, it is not unreasonable to suppose that he had told the Thessalonians what happened to him. Indeed, it is difficult to imagine that he did not.

In 1 Cor 15:10, at the end of a section in which he recounts a series of appearances by the risen Lord, the last being to him, Paul writes: "But by the grace of God I am what I am, and his grace toward me has not been in vain. On the contrary, I worked harder than any of them — though it was not I, but the grace of God that is with me." In light of what Paul has written in v. 8 about the Lord appearing to him *(ōphthē kamoi)*, it is clear that "the grace of God" *(hē charis tou theou)* refers to the divine favor Paul experienced at that Christophany.

Paul makes a similar reference to the grace given him when he writes: "I have written to you rather boldly by way of reminder, because of the grace *(charin)* given me by God to be a minister of Christ Jesus to the Gentiles in the priestly service of the gospel of God, so that the offering of the Gentiles may be acceptable, sanctified by the Holy Spirit" (Rom 15:15-16). Here Paul alludes to the apostolic commission he mentioned in the letter opening: "through whom we have received grace and apostleship *(charin kai apostolēn)* to bring about the obedience of faith among all the Gentiles for the sake of his name" (1:5). In light of these more explicit texts, it is not too much to claim that Paul is also referring to his call in other texts in which he speaks of the grace given to him.[12]

Ephesians and Colossians also make use of the language of something having been "given" to Paul. In Eph 3:2 Paul reminds the Ephesians of the "commission of God's grace that was given me for you." According to v. 7,

---

Christian. This point is made by Peter T. O'Brien, "Was Paul Converted?" in *The Paradoxes of Paul,* 361-91, here 366.

12. Examples of such texts are the following: "For *by the grace given to me* I say to everyone among you not to think of yourself more highly than you ought to think" (Rom 12:3); "*According to the grace of God given to me,* like a skilled master builder I laid a foundation" (1 Cor 3:10); "Now concerning virgins, I have no command of the Lord, but I give my opinion as *one who by the Lord's mercy is trustworthy*" (1 Cor 7:25).

Paul has become a servant of the gospel "according to the gift of God's grace that was given me by the working of his power." Aware that he is the least of all the saints, Paul writes: "this grace was given to me *(emoi . . . edothē hē charis)* to bring to the Gentiles the news of the boundless riches of Christ" (v. 8). As in the non-disputed letters, the Paul of Ephesians and Colossians portrays himself as profoundly aware of the favor God bestowed on him at the Damascus road Christophany. This grace is the gift of the gospel and the commission he received to preach the gospel to the Gentiles.

To summarize, in the Pauline letters the expression "the grace given to me" frequently alludes to the gospel and apostleship that was entrusted to Paul at the Damascus road Christophany. It is because he has experienced God's saving grace in his life that the great apostle preaches the gospel of God's saving grace to others.

Paul's Ministry

When reflecting on the nature of the ministry or mystery that was entrusted to him, Paul often refers to the call that made it possible. In 2 Cor 3:4–4:6, for example, he provides the Corinthians with an extended description of his apostolic ministry. In doing so, he describes himself as the minister of a new covenant (3:6) who exercises a ministry of the Spirit (v. 8) and of righteousness (v. 9). Profoundly aware that no one is competent for such a ministry, he affirms that his competency does not come from himself but from God who has made him competent to be the minister of this new covenant, which is empowered by God's life-giving Spirit (vv. 5-6). Aware of his unworthiness to exercise this ministry, which he describes as more glorious than the ministry Moses exercised, Paul acknowledges that it is by God's mercy that he possesses this ministry (4:1). He does not preach Christ because of his own merits, but because of God, "who said, 'Let light shine out of darkness,' who has shone in our hearts to give the light of the knowledge of the glory of God in the face of Jesus Christ" (v. 6). These references to Paul's competency to be the minister of a new covenant, the mercy he has received, and the enlightenment he experienced are allusions to Paul's Damascus road Christophany.

Ephesians and Colossians also relate Paul's call and ministry when they portray him as the great apostle who reveals the mystery hidden for ages but now revealed to the church through his ministry. Paul became a servant of this mystery according to the "stewardship" or "commission" *(tēn oikonomian)* God gave to him (Col 1:25). In Ephesians, Paul assumes that his readers have heard of this stewardship that was given to him and how the mystery was made known to him by a revelation (*kata apokalypsin,* Eph 3:3). Paul has become a servant according to "the gift of God's grace" that was given to him (v. 7). As in 2 Corinthians, Paul is profoundly aware that the ministry he exercises in revealing God's mystery is something that was entrusted to him at a particular moment in his life.

In Defense of Paul's Gospel and Apostleship

On several occasions, Paul refers to his call to defend his apostolic credentials and the gospel he preaches. In 1 Cor 9:1 he defends his right to be called an apostle by asking the Corinthians: "Am I not free? Am I not an apostle? Have I not seen *(heoraka)* Jesus our Lord? Are you not my work in the Lord?" Given the rhetorical nature of Paul's questions, the answer he expects is clear. His defense against those who are passing judgment on him at Corinth is twofold. First, he has seen the risen Lord.[13] Second, his work among the Corinthians authenticates his apostleship.

In 1 Corinthians 15 Paul must defend what he and all the apostles preach, namely the resurrection of Christ and the resurrection of those who believe in him. To defend this common gospel, he reminds the Corinthians of the message he proclaimed to them: Christ's death and resurrection and the appearances of the risen Lord (vv. 1-11). As he comes to the end of this list, he writes: "Last of all, as to one untimely born, he appeared also to me" (*ōphthē kamoi,* v. 8). In this way, Paul grounds his gospel about the resurrection in a personal experience of the risen Lord.

Paul's most dramatic defense of his gospel and apostleship, as well as his most extensive statement about the Damascus Christophany, occurs in Galatians. Having learned that the gospel he preached to his Gentile converts at Galatia has been criticized by those who would require the Galatians to be circumcised and to submit to the rule of the Mosaic Law, in Gal 1:11–2:14 Paul employs an extended autobiographical statement to per-

---

13. In 1 Cor 9:1, in order to authenticate his apostleship, Paul emphasizes that he has seen the risen Lord. But there were others, such as the five hundred mentioned in 15:6, who had seen the risen Lord who were not apostles. Thus not all who saw the risen Lord were apostles. Paul was an apostle because the risen Christ commissioned him when he appeared to him.

suade his converts of "the truth of the gospel" he preached to them, namely that a person is justified by faith rather than by doing the works of the law. At the heart of this statement is Paul's most explicit account of his call and conversion.

> For I want you to know, brothers and sisters, that the gospel that was proclaimed by me is not of human origin; for I did not receive it from a human source, nor was I taught it, but *I received it through a revelation of Jesus Christ.* You have heard, no doubt, of my earlier life in Judaism. I was violently persecuting the church of God and was trying to destroy it. I advanced in Judaism beyond many among my people of the same age, for I was far more zealous for the traditions of my ancestors. *But when God, who had set me apart before I was born and called me through his grace, was pleased to reveal his Son to me, so that I might proclaim him among the Gentiles,* I did not confer with any human being, nor did I go up to Jerusalem to those who were already apostles before me, but I went away at once into Arabia, and afterwards I returned to Damascus. (Gal 1:11-17)

At the outset of this statement, Paul draws a relationship between the gospel he preaches and the Christophany he experienced (vv. 11-12). The gospel he proclaimed to the Galatians was not something he devised or received from others; it came through an *apokalypseōs Iēsou Christou* (v. 12), a phrase that can be construed as a revelation *from* Jesus Christ or as a revelation *about* Jesus Christ, which God granted Paul, as is implied in v. 15.[14] Having established the intimate relationship between this revelation and the gospel he preaches, Paul reminds the Galatians of his former way of life (vv. 13-14) before speaking of his Christophany (vv. 15-17). Previous to his call, he persecuted the church of God, and, because of his zeal for his ancestral traditions, he progressed in "Judaism" beyond his contemporaries. The church of God and the Judaism for which he was so zealous were polar opposites.

Paul's account of what happened to him is related in a single sentence

14. Although I interpret Gal 1:12 as an objective genitive, the distinction between the objective genitive and the genitive of origin should not be pressed. Although God revealed his Son to Paul in this "revelation of Jesus Christ," Paul writes that he saw the Lord (1 Cor 9:1), and he says that the risen Lord appeared to him (15:8). This suggests that "a revelation of Jesus Christ" may have a dual dimension: a revelation *about* Jesus Christ (objective genitive) and a revelation *from* Jesus Christ (genitive of origin).

(1:15-17). While the main clause explains what Paul did after this revelation ("I did not confer with any human being . . . but I went away at once to Arabia . . ."), the temporal clause ("But when God . . .") and the purpose clause ("so that I might proclaim him to the Gentiles") bear the weight of Paul's statement. Alluding to the call of the servant in Isaiah (Isa 49:1-6) and the call of the prophet Jeremiah (Jer 1:4-10), Paul describes the dramatic moment in which God revealed his Son to him (*en emoi*, Gal 1:16) as something God had planned before Paul was born.[15] Consequently, although God could have called Paul before he persecuted the church, God chose to reveal his Son at a particular moment when the persecutor sought to destroy the church. God's purpose in calling Paul had more than Paul's own welfare in view. God revealed his Son *so that* Paul might proclaim God's Son to the Gentiles, the very people from whom Paul zealously separated himself because of his zeal for the ancestral traditions of his people.[16]

According to Gal 1:16, then, Paul's Damascus Christophany had a twofold purpose. On the one hand, God revealed that the crucified one was none other than God's Son. On the other, God called Paul to proclaim the Son, the crucified Christ, to the Gentiles from whom Paul so zealously separated himself. Nothing would ever again be quite the same in Paul's life. The one who had been zealous for the law would now be zealous for the gospel of God's Son, and the one who had persecuted the church of God, which threatened the law and the ancestral traditions he so zealously defended, would now proclaim the gospel of a crucified Messiah. Paul's call was his conversion.

---

15. Seyoom Kim (*Paul and the New Perspective: Second Thoughts on the Origin of Paul's Gospel* [Grand Rapids: Eerdmans, 2002], 101-25) points to Isaiah 42 as another important Old Testament text for understanding Paul's call. The precise meaning of *en emoi* is disputed. It could mean "to me" or "in me." But given Paul's insistence that he "saw" the Lord (1 Cor 9:1) and that the Lord "appeared" to him (15:8), I understand the phrase as an indication of an appearance rather than an internal mystical experience.

16. Dunn ("Paul's Conversion: A Light to Twentieth Century Disputes," 360-62) provides a helpful description of the pre-Christian Paul's zeal for Israel's distinctiveness. In light of this description, Dunn views Paul's conversion as a movement from zeal for Israel's distinctiveness to equally zealous preaching to Gentiles. While I agree with Dunn's assessment of Paul's zeal, I do not think that this movement from zeal for Israel to preaching the gospel to the Gentiles is the full reality of Paul's call/conversion. There are Christological and soteriological dimensions that must also be taken into consideration.

The Change in Paul's Life

Although Paul speaks of his Damascus experience as a "call," this event resulted in a profound change in his life that can rightly be called a "conversion."[17] But it was not so much a conversion from a sinful way of life to a morally good way of life or from one religion to another as a total reorientation of Paul's life in terms of Christ rather than Torah. Accordingly, whereas his life was formerly defined by zeal for Torah, now it was defined by zeal for Christ. Paul's call to preach the gospel to the Gentiles resulted in a reorientation of his life and in a commission to preach the gospel to the Gentiles.

Paul hints at the change he experienced when he writes: "If I proclaim the gospel, this gives me no ground for boasting, for an obligation is laid on me, and woe to me if I do not proclaim the gospel!" (1 Cor 9:16). The "obligation" *(anankē)* imposed on Paul was his commission to preach the gospel to the Gentiles. Because of this obligation, the former zealot for the law made himself a slave to all so that he might win some for Christ. When with Jews, he lived under the law, and when with Gentiles he lived as one outside the law, so that he might gain both those under and outside the law for Christ (vv. 19-21). Paul understands that the occasion of his call/conversion was the moment when Christ conquered him. Consequently, in 2 Corinthians he presents himself as one who was taken captive by God who now leads him, in Christ, in a triumphal procession.

> But thanks be to God, who in Christ always leads us in triumphal procession, and through us spreads in every place the fragrance that comes from knowing him. For we are the aroma of Christ to God among those who are being saved and among those who are perishing; to the one a

17. Segal (*Paul the Convert*, 6-7) has provided a strong argument that Paul's Damascus road experience was a conversion. He writes: "I maintain, one must recognize that Paul was a Pharisaic Jew who converted to a new apocalyptic, Jewish sect and then lived in a Hellenistic community as a Jew among gentiles." O'Brien ("Was Paul Converted?" 390) also argues that Paul's experience must be understood as a conversion. He writes: "To describe the Damascus road experience as *simply* Paul's 'call' to the Gentiles does not account for the revelation of Christ and his gospel in which there was a radical change in Paul's thinking about Jesus as the Messiah and the Son, about the Torah, the messianic salvation, and not least Israel's and the Gentiles' place within the divine plan. In the Damascus encounter Paul underwent a significant 'paradigm shift' in his life and thought; his own self-consciousness was that of having undergone a conversion." The position of Segal and O'Brien stands in contrast to that found in the classic essay of Krister Stendahl, "Call Rather Than Conversion," in *Paul among Jews and Gentiles* (Philadelphia: Fortress, 1976), 7-23.

fragrance from death to death, to the other a fragrance from life to life. Who is sufficient for these things? (2 Cor 2:14-16)

In 2 Corinthians 5 Paul makes a number of other statements that point to the change that occurred in his life because of his encounter with Christ.[18] Convinced that Christ died for all (2 Cor 5:14), he writes: "From now on, therefore, we regard no one from a human point of view; even though we once knew Christ from a human point of view, we know him no longer in that way. So if anyone is in Christ, there is a new creation: everything old has passed away; see, everything has become new" (vv. 16-17)! Before the Damascus Christophany, Paul knew Christ *kata sarka*, by which he means that he understood the crucified Christ from a purely human perspective. But "from now on" *(apo tou nyn)*, after his call/conversion, he understands him in light of the Damascus Christophany. In the light of that experience, he affirms that whoever is in Christ belongs to the new creation; for the old has passed away, and God has made all things new in Christ (v. 17).

Phil 3:4-11 provides another description of the dramatic change that occurred in Paul's life because of the Damascus road experience. As in Galatians, there is a polemical tone to this passage since the Apostle must warn his Gentile converts not to have themselves circumcised. Pointing to his own life, Paul reminds the Philippians of his Jewish pedigree and the zeal that led him to persecute the church. Reflecting on his life under the law, he says that "as to righteousness under the law" he was "blameless" (v. 6). The righteousness that Paul attained under the law, however, pales in comparison to the righteousness he now knows in Christ. Accordingly, he writes: "Yet whatever gains I had, these I have come to regard as loss because of Christ" (v. 7). Paul's sole desire is to be found in Christ and experience the righteousness "that comes through faith in Christ" (v. 9). Although Paul never explicitly refers to his call and conversion in Phil 3:1-11, most scholars include this text with Gal 1:11-17 in their discussion of Paul's call and conversion, and with good reason, for it is only in light of that experience that this text makes sense.[19]

18. Kim (*Paul and the New Perspective*, 214-38, here 236) points to numerous connections between Paul's call and conversion on the one hand and 2 Cor 5:11-21 on the other. He writes: "2 Cor 5:11-21 is full of allusions to Paul's Damascus experience of conversion/call: what he is talking about in that passage is *what happened to him on the Damascus road*" (emphasis in the original).

19. Although Dunn and Kim disagree in the way they interpret the Damascus road event, both agree that the text of Philippians has Paul's call and conversion in view.

The Pauline text that most explicitly presents Paul's Damascus experience as a conversion is the account given in 1 Timothy.

> I am grateful to Christ Jesus our Lord, who has strengthened me, because he judged me faithful and appointed me to his service, even though I was formerly a blasphemer, a persecutor, and a man of violence. But I received mercy because I had acted ignorantly in unbelief, and the grace of our Lord overflowed for me with the faith and love that are in Christ Jesus. The saying is sure and worthy of full acceptance, that Christ Jesus came into the world to save sinners — of whom I am the foremost. But for that very reason I received mercy, so that in me, as the foremost, Jesus Christ might display the utmost patience, making me an example to those who would come to believe in him for eternal life. To the King of the ages, immortal, invisible, the only God, be honor and glory forever and ever. Amen. (1 Tim 1:12-17)

This autobiographical statement occurs toward the beginning of 1 Timothy, after an initial exhortation (vv. 3-11) in which Paul urges Timothy to warn people not to teach false doctrines (v. 3), which are contrary to the sound teaching (v. 10) that is in accord with the glorious gospel with which Paul was entrusted (v. 11). After Paul establishes this contrast between false teaching and the sound teaching of the gospel, he expresses his gratitude to Christ Jesus who appointed him to his service (v. 12). Paul acknowledges that, previous to that moment, he was a blasphemer, a persecutor, a violent man. But because he acted from ignorance and unbelief, he was treated mercifully and, through God's grace, was brought to faith and love. After introducing a statement he calls "trustworthy" (that Christ Jesus came into the world to save sinners), Paul describes himself as the "first," the "foremost" (*prōtos*, v. 15) of the sinners whom Christ came into the world to save. Reflecting on his past, Paul now understands that he was treated with such extraordinary mercy so that he might become the prototypical example (*hypotypōsin*, v. 16) of Christ's patience and mercy toward sinners.

Paul's description of himself as a persecutor in 1 Timothy echoes what he wrote in Gal 1:13 and Phil 3:6, but now he does not speak of the apostolic commission he received at the moment of his call to preach the gospel to the Gentles.[20] Instead, he focuses on the dramatic change that Christ

---

20. It should be noted, however, that 1 Tim 2:7 does make a connection between Paul's call and his commission to be a preacher, apostle, and teacher to the Gentiles.

brought about in his life in order to make his conversion a model and source of hope for others. By reminding Timothy of what happened to him, Paul provides him with an outstanding example of mercy and conversion that Timothy can use in his preaching and instruction. In effect, Paul hands on the story of his conversion as part of the sound teaching that Timothy and those whom he appoints must transmit to the next generation.

Paul's Call and Conversion according to Acts

Like the account of 1 Timothy, the three narrations of Paul's call in Acts 9, 22, and 26 belong to a later tradition. But whereas the tradition in the Pastorals presents Paul's conversion as an example of God's mercy toward sinners, Acts recounts Paul's Damascus road experience to demonstrate the power of Christ and the continuity of the Christian message with the law and the prophets. The first and most extensive narrative is told from the point of view of the Lukan narrator in order to show how Christ made the church's most fearsome persecutor his chosen instrument to bring his name to Gentiles, kings, and Israelites (9:1-19), whereas the second and third accounts are told from the point of view of Paul within the context of two speeches (22:1-21; 26:1-23) in which Paul must defend himself from charges that he speaks against the people of Israel, the law, and the temple (21:28). My purpose in this section is to examine this material in its literary context in order to understand the relationship Luke establishes between Paul's call and conversion on the one hand and the message Paul proclaims on the other.

The First Account

Before narrating Paul's call, Luke introduces Saul (Paul) as consenting to the execution of Stephen (8:1), a leader of the Hellenistic wing of the church who has been charged with speaking against the temple and the law (6:13). Zealous for Israel's temple and its law, Saul embarks upon a campaign to destroy the church (8:3). In ch. 9 he extends his campaign to the synagogues of Damascus. But before he can enter the city, he encounters the risen Jesus. A light appears from the sky, and a voice speaks to him. Unable to see because of the light, the would-be persecutor must be led into the city by his companions (vv. 3-9).

The account that follows the narration of the Christophany is longer and more instructive (9:10-19). The Lord commands Ananias to go to Saul and restore his sight because he is "an instrument whom I have chosen to bring my name before Gentiles and kings and before the people of Israel; I myself will show him how much he must suffer for the sake of my name" (vv.15-16). After being baptized, Saul preaches in the synagogues that Jesus is the Son of God, the Messiah (vv. 20-22).

In the narrative that follows, Luke portrays Paul as preaching to Gentiles and the people of Israel, in accordance with the commission he received through the mediation of Ananias.[21] In the synagogue of Antioch of Pisidia, Paul delivers an extensive sermon, proclaiming that God has fulfilled the promise he made to the ancestors by raising Jesus from the dead (13:33). Paul then proclaims, "by this Jesus everyone who believes is set free from all those sins from which you could not be freed by the law of Moses" (v. 39). When the members of the synagogue reject this message, Paul and Barnabas threaten to turn to the Gentiles: "For so the Lord has commanded us, saying, 'I have set you to be a light for the Gentiles, so that you may bring salvation to the ends of the earth'" (v. 47). Having presented a detailed account of Paul's preaching to Jews at Antioch, Luke is content to summarize Paul's preaching at Thessalonica by saying that he entered the synagogue and argued from the Scriptures, "explaining and proving that it was necessary for the Messiah to suffer and rise from the dead, and saying, 'This is the Messiah, Jesus whom I am proclaiming to you'" (17:3). Luke summarizes the content of Paul's preaching at Corinth in a similar manner by noting that Paul was "testifying to the Jews that the Messiah was Jesus" (18:5).

Having employed the sermon in the synagogue of Antioch to provide readers with an example of Paul's preaching to Jews, Luke uses Paul's speech at Athens (17:22b-31) to summarize the way in which Paul preaches to Gentiles. In the past, God overlooked sins, but now God requires all to repent "because he has fixed a day on which he will have the world judged in righteousness by a man whom he has appointed, and of this he has

---

21. In Paul's letters, most notably Galatians, there is no mention of Ananias. This, however, does not necessarily mean that Ananias is a fictitious character. Johannes Munck (*Paul and the Salvation of Mankind* [London: SCM, 1959], 17) notes: "It is possible that a man of that name made friends with Paul when the latter found himself in Damascus profoundly shaken and half blind, and that Jewish Christians imagined that he acquired more influence over Paul than the latter admitted." But since Paul argues in Galatians that his gospel and apostleship came from a revelation of Jesus Christ rather than from human beings, he is silent about Ananias, lest he give the impression that his gospel and commission were mediated by him.

given assurance to all by raising him from the dead" (17:31). Thus whereas Paul's employs the Scriptures when preaching to Jews to prove that Jesus is the Messiah, his preaching to Gentiles calls people to repent because Jesus' resurrection foreshadows the coming day of the Lord.

The literary-theological relationship Luke establishes between Paul's Damascus road experience as narrated in ch. 9 and his preaching among Jews and Gentiles can be summarized in this way: At the Christophany, Christ commissioned Paul (through Ananias) to preach to Jews and Gentiles. To the former he proclaimed that Jesus is the Messiah, the fulfillment of God's promises to Israel. To the latter he preached the need for repentance because God is about to judge the world through Jesus whom he has raised from the dead.

The Second Account

In his second account of Paul's call, Luke has Paul recount what happened to him on the Damascus road from his own point of view (Acts 22:1-21). The purpose of this account, however, is not merely to describe what happened, since the readers of Acts already know the story. Rather, Luke's purpose is to defend Paul from charges that the former Pharisee has apostatized from his ancestral faith.[22] Accordingly, Luke has Paul recount his call in a way that assures the readers of Acts, as well as Paul's audience, that Paul preaches what he formerly persecuted because he was called by the risen Lord. Rather than having abandoned his ancestral faith, he proclaims its fulfillment in Christ.

The defense speech in ch. 22 takes place in Jerusalem, where Paul has been arrested because of a riot caused by some who have accused him of teaching what is contrary to the people of Israel, the law, and the temple and of profaning the temple by bringing Gentiles into it (21:28). When the Roman commander allows him to speak, Paul begins his "defense" by pointing to his Jewish heritage, his education in the law under Gamaliel, and his zeal for God, which led him to persecute the Way (22:1-5). Next, he recounts his Damascus road experience (vv. 6-11) and the role of Ananias (vv. 12-16), whom he describes as "a devout man according to the law and well spoken

---

22. Jacob Jervell makes this point in "Paul: The Teacher of Israel: The Apologetic Speeches of Paul in Acts," in *Luke and the People of God: A New Look at Luke-Acts* (Minneapolis: Augsburg, 1972), 153-83.

of by all the Jews living there" (v. 12). Ananias continues to mediate the meaning of Paul's call by informing him that "the God of our ancestors" chose him to see "the Righteous One" and hear his voice (v. 14). But now, in a new episode, Paul recounts a vision he experienced in the temple when the risen Lord appeared to him and commissioned him to go to the Gentiles (vv. 17-21). The manner in which Paul constructs his defense is intended to prove to the Jerusalem audience that the accusations against him are false. It was the God of their ancestors who designated him to know "the Righteous One." It was in the very temple that Paul is accused of defiling that Jesus commissioned him to preach to the Gentiles.[23] Paul remains a loyal Jew who is as zealous for God as those who accuse him of speaking against Israel, its law, and its temple. But their zeal is as misguided as his was when he "persecuted this Way up to the point of death" (v. 4). In light of his Damascus road experience, he now realizes that the one whose followers he persecuted is "the Righteous One" who sent him to the Gentiles (v. 21).

In the chapters that follow (Acts 23–28), Luke portrays Paul as a prisoner who suffers for the Lord, thereby fulfilling what the Lord told Ananias (9:16). The most striking aspect of these chapters is the manner in which Paul makes "the resurrection of the dead" the central issue of his case. When he stands before the Sanhedrin (23:1-10), for example, he cries out that he is on trial for the resurrection of the dead (v. 6). When he stands before his Jewish accusers and the Roman governor Felix (24:1-21), he defends himself by saying that he worships the God of the ancestors, that he believes everything written in the law and the prophets, and that he has the same hope in God as his accusers: that there will be a resurrection of the righteous and unrighteous (v. 15). The issue, he asserts, is not the charges that have been brought against him: "It is about the resurrection of the dead that I am on trial before you today" (v. 21). Finally, after Paul appeals to Caesar (25:11), leaving the Roman governor Festus no recourse but to send him to Rome, Festus summarizes the case for King Agrippa by saying that the issue concerns a disagreement between Paul and the Jews over points of their religion "and about a certain Jesus, who had died, but whom Paul asserted to be alive" (v. 19).

The events that follow Paul's first defense speech in Jerusalem show that Luke's second account of Paul's call draws an intimate relationship between Paul's call and his faith in the resurrection of Jesus, which Paul views

---

23. Although Luke does not appear to allude to it, the prophet Isaiah also received a vision in the temple, according to Isaiah 6.

as the inauguration of the resurrection of the dead. Paul had already hinted at this in his speech at Athens when he drew a connection between the resurrection of Jesus and God's coming judgment (17:31). This relation, which Luke draws between Paul's call and the resurrection of the dead, coheres with his portrayal of Paul as a zealous Pharisee. Having hoped for the resurrection of the dead as a Pharisee, Paul interpreted the resurrection of Jesus as the beginning of the resurrection of the dead, an indication that the Day of Judgment is at hand.

The Third Account

Luke's third narration of the call occurs in Paul's last defense speech before he is sent to Rome (Acts 26:2-11). Paul now stands before King Agrippa, his sister Bernice, the Roman governor Festus, the Roman cohort commanders, and the prominent men of Caesarea. As in his first defense speech, he begins by recalling his former way of life, but this time he introduces what he perceives to be the real issue: the resurrection of the dead, which he equates with the promise made to the ancestors.

> And now I stand here on trial *on account of my hope in the promise made by God to our ancestors,* a promise that our twelve tribes hope to attain, as they earnestly worship day and night. It is for this hope, your Excellency, that I am accused by Jews! *Why is it thought incredible by any of you that God raises the dead?* (Acts 26:6-8)

Next, Paul recounts his experience on the Damascus road (vv. 12-18), but this time there is no mention of Ananias or the temple vision. Instead, the risen Lord directly commissions Paul, explaining that he has appeared to him *(ōphthēn)* so that Paul may be his servant and witness (v. 16). The Lord promises to deliver Paul from his own people and from the Gentiles, to whom "I am sending you" (v. 17). At the end of his speech Paul explains that he obeyed the vision, which led him to preach the need for repentance throughout Judea and to the Gentiles (vv. 19-23). What Paul teaches is in accord with what the prophets and Moses foretold: "that the Messiah must suffer and that, as the first to rise from the dead, he would proclaim light both to our people and to the Gentiles" (v. 23). The remark that the Messiah is the first to rise from the dead echoes what Paul said at the beginning of this speech: he is on trial for his hope in the promise God made to Israel, namely the resurrection of the dead. By the end of his defense speeches, it is apparent that Paul has drawn a close relationship between his Damascus road experience and his hope for the resurrection of the dead.

The relationship that Luke draws between Paul's Damascus road experience and his preaching can be summarized in two points. First, through that Christophany Paul was commissioned to be Christ's chosen instrument to carry his name before Gentiles, kings, and the people of Israel (9:15). Christ designated him to be a light to the Gentiles (13:47; 26:17-18), a servant and witness of what he had seen and would be shown (22:15; 26:16). Second, in light of the Damascus road experience, Paul understood that Jesus was Israel's promised Messiah, in whom God was fulfilling Israel's hope for the resurrection of the dead, which began with Jesus' resurrection. Because Luke limits the title "apostle" to the Twelve, he cannot draw a connection between Paul's Christophany and apostleship in the way that Paul does in his letters. And since, except in 20:24, he does not use the noun "gospel" to summarize the content of what Paul preaches, Luke does not draw a relationship between Paul's Christophany and "the gospel" he received, as Paul does in his letters.

Despite these differences, Acts and the Pauline letters draw a similar relationship between *Paul's call and conversion on the one hand and the content of his preaching and the commission he received* on the other. According to Acts, the Christophany Paul experienced was the moment when he was commissioned to proclaim to Gentiles and Jews that Jesus is the Messiah, the first to rise from the dead. Like the Pauline letters, the Acts of the Apostles grounds the content of what Paul preaches and the commission he received in the Damascus Christophany. Having reviewed how the letters and Acts present Paul's call, I now consider Paul's gospel and apostleship in light of his call.

Paul's Gospel

Ways of Speaking about the Gospel

The frequency with which the Pauline corpus employs "gospel" testifies to the word's importance.[24] Of the seventy-six uses in the NT, sixty occur in

---

24. For an overview of how "gospel" is used in the Pauline letters, see Friedrich Hauck, "*euangelizomai, euangelion,*" *TDNT* 2:707-37.

the Pauline letters. In most instances the Pauline corpus speaks simply of "the gospel." For example, Paul is not ashamed of the gospel because it is God's power, that which brings people to salvation (Rom 1:16). Although those who proclaim the gospel are entitled to get their living from it (1 Cor 9:14), Paul preaches the gospel free of charge to the Corinthians (2 Cor 11:7); for he does everything for the sake of the gospel (1 Cor 9:23). The Philippians participate in the gospel (Phil 1:5) by joining in the work of the gospel (Phil 2:22; 4:3). Paul defends the truth of the gospel for the sake of the Galatians (Gal 2:5, 14), suffers for the gospel (2 Tim 1:8), and is imprisoned for the gospel (Phil 1:16; Phlm 13).

Other expressions give further nuance and meaning to "the gospel." Some relate the gospel to God: "the gospel of God" (Rom 1:1; 15:16; 1 Thess 2:2, 8, 9) and "the glorious gospel of the blessed God" (1 Tim 1:11). Others relate the gospel to the Son, Christ, or the Lord Jesus: "the gospel of his Son" (Rom 1:9), "the gospel of Christ" (Rom 15:19; 1 Cor 9:12; 2 Cor 2:12; 9:13; 1 Thess 3:2), "the gospel of the glory of Christ" (2 Cor 4:4), and "the gospel of our Lord Jesus" (2 Thess 1:8). Still others draw a connection between Paul and the gospel: "my gospel" (Rom 2:16; 16:25; 2 Tim 2:8), and "our gospel" (2 Cor 4:3). Others describe the character or the nature of the gospel: "the gospel for the circumcised" and "the gospel for the uncircumcised" (Gal 2:7), "the gospel of your salvation" (Eph 1:13), and "the gospel of peace" (Eph 6:15).

Expressions such as "the gospel of God" and "the gospel of Christ" can be understood in different ways, depending on how one construes the genitive. Taken as a subjective genitive "the gospel of God" refers to God's own good news, but construed as an objective genitive it refers to the good news about God. Likewise, if "the gospel of Christ" is taken as a subjective genitive it refers to the good news Christ brings, but if it is construed as an objective genitive the focus is on the good news about Christ. While the meaning of each text must be decided in context, in most instances "the gospel of God" is God's good news, whereas "the gospel of Christ" points to the good news about Christ. Thus "the gospel" means God's good news about his Son, Jesus Christ, whom God raised from the dead. Other expressions such as "the gospel of peace" and "the gospel of your salvation" point to the soteriological effect of the gospel, which brings peace and salvation.

Although Paul sometimes speaks of "my gospel," "our gospel," "the gospel for the circumcised," and "the gospel for the uncircumcised," this does not mean that there are different gospels. To be sure, there were apostles and ministers of the gospel who contested the circumcision-free gospel Paul taught among the Gentiles or the manner in which he exercised his ministry. When this happened, as in Galatia and Corinth, Paul called into question the credentials and preaching of such people, whom he calls "agitators" in Galatians and "super-apostles" in 2 Corinthians. But in the midst of these polemics, Paul insisted that there is only one gospel. Consequently, although he speaks of "my gospel" and "our gospel," this does not mean that "his" gospel is different from the gospel preached by other apostles. All the apostles preach the same gospel (1 Cor 15:11). When Paul uses "my gospel" or "our gospel," then, he has in view the gospel of God, which is the gospel about Christ, that Paul preaches. Likewise, when he says that he was entrusted with "the gospel for the uncircumcised" and Peter with the "gospel for the circumcised" (Gal 2:7), he is referring to different mission fields rather than to different gospels. The essential content of the gospel, God's redemptive work in Jesus Christ, remains the same whether the gospel is proclaimed to Gentiles or to Jews.

The gospel is a power that brings salvation. In Rom 1:16 Paul writes: "it is the power of God for salvation to everyone who has faith, to the Jew first and also to the Greek." In recalling his preaching to the Thessalonians, he reminds them that the gospel did not come to them in word only "but also in power and in the Holy Spirit and with full conviction" (1 Thess 1:5), and they received it not as a human word but as God's word (2:13). Likewise, when recounting how he preached the gospel in Corinth, he tells the Corinthians that his speech and proclamation "were not with plausible words of wisdom, but with a demonstration of the Spirit and of power" (1 Cor 2:4). Finally, he asks the Galatians if they received the Spirit "by doing the works of the law or by believing what you heard" (Gal 3:2). In these and other ways, Paul indicates that when the preached word is received in faith the gospel brings people to salvation.

The Content of the Gospel

Although scholars debate the precise content of what was communicated to Paul at the moment of his call and conversion, there is no doubt that he draws a close relationship in his letters between that experience and the gospel he proclaims. In Gal 1:11-12 he insists on the divine origin of the gospel, which came to him through "a revelation of Jesus Christ," and in Rom 1:1 he identifies himself as a called apostle "set apart for the gospel of God." Consequently, even if we assume (as I believe we must) that Paul's insight into, and understanding of, the gospel grew throughout his ministry, he implies that the essential meaning of the gospel he preaches was communicated to him when he was commissioned to preach the gospel to the Gentiles.

Paul, however, rarely explains the content of the gospel. Since he or others have already proclaimed the gospel to those to whom he is writing, he assumes that those who read his letters understand what he means when he refers to "the gospel," which is his way of summarizing God's saving work in the death and resurrection of Jesus Christ. In 1 Cor 15:3-5 and Rom 1:3-4, however, Paul does outline the contours of the gospel he proclaims. Drawing from a tradition he received and then handed on to the Corinthians, he writes:

> For I handed on to you as of first importance what I in turn had received: that Christ died for our sins in accordance with the scriptures, and that he was buried, and that he was raised on the third day in accordance with the scriptures, and that he appeared to Cephas, then to the twelve. (1 Cor 15:3-5)

On first reading, Paul appears to contradict what he writes in Gal 1:11, where he insists that he did not receive his gospel from a human source. His statement in Galatians, however, does not mean that he did not draw upon the tradition of the church in his preaching of the gospel. In 1 Corinthians 15 he makes use of tradition to summarize the gospel because he wants to establish that the gospel he preaches is in accord with the gospel that all of the apostles proclaim (see 1 Cor 15:11), namely, that in accordance with the Scriptures, Christ died for sins and was raised from the dead.

In the letter to the Romans, Paul begins with an extended greeting (Rom 1:1-7) because he must introduce himself to a community he did not establish, some of whose members may have questioned the manner in which he preached the gospel. Therefore, in the midst of his greeting, he summarizes the essential content of the gospel he preaches:

> . . . set apart for the gospel of God, which he promised beforehand through his prophets in the holy scriptures, the gospel concerning his Son, who was descended from David according to the flesh and was declared to be Son of God with power according to the spirit of holiness by resurrection from the dead, Jesus Christ our Lord. (Rom 1:1b-4)

As he did in 1 Corinthians 15, Paul highlights the continuity between the gospel and Israel's Scriptures and the centrality of the resurrection. Unlike 1 Corinthians 15, however, the greeting of Romans does not explicitly refer to Christ's' salvific death.[25] Rather, it focuses on the one whose person defines the gospel: Jesus, the royal descendant of David, who was manifested as the Son of God in power by his resurrection from the dead.

These two texts show that Paul can employ different traditions to summarize the gospel. The formulations, however, always focus on the one whom God raised from the dead, which is the nonnegotiable content of the gospel to which the Scriptures testify.

The centrality of Christ's death for the gospel he preaches is evident in the opening chapter of 1 Corinthians when Paul reminds the Corinthians of the paradoxical message of the cross. Writing to a community in danger of falling into factions that identify themselves with those who baptized them, Paul insists that Christ did not send him to baptize but to proclaim the gospel. He then identifies the gospel with the message of the cross. Although "the message of the cross" is foolishness to those who are perishing, it is the "power of God" *(dynamis theou)* for those who are being saved (1 Cor 1:18). Consequently, while Jews demand signs and Greeks desire wisdom, the content of Paul's gospel is "Christ crucified" (*Christon estaurōmenon,* v. 23), whom Paul identifies as "the power of God and the wisdom of God" (v. 24). Thus the gospel paradoxically reveals God's power and wisdom in the weakness and folly of the cross. The Pauline gospel thus encompasses both the scandal of the cross (1 Cor 1 and 2) and the power of the resurrection (Rom 1; 1 Cor 15).

On several occasions, Paul and those who wrote in his name relate the gospel to the mystery of God, which is the divine economy of salvation. In 1 Corinthians, for example, he equates the paradoxical message of the cross that he preaches with the "the mystery of God" (*to mystērion tou theou,* 1 Cor 2:1). This wisdom, which is for the mature, is "God's wisdom, secret and hidden *(en mystēriǭ tēn apokekrymmenēn),* which God decreed before the ages for our glory" (v. 7). As an apostle, Paul is a steward of "the mysteries of God" (*mystēriōn theou,* 4:1).

Colossians and Ephesians develop this theme further. Paul has become a servant according to the commission given to him to make the word of God fully known, namely, "the mystery that has been hidden throughout

---

25. The death of Jesus, however, is presupposed in the reference to his resurrection from the dead. Moreover, Jesus' death plays a major role in the rest of the letter.

the ages and generations but has now been revealed to his saints" (Col 1:26). Paul then explains how great among the Gentiles are "the riches of the glory of this mystery, which is Christ in you, the hope of glory" (v. 27). Thus the content of the gospel is equated with the mystery of God's plan whereby Christ is present in the Gentiles. The mystery, which is the gospel, is Christ (2:2). It is on account of this mystery that Paul is a prisoner (4:3).

Ephesians develops this line of thought further in terms of the reconciliation of Gentile and Jew that God brought about through Christ. God has made known to Paul the mystery of his will, a plan to gather up all things in Christ (Eph 1:9-10). This mystery, which is the gospel that Paul proclaims, was made known to him by revelation (3:3), presumably at his call. Paul has been given the grace to preach to the Gentiles "and to make everyone see what is the plan of the mystery hidden for ages in God who created all things" (v. 9). In former times this mystery was not made known, but now it has been revealed to the apostles and prophets, namely, that "the Gentiles have become fellow heirs, members of the same body, and sharers in the promise in Christ Jesus through the gospel" (v. 6).

The Pastoral Epistles portray Paul as instructing Timothy and Titus to guard what Paul entrusted to them (1 Tim 6:20; 2 Tim 1:14). He entrusted to them what was entrusted to him, namely, "the glorious gospel of the blessed God" (1 Tim 1:11; see also 2 Tim 1:12; Tit 1:3). It was for this gospel that Paul "was appointed a herald and apostle and a teacher" (2 Tim 1:11). This gospel is the proclamation of what Paul calls "the mystery of the faith" (1 Tim 3:9) and "the mystery of our religion," which Paul summarizes in a brief hymn-like passage: "He was revealed in the flesh, vindicated in the spirit, seen by angels, proclaimed among Gentiles, believed in throughout the world, taken up in glory" (1 Tim 3:16).

Although the Pastorals do not provide a formal definition of the gospel, a number of texts allude to its content. For example, after instructing Timothy that prayers should be offered for everyone, Paul explains, "there is one God; there is also one mediator between God and humankind, Christ Jesus, himself human, who gave himself for all — this was at the right time." Paul then adds, "for this I was appointed a herald and an apostle . . . a teacher of the Gentiles in faith and truth" (1 Tim 2:5-7). In this way he indicates that what he has just said is the content of the gospel he preaches. In another text, Paul exhorts Timothy not to be ashamed "of the testimony about our Lord or of me his prisoner but join with me in suffering for the gospel, relying on the power of God who saved us and called us with a holy calling, not according to our works but according to his own purpose and grace" (2 Tim 1:8-9). He then adds, "This grace was given to us in Christ Jesus before the ages began, but has now been revealed through the appearing of our Savior Christ Jesus, who abolished death and brought life and immortality to light through the gospel" (v. 10). In this statement, Paul summarizes the gospel in terms of God's grace and purpose revealed in Christ who destroyed death and brought life. Finally, in a text reminiscent of Rom 1:3-4, Paul summarizes the gospel for Timothy: "Remember Jesus Christ, raised from the dead, a descendant of David — *that is my gospel,* for which I suffer hardship, even to the point of being chained like a criminal" (2 Tim 2:8-9).

Although the Pastorals are often accused of turning the gospel into a frozen "deposit of faith," these passages show that they present the gospel in terms of Jesus' death and resurrection, an act of God's grace whereby Christ destroyed death and brought life. Whereas the sound teaching of the gospel brings life, false knowledge and teaching lead to destruction and death. Accordingly, Timothy and Titus must combat error by handing on to others what Paul handed on to them — the sound teaching of the gospel.

The non-disputed Pauline letters, Colossians and Ephesians, and the Pastorals all relate Paul's gospel to his call and conversion. In doing so, they ground the gospel he preaches in the call he received to proclaim the gospel to the nations. Although these letters do not provide a uniform definition of the gospel, the event of Christ's death and resurrection remains a constant element in their descriptions of the gospel. The non-disputed Pauline letters highlight the scandal of the cross, Colossians and Ephesians focus on the mystery that the gospel reveals, and the Pastorals present the gospel as sound teaching that must be handed on to the next generation.

Paul's Apostleship

Like his gospel, Paul's apostleship is rooted in his call. He has been called to be an apostle (Rom 1:1) "by the will of God" (1 Cor 1:1). He is an apostle because he has seen the Lord (1 Cor 9:1; 15:8). In revealing his Son to Paul, God set Paul apart to preach among the Gentiles (Gal 1:15-16). Having received the grace of apostleship to bring about the obedience of faith among the Gentiles (Rom 1:5), Paul understands that he is an apostle to the Gentiles (Rom 11:13) who exercises his ministry among the uncircumcised (Gal 2:8). Paul, then, views his apostleship in terms of his call and commission to preach the gospel among the Gentiles. Not only has he seen the Lord, he was called and commissioned by the Lord to preach the gospel among the Gentiles. Paul is insistent, then, that just as his gospel came from a revelation of Jesus Christ, so his apostleship came from Jesus Christ and God the Father (Gal 1:1).

Paul's call, his gospel, and his apostleship are intimately related to each other. Consequently, those who oppose his right to be called an apostle implicitly question the gospel he preaches and his claim to have seen the Lord.[26] For if Paul received his gospel and apostleship from the Lord, one can dispute neither his claim to be an apostle nor the truth of the gospel he preaches. But if Paul has not seen the Lord, there are no grounds for the gospel he preaches or for his claim to be an apostle. Paul's claim to have seen Christ is the "doctrine" by which Pauline theology stands or falls. Just as the truth of the Four Gospels depends on whether their witness to the resurrection is true or false, so the truth of Pauline theology depends upon whether or not Paul saw the Lord.

The question of Paul's apostleship arises primarily in Galatians and the Corinthian correspondence. In the former, the central issue has to do with the circumcision-free gospel he preaches to the nations. While Paul grounds this gospel in his apostolic call, his opponents criticize his teaching by questioning his right to be called an apostle. Although it is difficult to know precisely what the agitators told the Galatians, the manner in which Paul employs autobiographical information to defend "the truth of the gospel" (Gal 2:5, 14) suggests that they questioned the legitimacy of his gospel by disputing his right to call himself an apostle equal in status to the Jerusalem apostles. This is why Paul insists on the divine origin of his call. Although he is not one of the Twelve, his apostleship is equal to theirs because he was commissioned by the Lord.

At Corinth the issue is not so much the gospel Paul preaches as it is the manner in which he exercises his apostleship. In 1 Corinthians 1–4 he must deal with the divisions within the community because different factions have aligned themselves with other apostolic ministers (1 Cor 1:12). To respond to this problem, Paul reminds the Corinthians of the authentic na-

26. This is, of course, not true of Acts, where Luke restricts the title "apostle" to the Twelve. Paul's call, however, remains central to Luke's understanding of Paul and his message. Consequently, to deny that Paul saw the risen Lord is to deny the message he proclaims. This is why Luke is so intent on defending Paul against accusations that he is an apostate from Judaism. Luke's defense of Paul is that he has seen the Lord, who commissioned him to be his chosen instrument to carry his name before Gentiles, kings, and Israelites.

ture of apostolic ministry, which should reflect the gospel it proclaims. Since the central content of the gospel is Christ crucified, apostles must embody this gospel in their ministry. To make this point, Paul draws a contrast between the Corinthians, who mistakenly view themselves as having already attained the fullness of the Christian life, and the apostles, whose lives embody the gospel of Christ crucified.

> Already you have all you want! Already you have become rich! Quite apart from us you have become kings! Indeed, I wish that you had become kings, so that we might be kings with you! For I think that God has exhibited us apostles as last of all, as though sentenced to death, because we have become a spectacle to the world, to angels and to mortals. We are fools for the sake of Christ, but you are wise in Christ. We are weak, but you are strong. You are held in honor, but we in disrepute. (1 Cor 4:8-10)

The issue of apostolic ministry becomes more acute in 2 Corinthians. Apostles whom Paul sarcastically dubs "super-apostles" (2 Cor 11:5; 12:11) have come to Corinth and criticized his ministry. According to them, Paul is not the skilled and eloquent preacher they are (10:10; 11:6). Moreover, unlike them he refuses to allow the community to support him. In response to the criticism that comes from these "super-apostles," Paul defends himself by showing the correspondence between the gospel he preaches and the apostolic ministry he exercises. In a "fool's speech" he purposely highlights the sufferings and weaknesses of his ministry to show the correspondence between the gospel he preaches and the ministry he exercises (11:16–12:10). Just as Christ was crucified in weakness and now lives by the power of God (13:4), so Paul gladly boasts in his weakness so that Christ's power might reside in him (12:9). For Paul, authentic apostolic ministry reflects the paradoxical gospel of the crucified Christ so that the power of God can be seen in the weakness of the apostolic minister. Paul carries in his body "the death of Jesus so that the life of Jesus may be made visible in our body" (4:10). By this, Paul means that he embraces the suffering and dying of Jesus in his life so that he can attain resurrection life. By doing so, he brings life to those for whom he is an apostle (v. 12).

Whereas in Galatians Paul defends his gospel and apostleship by referring to his call, in the Corinthian correspondence he shows that his apostolic ministry embodies the gospel he preaches. Accordingly, the way in which he lives his apostolic ministry proclaims the gospel he preaches.

Colossians and Ephesians portray Paul's apostleship in a slightly different way than the non-disputed letters do. In Colossians he writes that his "sufferings" *(pathēmasin)* are filling up what is lacking "in Christ's afflictions *(tōn thlipseōn tou Christou)* for the sake of his body, that is, the church" (Col 1:24). Here, "Christ's afflictions" refer to what the church must endure for the sake of Christ. In saying that he is filling up what is lacking in Christ's afflictions, then, Paul is not implying that something is lacking in Christ's redemptive sufferings. Rather, he is referring to the afflictions the church must endure on behalf of Christ before the end.

As an apostle, Paul is a "minister" *(diakonos)* of the church in accordance with God's "stewardship" or "commission" *(oikonomian tou theou)* that was given to him to bring the word of God to completion (Col 1:25). This word is the hidden mystery, which God has now revealed because God wants to make known "how great among the Gentiles are the riches of the glory of this mystery, which is Christ in you, the hope of glory" (v. 27). Whereas in the non-disputed Pauline letters, the Apostle points to his sufferings to show the correspondence between the gospel he preaches and the ministry he exercises, in Colossians he emphasizes the importance of his suffering for bringing to completion what is lacking in the church's afflictions on behalf of Christ and speaks of the gospel in terms of a hidden mystery that has now been revealed (1:26-27; 2:2).

Ephesians makes the relationship between Paul's call, his apostleship, and the mystery that has been revealed through the gospel more explicit. Echoing the language of Colossians, Paul assumes that his Gentile audience has heard of the "stewardship" or "commission" *(oikonomian,* Eph 3:2) of God's grace that was given to him for their benefit. It was "by revelation" *(kata apokalypsin,* v. 3) that "the mystery" was made known to him: "that is, the Gentiles have become fellow heirs, members of the same body, and sharers in the promise in Christ Jesus through the gospel" (v. 6). Paul has been made a "minister" or "servant" *(diakonos)* of this gospel by God's grace (v. 7). Echoing 1 Cor 15:9 he says that although he is the "least of the saints," he was chosen to bring to the Gentiles "the news of the boundless riches of Christ" (Eph 3:8). Thus, his role as an apostle is "to make everyone see what is the plan of the mystery *(hē oikonomia tou mystēriou)* hidden for ages in God who created all things" (v. 9).

Although Paul also speaks of the mystery in the non-disputed correspondence (Rom 11:25; 16:25; 1 Cor 2:1, 7; 4:1; 15:51), the relationship between call, mystery, and apostleship looms larger in Colossians and Ephesians. What was revealed to Paul at his call or commission was the mystery of the gospel, which reveals the role of the Gentiles in God's plan, a theme Paul foreshadowed when he told the Galatians that God announced the gospel in advance to Abraham: "All the Gentiles shall be blessed in you" (Gal 3:8).

The Pastorals present Paul as an apostle *(apostolos)*, herald *(kēryx)*, and teacher *(didaskalos)* of the Gentiles. In the letter openings of 1 and 2 Timothy, Paul introduces himself as "an apostle of Christ Jesus by the command of God our Savior and of Christ Jesus our hope" (1 Tim 1:1), and as "an apostle of Christ Jesus by the will of God, for the sake of the promise of life that is in Christ Jesus" (2 Tim 1:1). But in addition to introducing himself as an apostle of Christ Jesus, Paul says that he was appointed a herald, an apostle, and a teacher of the Gentiles (1 Tim 2:7). In 2 Timothy, when speaking of the gospel, he says that "this grace was given to us in Christ Jesus before the ages began, but it has now been revealed through the appearing of our Savior Christ Jesus, who abolished death and brought life and immortality to light through the gospel" (2 Tim 1:9b-10). He adds that it was *for this gospel* that he was appointed a herald, apostle, and teacher. The Pastorals continue to maintain the connection between Paul's call, the gospel he preaches, and his commission to be the apostle to the Gentiles, and they are aware that this gospel is a gospel of grace previously hidden. But since their purpose is to instruct Timothy and Titus to combat false teaching and hand on the sound teaching they received from Paul, they present the Apostle as the great teacher of the Gentiles.

Coherence and Meaning in Paul's Call

In this chapter I have tried to show the relationship between Paul's Damascus road experience on the one hand and his gospel and apostleship on the other *as reflected in the Pauline letters*. My thesis has been that the Pauline corpus grounds Paul's gospel and commission in the Damascus road Christophany. The same can be said for the Acts of the Apostles, even though Luke does not grant Paul the title of apostle (which it reserves for the Twelve) and does not regularly employ the term "gospel" to denote Paul's preaching.

Although the Pauline letters were not written to present a systematic account of Paul's theology, and although some of them may have been written in his name rather than by him, they testify that the Apostle's gospel of God's saving grace is rooted in a personal experience of God's grace that occurred at his call. At that moment, the former persecutor understood that God had rescued him from a misguided zeal that had led him to persecute the church of God. He understood that the crucified one was God's son. Although we will never know what Paul saw and heard, the Pauline letters testify that he understood his gospel and commission in light of that experience. The Pauline Corpus, then, grounds the Apostle's theology in his Damascus road experience.

According to the Pauline Corpus, it was at the Damascus road Christophany that Paul understood that the crucified one is God's Messiah, the exalted Lord. He comprehended that Jesus' death was salvific, that Jesus had died for sins. Because of this Christophany, Christ became the focal point of Paul's life. With Christ as the focal point of his life, Paul joined the community he formerly persecuted and lived his new life in terms of Christ. In light of this Christophany, Paul comprehended the mystery of God, the plan hidden for ages but now revealed in Christ. Through this Christophany, he saw that the end of the ages had begun, since Christ's resurrection was the first fruits of the general resurrection of the dead. Paul's personal experience of God's saving grace, then, has christological, soteriological, ecclesiological, ethical, and eschatological implications.[27] I am not claiming that Paul fully comprehended all these realities at the moment of his call and conversion. I assume that he grew in his understanding of the Christophany, the gospel, and his commission. But I am suggesting that inasmuch as the Pauline writings and the Acts of the Apostles draw a relation between Paul's Christophany, gospel, and commission, he developed his understanding of Christ, Christ's benefits, the church, the moral life, and the parousia in light of his call and conversion.

Building on this chapter, the chapters that follow will explore how the Pauline letters develop the experience of the saving grace that Paul encountered at the Damascus road Christophany in terms of Christology, soteriology, ecclesiology, the moral life, eschatology, and theology.

---

27. The essays in the volume edited by Longenecker *(The Road from Damascus)* draw out the relationship between Paul's call on the one hand and his understandings of Christology, eschatology, Gentile mission, justification, reconciliation, covenant theology, the Mosaic law, the Holy Spirit, women, and ethics, on the other.

For Further Reading

Becker, Jürgen. *Paul: Apostle to the Gentiles.* Louisville: Westminster John Knox, 1993. Pages 57-81.

Dietzfelbinger, T. L. *Die Berufung des Paulus als Ursprung seiner Theologie.* Neukirchen-Vluyn: Neukirchener Verlag, 1985.

Donaldson, Terence L. "Zealot and Convert: The Origin of Paul's Christ-Torah Antithesis." *CBQ* 51 (1989): 655-82.

Dunn, James D. G. *Beginning from Jerusalem.* Christianity in the Making, vol. 2. Grand Rapids: Eerdmans, 2009. Pages 322-77.

―――. "'A Light to the Gentiles', or 'The End of the Law'? The Significance of the Damascus Road Christophany for Paul." Pages 89-107 in *Jesus and the Law: Studies in Mark and Galatians.* Louisville: Westminster, 1990.

―――. "Paul's Conversion — A Light to Twentieth Century Disputes." Pages 347-65 in *The New Perspective on Paul.* Revised Edition. Grand Rapids: Eerdmans, 2005.

Finny, Philip. *The Origins of Pauline Pneumatology.* WUNT 194; Tübingen: Mohr Siebeck, 2005.

Gaventa, Beverly R. *From Darkness to Light: Aspects of Conversion in the New Testament.* Philadelphia: Fortress, 1986.

Hengel, Martin. "The Stance of the Apostle Paul toward the Law in the Unknown Years between Damascus and Antioch." Pages 75-103 in *Justification and Variegated Nomism.* The Paradoxes of Paul, vol. 2, ed. D. A. Carson, Peter T. O'Brien, and Mark A. Seifrid. Grand Rapids: Baker Academic, 2004.

Hengel, Martin, and Anna Maria Schwemer. *Paul between Damascus and Antioch: The Unknown Years.* Louisville: Westminster John Knox, 1997.

Kim, Seyoon. *The Origin of Paul's Gospel.* 2nd ed. Tübingen: Mohr-Siebeck, 1984.

―――. *Paul and the New Perspective: Second Thoughts on the Origin of Paul's Gospel.* Grand Rapids: Eerdmans, 2002.

Longenecker, Richard N., ed. *The Road from Damascus: The Impact of Paul's Conversion on His Life, Thought, and Ministry.* Grand Rapids: Eerdmans, 1997.

Munck, Johannes. "The Call." Pages 11-35 in *Paul and the Salvation of Mankind.* London: SCM, 1959.

Newman, Carey C. *Paul's Glory-Christology: Tradition and Rhetoric.* NovTSup 69. Leiden: Brill, 1992. Pages 165-212.

O'Brien, Peter T. "Was Paul Converted?" Pages 361-91 in *Justification and Varie-*

gated Nomism. The Paradoxes of Paul, vol. 2, ed. D. A. Carson, Peter T. O'Brien, and Mark A. Seifrid. Grand Rapids: Baker Academic, 2004.

Räisänen, Heikki. "Paul's Conversion and the Development of His View of the Law." *NTS* 33 (1987): 404-19.

Schnelle, Udo. *Apostle Paul: His Life and Theology.* Grand Rapids: Baker Academic, 2003. Pages 87-102.

Segal, A. F. *Paul the Convert: The Apostolate and Apostasy of Saul the Pharisee.* New Haven: Yale University Press, 1990.

Stendahl, Krister. "Call Rather than Conversion." Pages 7-23 in *Paul among Jews and Gentiles and Other Essays.* Philadelphia: Fortress, 1976.

Stuhlmacher, P. "'The End of the Law': On the Origin and Beginning of Pauline Theology." Pages 134-54 in *Reconciliation, Law, and Righteousness: Essays in Biblical Theology.* Philadelphia: Fortress, 1986.

3. Christ the Embodiment of God's Saving Grace

Introduction

In the last chapter I proposed that Pauline theology begins with the experience of God's saving grace that informed Paul's call and conversion. At that moment God revealed his Son to Paul, thereby changing and transforming the life of the former persecutor. The one who previously understood himself in relation to the law now defined his life in terms of Christ, whom he experienced as the embodiment of God's grace. The centrality of God's grace for Paul is apparent from the greeting of grace that he regularly extends to the recipients of his letters: "Grace to you and peace from God our Father and the Lord Jesus Christ" (1 Cor 1:3).[1] Given the importance of this theme in Pauline theology, in this chapter I will consider the Pauline understanding of Christ as the embodiment of God's saving grace.[2]

Those who study Pauline Christology face two challenges: the occasional nature of the Pauline correspondence and its focus on soteriology. The first of these challenges is the more difficult. Paul (and those who may have written in his name) wrote as occasion demanded. Rather than develop a systematic theology, then, the Pauline letters respond to the ques-

---

1. This greeting is found in every Pauline letter. In 1 and 2 Timothy, however, the greeting includes a reference to "mercy." "Peace" has in view the reconciliation that God has effected in Christ, whereas "grace" points to the extraordinary favor God extends to humanity in Christ.

2. I refer to "the Pauline understanding of Christ" rather than to "Paul's understanding of Christ" since my purpose is to summarize the Christology of the Pauline corpus rather than reconstruct the Christology of the historical person Paul.

tions and needs of their audiences.[3] This means that even when the letters introduce new themes, they presuppose that their audiences have already been instructed in the faith. Their purpose, then, is not so much to teach and instruct as it is to remind and encourage. Given the occasional nature of the Pauline correspondence, it is not surprising that these letters present Christ in different ways. For example, whereas the Corinthian correspondence highlights the crucified Christ who is the first fruits of the general resurrection of the dead, the letter to the Philippians presents him in terms of his self-abasement and exaltation. And whereas Colossians and Ephesians speak of the cosmic Christ who is the head of the body that is the church, the Pastoral letters present Christ as the epiphany or manifestation of the Savior God. Consequently, apart from their common use of "Christ" and "Lord," the Pauline Epistles can portray Christ in varying ways. Given the occasional nature of Paul's correspondence, then, we will not find a systematic presentation of the person of Christ, although we will discover reoccurring themes and emphases.

The second challenge to Pauline Christology may be surprising to some. Despite the central role that Christ plays in the Pauline correspondence, there is little discussion about his identity (Christology). Instead the focus is on the nature and benefits of Christ's redemptive work (soteriology). There are two reasons for this. First, there appears to have been surprisingly little controversy in the Pauline communities about the person and identity of Christ.[4] The recipients of Paul's letters confessed that the one in whom they put their faith was the Son of God and exalted Lord. Second, although Paul's converts confessed Jesus as their Lord and Messiah, they did not always appreciate the full significance of his death and resurrection for their lives. Consequently, Paul and those who may

3. This statement about the occasional nature of the Pauline correspondence is true for the disputed as well as for the non-disputed correspondence. It even applies to Ephesians, which, on first reading, may appear to have little or no specific occasion. A closer reading, however, suggests that Paul (or the one writing in his name) is addressing a new generation of believers who are in danger of forgetting their relationship to Israel.

4. At least this appears to be the situation from what can be known from the letters themselves. We do not find controversies about the person of Christ as much as misunderstandings about the meaning and significance of his work. Gordon Fee (*Pauline Christology: An Exegetical-Theological Study* [Peabody: Hendrickson, 2007], 3-5, here pp. 3 and 4) notes that the Pauline letters "are filled with christological presuppositions." He writes that we are seldom reading "Paul's *argued* Christology, but rather his *assumed* Christology, and in these letters a Christology that he also assumed on the part of his readers." In other words, Paul seems to assume that he and his readers share a common Christology.

have written in his name found it necessary to remind their audiences of the significance of God's redemptive work in Christ. For example, Galatians presents Christ's redemptive work in terms of justification in order to combat those who would require the Galatians to be circumcised and adopt a Jewish way of life *in addition* to believing in Christ. For its part, Colossians presents Christ's redemptive work in terms of cosmic reconciliation in order to deal with a teaching that would require obedience and subservience to powers that were thought to control the cosmos. The Pauline corpus, then, is a much richer field for harvesting soteriology than it is for reaping Christology.[5]

Although I have made a distinction between Christology and soteriology, these topics are closely related to each other.[6] The benefits of Christ's redemptive work cannot be separated from his person any more than his person can be separated from his redemptive benefits. If Jesus were not the Christ, the Son of God, his crucifixion would not have been a redemptive death. But inasmuch as he is the Son of God whom God sent into the world, his death has a salvific value, which I will discuss in the next chapter.

In this chapter, my focus is on what the Pauline Corpus teaches about the identity of Christ. The chapter has three parts: (1) How Paul Identifies the One Whom He Proclaims, (2) The One Who Preexisted and Exists with God, and (3) The Corporate Christ.

How Paul Identifies the One Whom He Proclaims

Although Paul identifies the one whom he proclaims in several ways, he is not as interested in christological titles as are the Synoptic writers.[7] Pre-

---

5. In contrast to the Pauline letters, the Synoptic Gospels give more attention to the person of Christ than to his redemptive work. Although they are interested in soteriology, they are more intent on showing that Jesus is the Messiah, the Son of God, the one who will return as the glorious Son of Man. In the Johannine Gospel, Christology and soteriology are more integrated since anyone who believes that Jesus is the one whom the Father sent into the world has already passed from death to life.

6. This is a point made by Arland J. Hultgren, *Christ and His Benefits: Christology and Redemption* (Philadelphia: Fortress, 1987), 4. He writes: "Christology can hardly be thought to have developed in a speculative vacuum simply for its own sake. . . . It developed rather through a process of seeking to explicate the fullness of who Christ is in light of the benefits which he has secured for humanity. What he has done, his function or work, gives rise to questions of his person (ontological christology)."

7. The Synoptic Gospels employ their narratives to show that Jesus is the Messiah, the

supposing that the recipients of his letters know *who* Christ is, Paul proclaims *what* God has done in Christ so that his converts can grow in their new life. Consequently, he uses titles to talk about Christ rather than to make specific christological statements. For example, he speaks of Jesus as "the Son of God" to highlight the unique relationship Jesus enjoys with God, which gives meaning and significance to his suffering and death. Likewise, he tends to employ "Christ," "Jesus Christ," and "Christ Jesus" when he speaks of Jesus' death and resurrection. Finally, he calls Jesus "the Lord" or "our Lord" to highlight the exalted status of the risen one to whom believers submit themselves. In addition to referring to Jesus as "Son," "Christ," and" Lord," Paul identifies him in relationship to Adam, Abraham, David, the church, creation, and redemption. Accordingly, Paul speaks of Christ as the eschatological Adam, the singular seed of Abraham, the royal descendant of David, the head of the body that is the church, the firstborn of creation, and the firstborn from the dead. On a few occasions, he also identifies Jesus as savior, and possibly as God. In this section, I will deal with three ways that the Pauline letters most frequently identify Jesus: "Son," "Christ," and "Lord."

Son/Son of God

The designation of Jesus as Son or Son of God does not occur frequently in the Pauline letters, nor is it present in every letter. Moreover, when Paul does use this title, he tends to speak of "his Son" or "his own Son," employing "the Son of God" only four times.[8] Despite the relatively few times that the language of Son/Son of God occurs in the Pauline writings, it plays a central role in Paul's preaching. For example in 2 Cor 1:19-20 he writes: "For the Son of God, Jesus Christ, whom we proclaimed among you, Silvanus and Timothy and I, was not 'Yes and No'; but in him it is always 'Yes.' For in him every one of God's promises is a 'Yes.'" In this text, which views Christ

---

Son of God, the Son of David, the Son of Man, the Lord. While they are interested in soteriology, their soteriology is subservient to their Christology and less developed than Paul's soteriology. The Johannine Gospel has a more integrated Christology and soteriology.

8. The use of "Son" and "Son of God" is found in the following texts of the Pauline corpus: "his Son" (Rom 1:3), "Son of God" (v. 4), "his Son" (v. 9), "his Son" (5:10), "his own Son" (8:3), "his Son" (v. 29), "his own Son" (v. 32), "his Son" (1 Cor 1:9), "the Son" (15:28), "the Son of God" (2 Cor 1:19), "his Son" (Gal 1:16), "the Son of God" (2:20), "his Son" (4:4), "his Son" (v. 6), "the Son of God" (Eph 4:13), "his beloved Son" (Col 1:13), "his Son" (1 Thess 1:10).

as the culmination of God's promises, Paul indicates that "the Son of God," whom he identifies as Jesus Christ, is the content of his preaching. Consequently, even though the title does not occur frequently in Paul's letters, it is evident that when he speaks of Jesus Christ he is referring to the Son of God. The text of Gal 1:16 makes a similar point. Reflecting on the significance of his apostolic call, Paul says that God revealed his Son to him so that he might proclaim God's Son among the Gentiles. Like 2 Cor 1:19 this text shows that the subject of Paul's preaching is the Son of God. The manner in which Paul describes his gospel makes a similar point. He proclaims that he has been set aside for "the gospel of God" (Rom 1:1), which he equates with "the gospel of his Son" (1:9). God's own good news, which Paul proclaims, is the good news *about* God's Son, Jesus Christ.

But what does Paul mean when he calls Jesus the Son of God? In the Hellenistic world the title pointed to certain individuals who were viewed as divine because of the power they manifested in their lives. Rudolf Bultmann maintained that "Son of God" took on a new meaning in the Hellenistic churches vis-à-vis its use in the Old Testament. "Now it comes to mean *the divinity of Christ, his divine nature,* by virtue of which he is differentiated from the human sphere; it makes the claim that Christ is of divine origin and is filled with divine 'power.'"[9] While the title does point to Jesus' divinity, others have argued — correctly in my view — that Paul's understanding of the title is more indebted to Israel's sacred writings, in which "son of God" was applied to angelic beings (Gen 6:2), the people of Israel (Exod 4:22-23; Hos 11:1), the king (2 Sam 7:14; Ps 2:7), and the suffering righteous one vindicated by God (Wisdom 2 and 5).[10] The people of Israel and the kings of Israel were called God's son in an adoptive sense because they were chosen and set apart for service to God, which required the absolute obedience and loyalty of a son. The case of the suffering righteous adds a new dimension. Oppressed by the wicked because of their righteousness (Wis 2:12-20), the righteous are vindicated by God and numbered among the sons of God (5:5). Accordingly, whereas the Hellenistic understanding of Son of God focused on the manifestation of divine power in the individual, Israel's Scriptures highlight the concepts of call

9. Rudolf Bultmann, *The Theology of the New Testament,* 2 vols. (New York: Charles Scribner's Sons, 1951), 1:128-29.

10. This approach to the background of the title is adopted by Oscar Cullmann, *The Christology of the New Testament* (London: SCM, 1963), 271-75, and Leonhard Goppelt, *Theology of the New Testament,* vol. 2: *The Variety and Unity of the Apostolic Witness* (Grand Rapids: Eerdmans, 1982), 69-71.

and obedience and, in the Book of Wisdom, divine vindication. Although the background of Israel's sacred writings may not account for the whole of the Pauline understanding of Jesus' sonship (which includes suffering, death, and resurrection), it provides us with several concepts that occur in the Pauline letters but are absent from the Hellenistic understanding of "Son of God," namely, the call to mission, absolute loyalty and obedience to God, and divine vindication. A number of texts illustrate this point.

In his greeting to the Romans, Paul summarizes his gospel about God's Son in two ways. In terms of his human origin, the Son of God was "descended from David according to the flesh" (Rom 1:3); that is to say, the Son of God was the promised royal Messiah of David's line. In terms of his resurrection from the dead, however, he "was declared to be Son of God with power according to the Spirit of holiness" (1:4). While this may suggest that Jesus *became* the Son of God in virtue of his resurrection, the qualifying phrase "with power according to the spirit of holiness" *(en dynamei kata pneuma hagiōsynēs)* indicates otherwise. Paul means that the one who was already God's Son during his earthly life has been exalted and enthroned *in power*. Having obediently completed the mission entrusted to him, the Son has been raised from the dead. From this text it is clear that the manner in which Paul views sonship has little to do with the Hellenistic notion of divine sonship. Whereas the later emphasized the divine power in the earthly life of the "Son of God," the Pauline notion highlights God's vindication of his Son. By raising his Son from the dead, God publicly declares him to be *Son of God in power*. It is in virtue of his resurrection, then, that the Son of God reigns in power, as Colossians affirms when it says that God "rescued us from the power of darkness and transferred us into the kingdom of his beloved Son" (Col 1:13).

Several texts indicate that Paul does not restrict Jesus' sonship to the period after his resurrection. In Galatians he writes: "But when the fullness of time had come, God *sent* his Son, born of a woman, born under the law, in order to redeem those who were under the law, so that we might receive adoption as children" (Gal 4:4-5). This sending formula suggests that Paul views the Son as preexistent.[11] A similar formula occurs in Rom 8:3: "For God has done what the law, weakened by the flesh, could not do: by send-

---

11. Although some dispute this interpretation, arguing that Paul is simply referring to the mission that God bestowed on Jesus, the manner in which Paul emphasizes that the Son was born of a woman and born under the law suggests that he is highlighting the entrance of the preexistent Son into the world.

ing his own Son in the likeness of sinful flesh, and to deal with sin, he condemned sin in the flesh." In this formula the phrase "in the likeness of sinful flesh" approaches what later theology would call the incarnation, thereby highlighting the preexistence of the Son.[12]

It is in light of these sending formulas that I now interpret three texts about the Son that speak of his death. In the first, Paul writes: "For if while we were enemies, we were reconciled to God through the death of his Son, much more surely, having been reconciled, will we be saved by his life" (Rom 5:10). Here, the identification of Jesus as God's Son ("his Son") highlights the significance of his death. The one who died was not just another human being but one who stood in the closest possible relationship to God, a relationship as intimate as that between a father and his son. A similar text occurs in Rom 8:32: "He who did not withhold his own Son, but gave him up for all of us, will he not with him also give us everything else?" Once more Paul's statement derives its force by identifying Jesus as "God's own Son," a phrase that echoes the story of Abraham not withholding his own son (Gen 22:16). Whereas the first two statements point to the death of the Son as proof of God's love, the third is more personal. Aware of what Christ has done for him, Paul writes, "it is no longer I who live, but it is Christ who lives in me. And the life I now live in the flesh I live by faith in the Son of God, who loved me and gave himself for me" (Gal 2:20). The Son of God, then, is the one who loved Paul personally (as the Apostle now realizes in light of his call/conversion) and handed himself over for Paul's sake. This, of course, is the supreme expression of the grace of God that Paul experienced in Christ. In light of the sending formulas of Gal 4:4 and Rom 8:3, these three statements (Rom 5:10; 8:32; Gal 2:20) take on their full meaning: the one whom God did not spare and who handed himself over for others was the preexistent Son of God who faithfully carried out the mission God entrusted to him. This is why God vindicated and established him as *Son of God in power* by raising him from the dead.

In addition to these texts highlighting what the Son has done, Paul points to the future work of God's Son. In 1 Thess 1:10 he notes that the Thessalonians, having turned to the living God, now "wait for his Son from heaven, whom he raised from the dead." In 1 Cor 15:28, after speaking of Christ's resurrection and parousia, Paul reveals that when everything

---

12. The expression means that the Son entered into the fullness of the human condition so that he could deal with sin on its own battleground — the flesh. It does not mean that he became *like* a human being without becoming a human being.

has been subjected to the Son, "then the Son himself will also be subjected to the one who put all things in subjection under him, so that God may be all in all." The Son who was obedient to the point of dying on the cross will be subjected to God as an obedient son is subjected to his father. In Ephesians, Paul anticipates the moment when believers will "come to the unity of the faith and of the knowledge of the Son of God, to maturity, to the measure of the full stature of Christ" (Eph 4:13). Here, Ephesians presupposes that the Son of God has already attained the eschatological goal toward which believers strive. Rom 8:29 presents a similar idea: "For those whom he foreknew he also predestined to be conformed to the image of his Son, in order that he might be the firstborn within a large family."

The texts I have examined indicate that when the Pauline letters speak of Jesus as the Son of God they have the full scope of his "career" in view: his preexistence, his being sent into the world, his death on behalf of others, his enthronement in power at the resurrection, his present rule as God's Messiah, and the eschatological work he has yet to accomplish.

In addition to calling Christ the Son/Son of God, Paul frequently speaks of God as the Father of Jesus Christ. For example he writes "the God and Father of our Lord Jesus Christ" (Rom 15:6; Eph 1:3) and "the God and Father of the Lord Jesus" (2 Cor 1:3). Furthermore, in the openings of his letters he extends grace and peace from "God our Father *and* the Lord Jesus Christ." Although this second formula does not identify God as the Father of Jesus Christ as does the first, the references to God as Father in the Pauline letters presuppose that Jesus Christ is God's Son; for it is in virtue of Jesus' sonship that believers call God *Abba*, Father (Rom 8:15; Gal 4:6) and that they wait to be conformed "to the image of his Son" (Rom 8:29). The use of "Father" as a designation for God, then, is the result of Paul's firm conviction that Jesus is the Son of God. Stated negatively, if Paul did not view Jesus as the Son of God, he would not have called God "Father."

Christ/Messiah

Paul's use of "Christ" is puzzling and paradoxical.[13] Puzzling because, despite the frequency with which "Christ" occurs in the Pauline corpus, it is

13. For two seminal essays on Paul's use of "Christ," see Nils Alstrup Dahl, "The Messiahship of Jesus in Paul," in *The Crucified Messiah and Other Essays* (Minneapolis: Augsburg, 1974), 37-47, and Martin Hengel, "'Christos' in Paul," in *Between Jesus and Paul:*

difficult to determine the significance Paul gives to this term, which functions as a messianic title in the Gospels, Acts, 1 John, and Revelation but tends to be used as a name in the Pauline letters. Paradoxical because, even though Paul's conversion led him to proclaim that Jesus is the Messiah, he does not develop the messianic dimension of this name in his letters. Accordingly, most scholars agree that this term begins to take on the character of a name in the Pauline Corpus. This is not to say that Paul ignored or dispensed with its original meaning. Rom 9:5 indicates that he understood its messianic connotation, and Rom 1:3 and 2 Tim 2:8 witness to Jesus' Davidic descent. But as Nils Dahl notes, "it is not necessary for Paul's readers to know that *Christos* is a term filled with content and pregnant with meaning. Even if one understands Christ only to be a surname of Jesus, all the statements of the epistle make good sense."[14] And yet, it is evident that "Christ" is more than a surname for Paul since he can use "Jesus Christ" and "Christ Jesus" interchangeably. Moreover, although he speaks of "Jesus," "Jesus Christ," or "Christ Jesus" as Lord, he refers to "the Lord Christ" only in Rom 16:18 and Col 3:24.[15] As we shall see, "Christ" points to the one in whom God has carried out his redemptive work. Accordingly, just as "gospel" summarizes the content of Paul's preaching, so "Christ" summarizes the content of his Christology.[16]

"Christ" appears in a number of different combinations in the Pauline corpus: "Christ" occurs 211 times, "Jesus Christ" 25 times, "Christ Jesus" 78 times, "Lord Jesus Christ" 48 times, "Jesus Christ Lord" 5 times, and "Christ Jesus Lord" 7 times.[17] Here I limit my remarks to "Christ," "Jesus Christ," and "Christ Jesus."

Studies in the Earliest History of Christianity (Minneapolis: Fortress, 1983), 67-77. For an overview of the title "Messiah," see Cullmann, *The Christology of the New Testament*, 111-36, which should be supplemented by the background study Joseph A. Fitzmyer, *The One Who Is to Come* (Grand Rapids: Eerdmans, 2007).

14. Dahl, "The Messiahship of Jesus in Paul," 37.

15. Dahl, "The Messiahship of Jesus in Paul," 38.

16. Lucien Cerfaux (*Christ in the Theology of St. Paul* [New York: Herder and Herder, 1959], 480-81) highlights the significance of the term when he writes, "Surely, it ['Christ'] designates rather a heavenly being who was called 'Christ' in his pre-existence, and who was given the name Jesus during his life on earth while waiting to bear the name and title of Kyrios." On page 488, he notes: "When we speak of Jesus, we think of Christ in his mortal life, but when we speak of 'Lord' we think of his risen life and of his life in the community. When we mean the person whose history began in eternity and continued in his presence among us, we use the word 'Christ.'"

17. I have taken these statistics from Fee, *Pauline Christology,* 26.

Christ The Pauline letters employ "Christ" alone in statements that (1) have soteriological import, (2) identify Christ in some way, (3) describe his love and self-giving, or (4) establish an intimate relationship between him and believers by the formulas "in Christ" and "with Christ." Given the importance of these formulas, I will deal with them in a separate section.

On several occasions, Paul refers to Christ as the one who died for the sake of others, for example, "Christ died *for* the ungodly" (Rom 5:6), "Christ died *for* us" (v. 8), "*for* whom Christ died" (Rom 14:15; 1 Cor 8:11), "Christ died *for* our sins" (1 Cor 15:3). In one instance, when refuting those who would require his Gentile converts to be circumcised, Paul notes that if they could have been justified on the basis of legal observance then "Christ died for nothing" (Gal 2:21), the implication being that Christ's death was necessary to bring about the justification of sinners. Closely related to these statements are a number of others that identify "Christ" as the one whom God *raised* from the dead: "just as Christ was *raised* from the dead" (Rom 6:4), "Christ being *raised* from the dead" (v. 9), "he who *raised* Christ from the dead" (8:11), "but in fact Christ has been *raised* from the dead" (1 Cor 15:20), "God put this power to work in Christ when he *raised* him from the dead and seated him at his right hand in the heavenly places" (Eph 1:20), "remember Jesus Christ, *raised* from the dead, a descendant of David" (2 Tim 2:8). The manner in which Paul employs "Christ" in these texts is a constitutive element of his Christology: the one whom Paul calls "Christ" is the subject of God's redemptive work because he died for others, and God raised him from the dead. The distinctive character of the Messiah Paul proclaims, then, is his death and resurrection.

In addition to statements that focus on Christ's death and resurrection, Paul speaks of Christ as the agent of God's redemptive work: "God, who reconciled us to himself through Christ" (2 Cor 5:18), "in Christ God was reconciling the world to himself" (v. 19). In still other instances, Christ is the subject of this redemption, as when Paul writes: "Christ redeemed us from the curse of the law" (Gal 3:13), "for freedom Christ has set us free" (5:1), "Christ loved the church and gave himself up for her" (Eph 5:25). In other texts, Paul speaks of Christ in connection with the day of redemption, "the day of Christ" (Phil 1:10; 2:16), when Christ will be revealed (Col 3:4). In all of these examples, the manner in which Paul uses "Christ" indicates that the one who bears this name is the one whom God designated or "anointed" (the root meaning of "Christ") to bring salvation. "Christ" is more than the name of an individual: it is the name of God's eschatological agent of salvation.

On several occasions Paul employs "Christ" in statements that identify him in a particular way. Although these are not formal christological definitions of who Christ is, they indicate how Paul understood the significance of "Christ." Since I will discuss some of them at greater length below, here I simply list and briefly comment on them. In a statement that has important implications for Paul's understanding of Christ's role in Israel's history, Paul affirms that "Christ is *the end of the law* so that there may be righteousness for everyone who believes" (Rom 10:4). When explaining the paradoxical nature of the message of Christ crucified, Paul identifies Christ as *"the power of God and the wisdom of God"* (1 Cor 1:24). In a moral exhortation in which he calls upon the Corinthians to live in a way appropriate to their calling, he writes, "for our *paschal lamb,* Christ, has been sacrificed (1 Cor 5:7). When recounting the period of Israel's wandering in the wilderness, Paul provides an allegorical interpretation of the rock from which Israel drank: "For they drank from the spiritual rock that followed them, and *the rock* was Christ" (10:4). In his discussion of the resurrection from the dead, he calls Christ *"the first fruits"* of those who will be raised from the dead (15:23). When defending himself from those who portray his gospel as veiled and obscure, he writes, "In their case the god of this world has blinded the minds of the unbelievers, to keep them from seeing the light of the gospel of the glory of Christ, who is *the image of God*" (2 Cor 4:4). In Galatians he argues that God's promise to Abraham had a singular "offspring" in view. Identifying Christ as that offspring he writes: "Now the promises were made to Abraham and to *his offspring;* it does not say, 'And to offsprings,' as of many; but it says, 'And to your *offspring,*' that is, to one person, who is Christ" (Gal 3:16). When discussing the nature of marriage the Apostle identifies Christ as the head of the church, its Savior: "For the husband is the head of the wife just as Christ is *the head of the church,* the body of which he is the Savior" (Eph 5:23). Finally, when referring to the mystery of God, he identifies this mystery with Christ: "I want their hearts to be encouraged and united in love, so that they may have all the riches of assured understanding and have the knowledge of *God's mystery,* that is, Christ himself" (Col 2:2). Although some of these statements have greater christological import than others, all of them show that Paul could identify Christ in a variety of ways as the occasion required. Inasmuch as some of these statements focus on Christ's distinctive role in Israel's history (the singular offspring of Abraham, the end of the law) and others point to his distinctive relationship with God (power and wisdom of God, the image of God, the mystery of God), it is apparent that "Christ" designates the one in whom God's redemptive purpose finds it goal.

On a few occasions Paul employs "Christ" when he makes statements about Christ's love and self-giving behavior. In doing so his purpose is not so much to highlight the humanity of Christ as it is to point to the love and selflessness of God's redemptive agent, the one Paul calls "Christ." The one who is the subject of these statements, then, is the redemptive figure whom Paul portrays in his other statements about Christ. For example, in Rom 8:35 he refers to "the love of Christ," by which he means the love that Christ manifested for believers by dying for them. This is made explicit in Eph 5:2, where the Apostle exhorts believers to "live in love, as Christ loved us and gave himself up for us, a fragrant offering and sacrifice to God." At the conclusion of a long discussion, in which he arbitrates between opposing factions within the Roman congregations, Paul provides the Romans with an example to imitate: "for Christ did not please himself; but, as it is written, 'The insults of those who insult you have fallen on me'" (Rom 15:3). It is on the basis of Christ's own behavior that Paul then exhorts the Romans to "welcome one another, therefore, just as Christ has welcomed you, for the glory of God" (v. 7) and reminds them that "Christ has become a servant of the circumcised on behalf of the truth of God" (v. 8). Finally, when he must defend himself because some have called into question his apostolic integrity, Paul appeals to the Corinthians by "the meekness and gentleness of Christ" (2 Cor 10:1). Although Paul may be describing Jesus' human qualities in these cases, the context indicates that he is also highlighting the self-giving that characterizes the redemptive figure he calls "Christ."

To summarize, although Paul uses "Christ" as a name, the manner in which he employs it includes an understanding of its bearer as the eschatological agent of God's redemptive work.

Christ Jesus/Jesus Christ What has been said about "Christ" applies also to "Christ Jesus" and "Jesus Christ." As he does with "Christ," Paul employs these expressions to name God's redemptive agent. By coupling "Christ" with "Jesus," however, he indicates that God's redemptive agent, Christ, is one with the pre-Easter Jesus. Consequently, although the recipients of Paul's letters were already employing "Christ" as a way of naming Jesus, these formulas show that *Jesus* was God's anointed redemptive agent. Or to put it differently, God's anointed redemptive agent *is* Jesus. Moreover, since Paul can alternate between "Jesus Christ" and "Christ Jesus," it is apparent that "Christ" is more than a name, even when it functions as a name.

Although it is sometimes suggested that Paul employs "Christ Jesus" to highlight Jesus' messiahship, the sense being "Messiah-Jesus," the contexts in which this expression occurs do not support this claim. "Christ Jesus" has essentially the same meaning as "Jesus Christ." But whereas Paul tends to link "Jesus Christ" with "Lord," for example, "the Lord Jesus Christ," he rarely uses "Lord" with "Christ Jesus."[18] "Christ Jesus" and "Jesus Christ" appear to be Paul's way of affirming that Christ, who is God's redemptive agent, is Jesus.

The expression "Christ Jesus" frequently occurs with the preposition "in" *(en Christō Iēsou)*.[19] In such expressions "Christ Jesus" is the sphere where certain activity occurs, a topic to which I will return. For example, "the redemption that is *in Christ Jesus*" (Rom 3:24), "alive to God *in Christ Jesus*" (6:11), "no condemnation for those who are *in Christ Jesus*" (8:1).[20] In addition to phrases such as these, which present Christ as a sphere or realm in which things occur or in which believers dwell, Paul employs "Christ Jesus" when speaking of what Jesus has done. For example, in a phrase that encompasses the whole work of redemption, he writes: "It is Christ Jesus, who died, yes, who was raised, who is at the right hand of God, who indeed intercedes for us" (8:34). Such phrases occur even more frequently in the Pastorals: "Christ Jesus came into the world to save sinners" (1 Tim 1:15), "for there is one God; there is also one mediator between God and humankind, Christ Jesus, himself human" (2:5), "In the presence of God, who gives life to all things, and of Christ Jesus, who in his testimony before Pontius Pilate made the good confession, I charge you" (6:13), "the appearing of our Savior Christ Jesus, who abolished death and brought life and immortality to light through the gospel" (2 Tim 1:10).

Paul also employs "Jesus Christ" in several ways, the most frequent being in conjunction with a greeting of grace and peace. For example, when greeting the Romans he writes: "Grace to you and peace from God our Father and the Lord Jesus Christ" (Rom 1:7; see also 16:20; 1 Cor 1:3; 2 Cor 1:2; 13:13; Gal 1:3; 6:18). At other times, he employs "Jesus Christ" to

18. Exceptions to this are Rom 8:39; 1 Cor 15:31; Eph 3:11; Phil 3:8; 1 Tim 1:2, 12; 2 Tim 1:2.

19. See Rom 3:24; 6:11, 23; 8:1-2, 39; 15:17; 16:3; 1 Cor 1:2, 4, 30; 4:17; 15:31; 16:24; Gal 2:4; 3:14, 26, 28; Eph 1:1; 2:6-7, 10, 13; 3:6, 21; Phil 1:1, 26; 2:5; 3:3, 14; 4:7, 19, 21; Col 1:4; 1 Thess 2:14; 5:18; 1 Tim 1:14; 3:13; 2 Tim 1:1, 9, 13; 2:1, 10; 3:12, 15; Phlm 23.

20. Other examples are "to those who are sanctified *in Christ Jesus*" (1 Cor 1:2), "the freedom we have *in Christ Jesus*" (Gal 2:4), "raised us up with him and seated us with him in the heavenly places *in Christ Jesus*" (Eph 2:6), "the heavenly call of God *in Christ Jesus*" (Phil 3:14), and "This grace was given to us *in Christ Jesus before the ages began*" (2 Tim 1:9).

conclude important sections of his argument: "Thanks be to God through Jesus Christ our Lord! So then, with my mind I am a slave to the law of God, but with my flesh I am a slave to the law of sin" (Rom 7:25; also see 5:11, 21; 1 Cor 15:57). In other instances, "Jesus Christ" occurs in conjunction with "the name." For example, "Now I appeal to you, brothers and sisters, by the name of our Lord Jesus Christ" (1 Cor 1:10; see also 1:2; 6:11; Eph 5:20; 2 Thess 3:6). It also occurs when Paul speaks of faith: "the righteousness of God through faith in Jesus Christ for all who believe" (Rom 3:22; see also Gal 2:16; 3:22), or when he refers to the day of the Lord or his future manifestation: "He will also strengthen you to the end, so that you may be blameless on the day of our Lord Jesus Christ" (1 Cor 1:8, see also 1 Thess 5:23; 2 Thess 2:1). In the Pastorals, the "day of the Lord Jesus Christ" is Christ's "manifestation": "until the manifestation of our Lord Jesus Christ" (1 Tim 6:14; see also Tit 2:13). In his discussion of Adam and Christ, Paul compares Adam's transgression with the work of "the one man, Jesus Christ" (Rom 5:15, 17). Finally, on a few occasions he combines "Jesus Christ" with other important titles such as "Son of God" and "Savior." For example, he writes, "For *the Son of God,* Jesus Christ, whom we proclaimed among you" (2 Cor 1:19), "But our citizenship is in heaven, and it is from there that we are expecting a *Savior,* the Lord Jesus Christ" (Phil 3:20; see also Tit 3:6). Since it is often coupled with other titles or used in grace wishes, "Jesus Christ" has a solemn, liturgical sound in Paul's letters. Its christological content, however, is consonant with "Christ" and "Christ Jesus." Jesus Christ is God's redemptive agent, the crucified one (1 Cor 2:2; Gal 3:1); and even though it is not a title, it carries christological implications.

Lord The most frequent way in which the Pauline letters name Jesus, apart from designating him as "Christ," is "Lord." In doing so, they highlight the exalted status of the risen Christ, who has been appointed to his messianic office as *Son of God in power.* However, whereas "Son of God" defines the relationship between Christ and God, "Lord" defines the relationship between Christ and the believer. In relationship to God, Christ is God's Son; in relationship to believers, he is their exalted Lord.

Several texts point to the centrality of this title for Pauline Christology. The most important occurs in 1 Corinthians. Before embarking upon a discussion of whether believers can participate in sacral banquets that involve worshiping other gods, Paul summarizes what those who believe in Christ confess:

> Indeed, even though there may be so-called gods in heaven or on
>> earth
> — as in fact there are many gods and many lords —
> yet for us
> *there is one God, the Father,*
>> from whom are all things
>>> and for whom we exist,
>> *and one Lord, Jesus Christ,*
>>> through whom are all things
>>> and through whom we exist. (1 Cor 8:5-6)

In this creed-like statement, which he may have received from an earlier tradition, Paul echoes the opening of Israel's foundational creed, the *Shema,* "The Lord is our God, the Lord alone" (Deut 6:4, "Lord" referring to Yhwh). But instead of identifying God as the Lord/Yhwh, Paul identifies God as "the Father" and Jesus Christ as "the Lord," thereby applying a name to Jesus that belongs to God.

If we ask how Christ attained this exalted status, we must turn to the second part of the "Christ hymn" in Phil 2:6-11 for an answer. Because Christ Jesus abased himself to the point of death on the cross, God exalted him with the name that is above every other name, so that every tongue should "confess that Jesus Christ is Lord" (v. 11). The confession that Jesus Christ is Lord functions as a summary of Christian faith that only those under the power of God's Spirit can make (1 Cor 12:3). This confession leads to salvation "because if you confess with your lips that Jesus is Lord and believe in your heart that God raised him from the dead, you will be saved" (Rom 10:9). Because of the importance of this confession, Paul regularly speaks of "the Lord Jesus" or "Jesus our Lord."[21] Convinced that God exalted Jesus by raising him from the dead and bestowing upon him the name "Lord," believers confess one God, who is the Father, and one Lord, who is Jesus Christ, the one they now serve.

Leonhard Goppelt noted that in the ancient Near East "*ho kyrios* became a standard designation for the salvation deities that were looked upon by their devotees exclusively as their patrons and commanders."[22]

---

21. For examples of "the Lord Jesus," see 1 Cor 5:4; 11:23; 16:23; 2 Cor 1:14; 4:14; 11:31; Eph 1:15; Phil 2:19; Col 3:17; 1 Thess 2:15; 1 Thess 4:1, 2; 2 Thess 1:7; 2:8; Phlm 5. For examples of "Jesus our Lord," see Rom 4:24; 6:23; 8:39; 1 Cor 9:1; 15:31; Eph 3:11; 1 Tim 1:2, 12; 2 Tim 1:2.

22. Goppelt, *Theology of the New Testament,* 2:82.

Paul is aware of this understanding when he grants that "there may be so-called gods in heaven or on earth — as in fact there are many gods and many lords" (1 Cor 8:5). It is not this Hellenistic usage that defines his understanding of "Lord," however, but his Jewish background.[23] Two data point to this. First, when "Lord" occurs within a scriptural quotation in the Pauline letters, it usually refers to God. For example, Paul writes, "And as Isaiah predicted, 'If the Lord of hosts *(kyrios sabaōth)* had not left survivors to us, we would have fared like Sodom and been made like Gomorrah'" (Rom 9:29).[24] This use of "Lord" in Paul's scriptural quotations suggests that his Bible, the Septuagint, was already using *Kyrios* in place of the divine name (Yhwh) as a translation for *Adonai,* which replaced the divine name in the Hebrew Bible. However, when Paul employs "Lord" apart from a scriptural quotation, it usually refers to Christ. Thus the name Paul applies to Jesus, "Lord," is the same name that refers to God in Paul's scriptural quotations.

Second, at the end of 1 Corinthians Paul retains an Aramaic phrase with which his Gentile converts were familiar since he saw no need to translate it for them: *marana-tha* (1 Cor 16:22, "Our Lord, come!"). If this phrase was used in the worship services of Corinth as a prayer for the Lord's return (as many believe), this indicates that the Gentile Corinthians were invoking Jesus as "Lord" not as another Hellenistic god but as the one who bore the name *Adonai/Mari,* which Israel read in place of the divine name (Yhwh).

The Pauline letters tend to use "Lord" in three contexts.[25] First, they employ it in statements that anticipate the Lord's return, as in the prayer, *marana-tha,* "Our Lord, come!"[26] This is evident from the following examples: "on the day of our Lord Jesus Christ" (1 Cor 1:8), "do not pronounce judgment before the time, before the Lord comes" (4:5), "on the

23. Among the many scholars who make this point are Cullmann, *The Christology of the New Testament,* 195-237; Goppelt, *Theology of the New Testament,* 2:79-87; Joseph A. Fitzmyer, "New Testament *Kyrios* and *Maranatha* and Their Aramaic Background," in *To Advance the Gospel: New Testament Studies* (New York: Crossroad, 1981), 218-35; Larry W. Hurtado, *Lord Jesus Christ: Devotion to Jesus in Earliest Christianity* (Grand Rapids: Eerdmans, 2003), 108-18.

24. For other examples of this usage, see Rom 10:13; 11:34; 14:11; 15:11; 1 Cor 2:16; 3:20; 2 Cor 6:17; 2 Tim 2:19.

25. Here I am following the three categories identified by Hurtado, *Lord Jesus Christ,* 115-17.

26. The phrase could also be construed *maran-atha,* giving the sense, "Our Lord comes." But even if it is, it remains a statement about the Lord's parousia.

day of the Lord Jesus" (2 Cor 1:14), "the Lord is near" (Phil 4:5), "before our Lord Jesus at his coming" (1 Thess 2:19), "at the coming of our Lord Jesus" (3:13), "the Lord himself . . . will descend from heaven" (4:16), "as to the coming of our Lord Jesus Christ" (2 Thess 2:1), "until the manifestation of our Lord Jesus Christ" (1 Tim 6:14), "the crown of righteousness, which the Lord, the righteous judge, will give me on that day, and not only to me but also to all who have longed for his appearing" (2 Tim 4:8). While Paul also employs "Son" in an eschatological context (1 Thess 1:10) and speaks of "the day of Christ" (Phil 1:10; 2:16) and "the day of Jesus Christ" (1:6), he uses "Lord" more frequently since it is precisely as the exalted Lord that Christ, the Son of God, will return.

Second, since Jesus is the exalted Lord through whom they have been redeemed, believers owe him the obedience of faithful and loyal servants. Consequently, Paul employs "Lord" in the context of moral exhortation. When adjudicating between the strong and the weak at Rome, he reminds them: "If we live, we live to the Lord, and if we die, we die to the Lord; so then, whether we live or whether we die, we are the Lord's" (Rom 14:8). When exhorting the Corinthians to avoid immorality, he instructs them: "The body is meant not for fornication but for the Lord, and the Lord for the body" (1 Cor 6:13). In his instructions about marriage and virginity, he says: "I want you to be free from anxieties. The unmarried man is anxious about the affairs of the Lord, how to please the Lord" (7:32). In Ephesians, he urges his audience: "Try to find out what is pleasing to the Lord" (Eph 5:10), and "do not be foolish, but understand what the will of the Lord is" (v. 17). In Colossians, he prays for the recipients of his letter: "that you may lead lives worthy of the Lord, fully pleasing to him, as you bear fruit in every good work and as you grow in the knowledge of God" (Col 1:10). In the household code of that same letter (3:18-25), he employs "Lord" seven times to motivate the Colossians to conduct themselves in a way fitting and pleasing to the Lord. In these and other exhortations, Paul reminds believers that they must live as obedient servants of their exalted Lord who will return as their judge.

Third, "Lord" occurs in a number of liturgical settings, the most important in Paul's instructions about participation in the Lord's Supper (1 Cor 10:14-22; 11:17-34). Because they belong to the Lord, believers are not permitted to "drink the cup of the Lord and the cup of demons" (10:21). Those who participate in the table of demons (idol worship) disqualify themselves from the table of the Lord. The Lord's Supper is a participation in the body and blood of the Christ (10:16) whereby believers "proclaim the Lord's death until he comes" (11:26). At this supper believers remember the death of the Lord, whom Paul calls "the Lord of Glory" in 2:8, as they wait in fervent hope for his return. Little wonder, then, that the community cries out *marana-tha!*

To summarize, whereas "Son/Son of God" points to the unique relationship between Christ and God, and whereas "Christ" identifies Jesus as the redemptive agent of God's work, "Lord" highlights the exalted status of Christ whom the community serves as its Lord until he returns. The one whom Paul proclaims is Christ, the Son of God, who, in virtue of his exaltation, is Lord.

The One Who Preexisted and Exists with God

Having summarized Paul's preaching about Christ and highlighted the principal ways in which he names him, in this section I will focus on Christ as the one who preexisted and exists with God. To do so, I will look at three hymn-like passages in Philippians, Colossians, and 1 Timothy.

Although the primary concern of this section is the preexistence of Christ, it is important to note that the Pauline letters give greater attention to the post-existence of Christ than to his preexistence. This is not surprising, given the prominence of Christ's death and resurrection in the Pauline kerygma. The central proclamation of the Pauline gospel is that Jesus Christ is Lord because God raised him from the dead. Consequently, whereas the Four Gospels devote their attention to Jesus' life and ministry, which culminates in his death and resurrection, the Pauline gospel begins with his death and resurrection, proclaiming the risen Christ to be the first fruits of the general resurrection that will occur at the parousia (1 Cor 15:20, 23). When speaking of Christ's post-existence with God, the Pauline gospel makes the following points: Having been raised from the dead, the risen Christ is presently enthroned at God's right, where he intercedes for the elect. During this period, his enemies are being subdued under his feet, until he returns at the parousia to hand over the kingdom to his Father. Although this is a composite description of Christ's post-existence drawn from several texts, it is a fair summary of how the Pauline gospel views the one who now exists with God.

Paul's most extensive description of Christ's post-existence occurs in 1 Corinthians, in the midst of a discussion of the general resurrection of the dead.

> But each in his own order: Christ the first fruits, then at his coming those who belong to Christ. Then comes the end, when he hands over the kingdom to God the Father, after he has destroyed every ruler and every authority and power. For he must reign until he has put all his enemies under his feet. The last enemy to be destroyed is death. For "God has put all things in subjection under his feet." But when it says, "All things are put in subjection," it is plain that this does not include the one who put all things in subjection under him. When all things are subjected to him, then the Son himself will also be subjected to the one who put all things in subjection under him, so that God may be all in all. (1 Cor 15:23-28)

This scenario envisions three moments: Christ's resurrection, the parousia, which ushers in the resurrection of the dead, and the end when Christ hands over the kingdom to his Father. The first of these events has already occurred, and at the present time Christ is already ruling, subjecting every ruler, authority, and power to himself. When the last and greatest enemy — death — is destroyed at the general resurrection of the dead, then the Son will hand over the kingdom to the Father, and God will be all in all.

Other texts contribute to an understanding of Christ's post-existence. Romans 8 affirms that the one who is now enthroned at God's right is presently interceding for the elect: "It is Christ Jesus, who died, yes, who was raised, who is at the right hand of God, who indeed intercedes for us" (v. 34). Colossians alludes to Christ's royal enthronement in heaven: "So if you have been raised with Christ, seek the things that are above, where Christ is, seated at the right hand of God" (Col 3:1). Ephesians is more expansive in its description of Christ's enthronement, which extends over every cosmic power and makes Christ the head over all things for the sake of his body, which is the church.

> God put this power to work in Christ when he raised him from the dead and seated him at his right hand in the heavenly places, far above all rule and authority and power and dominion, and above every name that is named, not only in this age but also in the age to come. And he has put all things under his feet and has made him the head over all things for the church, which is his body, the fullness of him who fills all in all. (Eph 1:20-23)

Since Christ is the head of the body, which is the church, Ephesians can even affirm that those who belong to the body of the church are raised up and seated with Christ in the heavenly places (2:6). The post-existence of Christ, then, is a period of enthronement, during which Christ intercedes for the elect until he returns at the parousia for the general resurrection of the dead.[27]

In addition to speaking of Christ's post-existence, the Pauline letters intimate that Christ enjoyed a preexistence with God.[28] For example, the sending formulas of Rom 8:3 and Gal 4:4 suggest that God sent the preexistent Son into the world (see also 1 Tim 1:15). The creedal statement of 1 Cor 8:6 proclaims that the one Lord whom the community confesses is the one through whom all things exist. The statement that Paul makes in 2 Corinthians, in the midst of a discussion about the collection for Jerusalem, points in a similar direction: "For you know the generous act of our Lord Jesus Christ, that though he was rich, yet for your sakes he became poor, so that by his poverty you might become rich" (2 Cor 8:9). Paul does not make these statements to teach the Corinthians about the preexistence of Christ. Rather, he presupposes that they already know that the one who presently exists with God in resurrection glory preexisted with God prior to coming into the world.

The Pauline notion of preexistence takes center stage in three hymn-like passages: Phil 2:6-11; Col 1:15-20; and 1 Tim 3:16. As in the passages noted above, it is not the explicit purpose of these texts (which I shall call hymns) to teach or proclaim Christ's preexistence.[29] In every instance the hymn plays a particular role in the letter in which it is embedded. For example, Paul employs the Philippians hymn to provide believers with a pattern of behavior for their lives. He introduces the Colossians hymn to combat certain teachers at Colossae whose doctrine he opposes. And he

27. While Ephesians and Colossians highlight Christ's enthronement at God's right, they do not explicitly speak of him interceding for the elect, nor do they speak of the general resurrection that will occur when he returns.

28. Whereas the Pauline conviction of Christ's post-existence is the logical outcome of the Pauline gospel of Christ's resurrection, the origin of the Pauline teaching on the preexistence of Christ is more difficult to determine. On the one hand, it is possible that Paul inherited this teaching from earlier tradition. On the other, he may have developed it on the basis of his understanding of Christ's post-existence: the one who presently exists with God must have already existed with God.

29. While it is likely that these passages are hymns that Paul (or those who wrote in his name) inherited, it is also possible that Paul or the authors of these letters composed these passages or edited earlier traditions. Given their poetic and hymn-like quality, I refer to them as hymns. My interest, however, is not in their prehistory but in the role they play in their canonical settings.

includes the hymn in 1 Timothy to remind Timothy of the mystery he is to proclaim. In each case, the preexistence of Christ is not a new teaching but something with which Paul's audience is familiar.

In the Form of God

The Philippians hymn (2:6-11) occurs in the middle of the letter, after Paul relates his current circumstances (1:12-26) and calls the community to live in accordance with the gospel it professes so that it can participate in his struggle (1:27-30). After summoning the Philippians to live as a united community (2:1-4) he calls on them to exhibit the attitude of Christ Jesus in their behavior toward each other (2:5).[30] The hymn that follows has two parts. In the first (vv. 6-8) Paul recounts the abasement of Christ Jesus. In the second (vv. 9-11) he describes Christ's exaltation. My concern is the first part of the hymn, in which Paul presents the self-abasement of the preexistent Christ.[31]

The first part of the hymn begins with a phrase that describes Christ's preexistent state: he was in the form of God (v. 6a). Paul immediately qualifies this by a statement that summarizes Christ's attitude: he did not regard equality with God as something to be exploited or insisted upon (v. 6b). Employing a strong adversative ("but"), the hymn insists that Christ emptied himself by taking the form of a slave. Qualifying this statement further, the hymn notes that he came in human likeness and was found to be in human form or appearance (v. 7). The hymn goes on to note that the one who took the form of a slave and came in human likeness abased himself to the point of death on a cross (v. 8). Thus the first half of the hymn moves from a description of Christ Jesus' original status of being in the form of and equal to God to his self-abasement, which resulted in

30. The text is notoriously difficult to translate since a verb must be supplied. For example, the NAB reads: "Have among yourselves the same attitude that is also yours in Christ Jesus." But the NET reads: "You should have the same attitude toward one another that Christ Jesus had." Whereas the former speaks of an attitude that belongs to the Philippians because they live in the sphere of Christ, the latter highlights Christ's own attitude. In my view, Paul is calling his audience to pattern their lives after the example of Christ's self-effacement. On this hymn, see Ralph P. Martin and Brian J. Dodd, eds., *Where Christology Began: Essays on Philippians 2* (Louisville: Westminster John Knox, 1998).

31. I speak of "Christ Jesus" as the subject of the hymn since "Christ Jesus" (v. 5) is the immediate referent of the pronoun "who" (v. 6).

his being in human likeness and appearance, in the form of a slave, to the point of dying on the cross. The movement between these two points (being in the form of God and taking on the form of a slave) is the result of a deliberate choice by Christ Jesus not to insist on his equality with God but to relinquish his divine prerogatives and abase himself.

In writing that Christ Jesus was "in the form of God" *(en morphḗ theou)* and that he was "equal to God" *(isa theǭ)*, Paul implies that the one whom he calls "Christ Jesus" already existed with God. In proclaiming that Christ did not regard this equality as something to be exploited *(harpagmon hēgēsato)* but emptied himself *(heauton ekenōsen)* by taking on the form of a slave *(morphēn doulou)*, Paul affirms what later theology would call the incarnation. This self-emptying or kenosis of Christ means that the one who was equal to God refused to insist on his divine status so that he could fully share in the nature and form of being human.[32] Finally, by saying that Christ Jesus came in human likeness *(en homoiōmati anthrōpōn)* and was found in human form *(schēmati heuretheis hōs anthrōpos)*, Paul does not mean that Christ appeared to be human but was not. Rather, the outward form points to and reveals the inner reality of the one who bears it. To say that Christ had the outward form of a slave, then, is to affirm that he fully participated in the human condition. And to affirm that he had the outward form of God is to say that he fully participated in the reality of God.

To summarize, although the Philippians hymn does not set out to explain or prove Christ's preexistence, it presupposes the preexistence of the one who made his appearance in human flesh. Unless one posits some notion of preexistence here, it is difficult to understand what the hymn means by Christ's self-abasement.

The Firstborn of Creation

Like the Philippians hymn, the Colossians hymn (1:15-20) plays an important role in the letter in which it is embedded. Paul writes to refute a teaching, which he views as a philosophy that is an empty deceit (2:8). The pro-

---

32. This does not mean that Christ Jesus emptied himself of his godly state so that he could no longer be called God's Son. If that were so, there would be no incarnation or redemption. Christ's self-emptying is his refusal to insist on and exploit his prerogative of being equal to God. This is clear from the way Paul encourages the Philippians to regard others as more important than themselves (Phil 2:3-4).

ponents of this teaching are urging the Colossians to adopt certain ascetic practices so that they can worship or enter into the worship of beings that Paul calls "the elemental spirits of the universe" (vv. 20-23). In response to this threat he reminds the Colossians of the cosmic scope of Christ's work, which has overcome the power of these elemental spirits. The hymn is at the heart of Paul's argument.

In introducing the hymn, Paul identifies God's "beloved Son" as the subject of what will follow: "He [God] has rescued us from the power of darkness and transferred us into the kingdom of his beloved Son, in whom we have redemption, the forgiveness of sins" (1:13-14). The hymn, which follows, has two parts. In the first, with which I am primarily concerned, Paul speaks of the work of the preexistent Son in the order of creation (vv. 15-18a). In the second, he refers to the Son's work in the order of redemption (vv. 18b-20). As with the Philippians hymn, it is not the purpose of this hymn to provide the Colossians with a doctrine of preexistence. Paul assumes that the preexistence of Christ is something with which the Colossians are familiar. But whereas the Philippians hymn focuses on the attitude of Christ, the Colossians hymn highlights what Christ has done.

The first part of the hymn begins with a statement that makes two claims about God's "beloved Son." First, he is the image of the invisible God; second, he is the firstborn of creation (v. 15). Having identified the Son in relationship to God and creation, the hymn describes the Son's role in three ways: *in him* all things were created, *through him* all things were created, *for him* all things were created (v. 16). Next, Paul makes two more statements about the relationship of the Son to creation: the Son is before all things, and in him everything holds together (v. 17). Thus the Son is the beginning and the end of creation. The first part of the hymn ends by relating the Son to the church: the Son is the head of the body, which is identified as the church (v. 18a).

The claims that the Colossians hymn makes for the Son echo what Paul writes in 1 Cor 8:6: "yet for us there is one God, the Father, from whom are all things and for whom we exist, and one Lord, Jesus Christ, through whom are all things and through whom we exist." Colossians, however, goes further in its description of Christ's role in creation by insisting that "all things in heaven and on earth . . . , things visible and invisible, whether thrones or dominions or rulers or powers" (Col 1:16) were created in, through, and for the Son. In calling the Son the "image of the invisible God" *(eikōn tou theou tou aoratou)*, the hymn affirms that the Son is the very likeness, the exact representation of God, a concept to which the second part of the hymn refers when it affirms that "all the fullness" (*pan to plērōma,* v. 19) was pleased to dwell in him. In 2:9 this fullness is described as "the whole fullness of deity." Finally, in calling the Son "the firstborn" (*prōtotokos*) of all creation, Colossians employs the metaphor of the firstborn son to affirm the preeminent status of the Son. Just as a firstborn son enjoys a status of preeminence in a human family, so the beloved Son is preeminent because he is the agent of God's creation.

To summarize, whereas the Philippians hymn employed preexistence as the starting point of its description of Christ Jesus' abasement, the Colossians hymn uses preexistence to show the preeminence of the Son over the order of creation, thereby disqualifying every appeal to the elemental spirits.

Revealed in the Flesh

1 Tim 3:16 provides another example of a hymn-like passage in which Paul (or someone writing in his name) appears to be drawing from material already familiar to his audience. Like the hymns in Philippians and Colossians, this passage is closely related to the overall argument of the letter, in which the Apostle instructs his delegate to combat false doctrine with the sound teaching that Paul has entrusted to him (1 Tim 1:3; 6:20). Having provided Timothy with instructions about how people should behave in the household of God (3:14-15), Paul introduces the hymn in this way: "Without any doubt, the mystery of our religion is great" (v. 16), thereby indicating that what he is about to say is a summary of this mystery.[33]

The hymn that follows consists of three strophes, each composed of two contrasting lines.

He was revealed in flesh,
    vindicated in spirit,

seen by angels,
    proclaimed among Gentiles,

---

33. The word that is translated here as "religion" (*eusebeia*) occurs frequently in the Pastoral Epistles (1 Tim 2:2; 3:16; 4:7, 8; 6:3, 5, 6, 11; 2 Tim 3:5; Tit 1:1). BDAG defines it as "awesome respect accorded to God, *devoutness, piety, godliness.*" In the Pastorals, this "awesome respect" is the result of the way in which God has been manifested in Christ Jesus.

believed in throughout the world,
    taken up in glory.

Although the subject of this passage ("he") is not identified, the context leaves no doubt that the subject is Christ Jesus, who "came into the world to save sinners" (1:15), the one mediator between God and humankind, who was truly human and "gave himself as a ransom for all" (2:6). In affirming that Christ Jesus was "revealed in flesh" *(ephanerōthē en sarki),* the hymn suggests what later theology calls the incarnation, which presupposes some form of preexistence. In saying that Christ was "vindicated in spirit" *(edikaiōthē en pneumati),* the hymn appears to have in view the resurrection, the moment when God vindicated the crucified Christ. The first strophe can be summarized in this way: the preexistent Christ was manifested in the flesh when he became human. Although Christ was rejected and put to death, God vindicated him by raising him from the dead. Accordingly, the one who made his appearance in the realm of the flesh now lives in the realm of God.

The second strophe affirms that the vindicated Christ was seen by the angels before being preached to the Gentiles. Thus whereas the first strophe moves from the realm of the flesh to the realm of the Spirit, the second begins in the realm of the Spirit and moves to the realm of the flesh where the vindicated Christ is preached among the Gentiles. The third strophe begins where the second ends, in the realm of the flesh. Having been believed in throughout the world, Christ Jesus is taken up into glory. The hymn can be outlined in this way:

The incarnation of the preexistent Christ
    The resurrection of Christ

The presentation of the risen Christ to the angels
    The proclamation of the risen Christ to the Gentiles

Faith in Christ throughout the world
    The ascension of Christ

The manner in which the hymn orders these events is not chronological since preaching about Christ begins after his ascension. By placing the ascension at the conclusion of the final strophe, however, the hymn establishes a contrast between Christ's appearance or descent on the one hand,

and his enthronement or ascent on the other hand.[34] Accordingly, remarks about the appearance of Christ (his descent) and his ascension (his ascent) bracket this hymn.

The appearance of the preexistent Christ in the flesh stands at the heart of "the mystery of our religion." Paul also refers to this appearance or epiphany in 2 Tim 1:9-10, when he writes: "who [God] saved us and called us with a holy calling, not according to our works but according to his own purpose and grace. This grace was given to us in Christ Jesus before the ages began, but it has now been revealed through the appearing *(epiphaneias)* of our Savior Christ Jesus, who abolished death and brought life and immortality to light through the gospel." Whereas the Paul of the Pastorals normally employs *epiphaneia* when referring to Christ's final appearance (1 Tim 6:14; 2 Tim 4:1, 8; Tit 2:13; see also 2 Thess 2:8), here he uses it in reference to the first appearance of Christ Jesus, whom he identifies as "our Savior."[35] Thus 1 and 2 Timothy present their understanding of Christ's preexistence within the context of an epiphany Christology: the preexistent Christ who appeared in the flesh will appear in glory at the end of the ages.

To summarize, the notion of preexistence in the Pauline letters is not as developed as it is in the Fourth Gospel. Whereas the Gospel of John grounds its understanding of preexistence in an explicit statement about the incarnation ("the word became flesh"), this is not the case in the Pauline letters. To be sure, they proclaim that God sent his Son into the world and the Son fully entered into the human condition. But there is no explicit statement of an incarnation as there is in the Fourth Gospel. In my view, the concepts of preexistence and incarnation have not been fully developed in the Pauline corpus. The reason for this may be the different theological starting points of the Johannine and Pauline traditions. Whereas the former begins with the incarnation of the preexistent Word in

34. This is reminiscent of Eph 4:9: "When it says, 'He ascended,' what does it mean but that he had also descended into the lower parts of the earth?"

35. "Savior" occurs frequently in the Pastorals, sometimes in reference to God (1 Tim 1:1; 2:3; 4:10; Tit 1:3; 2:10; 3:4), other times in reference to Christ (2 Tim 1:10; Tit 1:4; 2:13; 3:6). Tit 2:13 is a disputed text since it can be read as "our great God, and our Savior Jesus Christ" or "our great God and Savior Jesus Christ," the latter reading calling Christ "God." Whereas Fee (*Pauline Christology*, 440-48) maintains that Paul does not call Christ "God" here, I (*New Testament Christology* [Louisville: Westminster John Knox, 1999], 170-71) have argued that he does. However one construes the text, it is significant that the Pastorals apply the same title to Christ as to God, namely "Savior."

order to understand the death and resurrection of Christ, the latter begins with the death and resurrection of Christ, in light of which it begins to think about the preexistence of Christ.

The Corporate Christ

Thus far we have considered Christ as an individual: the preexistent Son of God, the exalted Lord. The most significant aspect of Pauline Christology, however, may be the manner in which the Pauline letters present Christ as a corporate figure in whom believers live and dwell.[36] Thus in addition to believing *in* Christ, believers dwell *in* Christ. In this section, I will look at this notion from two vantage points: (1) Paul's portrayal of Christ as the eschatological Adam, the New Human Being, and (2) Paul's conviction that believers live *in* and *with* Christ.

Eschatological Adam/New Human Being

Paul's Adam Christology is grounded in his Damascus road experience, that moment when God revealed his Son to him and he knew that the crucified one had been raised from the dead. Although we cannot know with historical certitude what Paul saw or experienced, the Acts of the Apostles and the Pauline corpus testify that he encountered the risen and glorified Christ. On the basis of that experience, he eventually understood that the crucified one was the "first fruits" of the general resurrection of the dead (1 Cor 15:20, 23), "the Lord of glory" (2:8), "the image of God" (2 Cor 4:4).[37]

---

36. In describing this phenomenon, C. F. D. Moule (*The Origin of Christology* [Cambridge: Cambridge University Press, 1977], 47-96, here 53) writes: "A person who had recently been crucified, but is found to be alive, with 'absolute' life, the life of the age to come, and is found, moreover, to be an inclusive, all-embracing presence — such a person is beginning to be described in terms appropriate to nothing less than God himself."

37. I am not claiming that Paul immediately understood all this at the moment of his call and conversion. But I am suggesting that it was on the basis of this experience that he eventually called Christ "the Lord of glory," "the image of God," "the first fruits from the dead." On Paul's glory Christology, see Carey C. Newman, *Paul's Glory-Christology: Tradition and Rhetoric* (NovTSup 69; Leiden: Brill, 1992). For an extended discussion of the origins of Paul's understanding of Christ as the image of God, see Seyoon Kim, *The Origin of Paul's Gospel* (2nd ed.; Tübingen: Mohr-Siebeck, 1984), 137-268.

Paul identifies Christ as the image of God when he draws a comparison between the glorious ministry of the old covenant that Moses exercised and the surpassing glory of his own new covenant ministry (2 Cor 2:14–4:6). In that discussion, Paul describes the new situation in which the recipients of the new covenant ministry find themselves: "And all of us, with unveiled faces, seeing the glory of the Lord [Christ] as though reflected in a mirror, are being transformed into the same image from one degree of glory to another; for this comes from the Lord, the Spirit" (3:18). A few verses later, in response to a criticism that his gospel is veiled or obscure, he affirms that it is only veiled to those whose minds have been blinded by "the god of this world," who prevents them from seeing "the light of the gospel of the glory of Christ, who is the image of God" (4:4). He then concludes with an allusion to his Damascus road experience: "For it is the God who said, 'Let light shine out of darkness,' who has shone in our hearts to give the light of the knowledge of the glory of God in the face of Jesus Christ" (4:6). This last text suggests that it was on the basis of his Damascus road experience that Paul eventually understood that the risen Christ, now bathed in God's glory, is the image of God.[38] This Christology occurs in other texts as well. In Col 1:15, Paul identifies the beloved Son as the image of God. In Rom 8:29 he affirms that believers will be conformed to the image of God's Son; and in 1 Cor 15:49 he says that they will bear the image of the man from heaven.

Paul's understanding of Christ as the image of God, on whose face shines the glory of God, is closely related to his Adam Christology, in which the Apostle presents Christ as the first fruits of the general resurrection of the dead, the progenitor of a new humanity. In 1 Cor 15:21-22 he explains that, since death came through a human being (Adam), it was fitting that the resurrection of the dead should also come through a human being (Christ); for just as in Adam all die, so in Christ all are made alive. Toward the end of his discussion of the resurrection of the dead, Paul returns to this Adam Christology:

Thus it is written, "The first man, Adam, became a living being"; the last Adam became a life-giving spirit. But it is not the spiritual that is first, but the physical, and then the spiritual. The first man was from the earth, a man of dust; the second man is from heaven. As was the man of

---

38. I employ the adverb "eventually" to stress that Paul's understanding of Christ grew and developed after his Damascus road experience.

dust, so are those who are of the dust; and as is the man of heaven, so are those who are of heaven. Just as we have borne the image of the man of dust, we will also bear the image of the man of heaven. (1 Cor 15:45-49)

In both texts, 2 Cor 2:14–4:6 and 1 Corinthians 15, Paul views Christ as a corporate figure whose actions have consequences for others. Previously humanity bore the image of Adam, but now it bears the image of the risen Christ.

Paul's most extensive discussion of Adam and Christ occurs in Rom 5:12-21, where he contrasts Adam's disobedience with Christ's obedience. Noting that sin entered the world through one man (Adam) and that with it came death (v. 12), Paul writes that just as Adam's transgression led to condemnation for all, so Christ's act of righteousness resulted in life for all (v. 18); and just as many were made sinners by Adam's disobedience, so many were made righteous through Christ's obedience (v. 19). Here, then, Paul views Adam as the progenitor of the old humanity, which dwells in sin and death, and Christ as the progenitor of the new humanity, which dwells in grace and life. Accordingly, whereas to be "in Adam" is to live in the realm of sin and death, to be "in Christ" is to live in the realm of life and grace.

The relationship between Paul's Damascus road experience and his understanding of Christ as the image of God, the eschatological Adam, can be summarized in this way. When God revealed his Son to him, Paul saw the risen Christ bathed in God's glory. On the basis of that experience, Paul eventually understood that the crucified Christ had become the Lord of glory, the image of God, the eschatological Adam who bears the image Adam tarnished by his transgression.[39] As the eschatological Adam, Christ is the progenitor of the new humanity, which draws its life from him and so is incorporated into him.

Although Romans and 1 Corinthians are the letters that explicitly employ an Adam Christology, echoes of this Christology are heard in Colossians and Ephesians, which present Christ as a cosmic figure, the "head" of the body that is the church (Eph 1:22; 4:15; 5:23; Col 1:18; 2:19). Closely related to this concept of Christ as the head of the body is an un-

---

39. I am aware that I am conflating the first and second creation accounts of Genesis. In the first, God creates humankind "in our image and likeness" (1:27). In the second, "God formed man from the dust of the ground, and breathed into his nostrils the breath of life; and the man became a living being" (2:7). Paul, however, does not make such neat distinctions.

derstanding of Christ as the "new human being" into whom believers are growing into full maturity (Col 1:28). For example, in his moral exhortation to the Colossians, Paul reminds them that since they have stripped off "the old self" *(ton palaion anthrōpon)* and clothed themselves with "the new self" *(ton neon),* with which they are being renewed, they ought to live in a way that reflects this new reality (Col 3:9-10). In Ephesians, the Apostle reminds his readers that Christ has broken down the barriers that once separated Gentile and Jew so that "he might create in himself one new humanity *(hena kainon anthrōpon)* in place of the two, thus making peace" (Eph 2:15). In that same letter, he reminds them how they were taught to put away their "old self" *(ton palaion anthrōpon,* 4:22) and clothe themselves with "the new self" *(ton kainon anthrōpon,* v. 24). Although these texts do not refer to Adam or Christ, I suggest that they are grounded in the Adam Christology of Romans and 1 Corinthians. Whereas the old self is indebted to Adam (the old human being), the new self draws its life from Christ (the new human being), the eschatological Adam.

Living in and with Christ

The manner in which Paul portrays Christ as the eschatological Adam, the new human, undergirds a series of statements in which he presents Christ as a corporate figure *in* and *with* whom believers live and dwell. Like Paul's Adam Christology, this understanding of Christ has its origins in the Damascus road experience that transformed Paul's life. As a result of that experience, the Apostle knows himself as intimately related to Christ: "it is no longer I who live, but it is Christ who lives in me. And the life I now live in the flesh I live by faith in the Son of God, who loved me and gave himself for me" (Gal 2:20). For Paul the risen Christ is an individual who transcends the boundaries of time and space. On the one hand, Paul can affirm that Christ died for him personally; on the other, he can claim that the risen one now lives in him. On the basis of this intensely personal experience, the Apostle speaks of Christ as someone *in* whom and *with* whom believers live, the sphere in which they live their lives.[40]

40. This understanding of Christ is also found in the Fourth Gospel, especially in its farewell discourse (John 13–17), where Jesus speaks of believers dwelling in him and of him dwelling in them. If we suppose, as I think we should, that neither John nor Paul depends on each other, then it is evident that the notion of a corporate Christ is not peculiar to either the Pauline or the Johannine tradition.

Paul makes extensive use of the expressions "in Christ" and "in the Lord," which James Dunn categorizes in three ways:

1. references to God's redemptive work in Christ, for example, "they are now justified by his grace as a gift, *through the redemption that is in Christ Jesus*" (Rom 3:24), "the free gift of God is eternal life in Christ Jesus our Lord" (6:23), "the love of God in Christ Jesus our Lord" (8:39), "sanctified in Christ Jesus" (1 Cor 1:2), "if anyone is in Christ, there is a new creation" (2 Cor 5:17), "the freedom we have in Christ Jesus" (Gal 2:4), and "for all of you are one in Christ Jesus" (3:28),

2. references to believers existing "in Christ" or "in the Lord," for example, "Greet Andronicus and Junia, my relatives who were in prison with me; they are prominent among the apostles, and *they were in Christ before I was*" (Rom 16:7), "as infants in Christ" (1 Cor 3:1), "those who have died in Christ" (15:18), "the churches of Judea that are in Christ" (Gal 1:22), "but now in Christ you who were once far off" (Eph 2:13), and "to all the saints in Christ Jesus" (Phil 1:1), and

3. references to Paul's own activity or his exhortation to believers to adopt a particular kind of behavior, for example, "*in Christ we speak as persons of sincerity,* as persons sent from God and standing in his presence" (2 Cor 2:17), "in Christ Jesus I became your father through the gospel" (1 Cor 4:15), and "we are speaking in Christ before God" (2 Cor 12:19).[41]

In addition to speaking of being *in Christ,* there are other occasions when Paul refers to believers participating *with Christ* in the events of his death, resurrection, and exaltation. For example, in Romans he says that believers have been *buried with* Christ through their baptism into his death (6:4), that their old self was *crucified with* him (v. 6), that they have *died with* Christ believing that they will be *raised with* him (v. 8), and that they are *co-heirs with* Christ so that if they *suffer with* him they will be *glorified with* him (8:17). In Galatians he writes that he has been *crucified with* Christ (2:19). In Ephesians, he says that God has *raised us up and seated us with* Christ in the heavenly places (2:6). In Colossians he writes that we were *buried with* Christ in baptism and raised up through faith in the power of God who raised Christ from the dead (2:12), that we were *made*

---

41. James D. G. Dunn, *The Theology of Paul the Apostle* (Grand Rapids: Eerdmans, 1998), 397-98.

alive together with Christ (v. 13), that *with Christ we died* to the elemental spirits (v. 20), that we have been *raised up with* Christ (3:1), that we have died and our life is *hidden with Christ* (v. 3), and that when Christ is revealed we will be *revealed with* him in glory (v. 4). Finally, in 2 Tim 2:11 the Apostle promises that if we have *died with* Christ we will *live with* him.

The frequency with which the Pauline corpus refers to believers being *in* Christ or *in* the Lord, or suffering, dying, rising, and being seated *with* Christ indicates that the risen Lord transcends the limitations of time and space. The personal Christ is the corporate Christ, the eschatological human being *with* whom and *in whom* believers dwell.

Coherence and Meaning in Pauline Christology

Pauline Christology identifies Christ as God's redemptive agent, the one whom God sent into the world to save sinners and reconcile the world to himself. Thus, even though "Christ" begins to function as a name in the Pauline letters, it is a name that identifies its bearer as God's redemptive agent, the one who suffered, died, and rose from the dead in accordance with God's redemptive plan. The very way in which the Pauline letters use "Christ," "Jesus Christ," and "Christ Jesus" points to the bearer of this name as God's redemptive agent.

In addition to naming the crucified and risen one as "Christ," the Pauline letters identify him as "the Son of God," thereby highlighting the intimate relationship that exists between him and the Father. Jesus Christ is not simply "a son of God" but the unique Son of God who makes it possible for others to call God "Father" in the way that he does.

Whereas "Christ" highlights Jesus' redemptive work and "Son" identifies his intimate relation to God, "Lord" points to the exalted status he enjoys in virtue of his resurrection from the dead. As the exalted Lord, Jesus shares God's own name. As the exalted Lord, he is the one to whom believers owe perfect obedience.

In addition to identifying Jesus as "Christ," "Son," and "Lord," the Pauline letters refer to him as "the image of God," "the eschatological Adam," "the new human being." Because he is the image of God, the eschatological Adam, the risen Christ has become a corporate figure "in whom" and "with whom" believers die and live. To be sure, Christ remains an individual, but in virtue of his resurrection from the dead he has become the one in whom others live and find their being.

The coherence of Pauline Christology, however, is found in Christ's death and resurrection rather than in these titles. Jesus is Christ, Son, and Lord in virtue of his saving death and life-giving resurrection. He has become the eschatological Adam, the image of God, a corporate person "in whom" and "with whom" believers live because God raised him from the dead. It was in light of the resurrection that Paul understood that the crucified one is the risen one, the "first fruits" of the general resurrection of the dead, the one who appeared in the flesh and will appear as God's eschatological agent at the end of the ages. In light of the resurrection, Paul understood that the one who exists with God in resurrection glory already existed with God before coming into the world.

To summarize, Pauline Christology is rooted in Paul's Damascus road experience, when God revealed his Son to the former persecutor. At that moment Paul understood the identity of the one whom he called Christ, Son, and Lord. The coherence of Paul's Christology, which is at the origin of the Christology of the letters that bear his name, is grounded in an experience of the crucified and risen Christ. If the Pauline letters express their understanding of Jesus' identity in diverse ways, it is because they are occasional in nature rather than theological treatises. These diverse presentations of Christ, however, are ultimately grounded in an experience of the crucified and risen Lord, and it is this experience that provides Pauline Christology with its coherence.

For Further Reading

Cerfaux, Lucien. *Christ in the Theology of St. Paul.* New York: Herder and Herder, 1959.

Dunn, James D. G. *Christology in the Making: A New Testament Inquiry into the Origins of the Doctrine of the Incarnation.* 2nd ed. Grand Rapids: Eerdmans, 1996.

————. *The Theology of Paul the Apostle.* Grand Rapids: Eerdmans, 1998. Pages 163-315.

Fee, Gordon D. *Pauline Christology: An Exegetical-Theological Study.* Peabody: Hendrickson, 2007.

Hultgren, Arland J. *Christ and His Benefits: Christology and Redemption in the New Testament.* Philadelphia: Fortress, 1987. Pages 47-57, 91-112.

Karris, Robert J. *A Symphony of New Testament Hymns.* Collegeville: Liturgical, 1996.

Kim, Seyoon. *The Origin of Paul's Gospel*. 2nd ed. Tübingen: Mohr-Siebeck, 1984.

————. *Paul and the New Perspective: Second Thoughts on the Origin of Paul's Gospel*. Grand Rapids: Eerdmans, 2002. Pages 165-213.

Longenecker, Richard N. "A Realized Hope, a New Commitment, and a Developed Proclamation: Paul and Jesus." Pages 18-42 in *The Road from Damascus: The Impact of Paul's Conversion on His Life, Thought, and Ministry*, ed. Richard N. Longenecker. Grand Rapids: Eerdmans, 1997.

Martin, Ralph P. "The Christology of the Prison Epistles." Pages 193-219 in *Contours of Christology in the New Testament*, ed. Richard N. Longenecker. Grand Rapids: Eerdmans, 2005.

Martin, Ralph P., and Brian J. Dodd, eds. *Where Christology Began: Essays on Philippians 2*. Louisville: Westminster John Knox, 1998.

Matera, Frank J. *New Testament Christology*. Louisville: Westminster John Knox, 1999. Pages 83-172.

Moo, Douglas J. "The Christology of the Early Pauline Letters." Pages 169-92 in *Contours of Christology in the New Testament*. Edited by Richard N. Longenecker. Grand Rapids: Eerdmans, 2005.

Navarro, Luis Sánchez, ed. *Pablo y Cristo. La centralidad de Cristo en el pensamiento de san Pablo*. Collectanea Matritensia 5. Madrid: Publicaciones San Dámaso, 2000.

Newman, Carey C. *Paul's Glory-Christology: Tradition and Rhetoric*. NovTSup 69. Leiden: Brill, 1992.

Ridderbos, Herman. *Paul: An Outline of His Theology*. Grand Rapids: Eerdmans, 1975. Pages 169-244.

Schnelle, Udo. *Apostle Paul: His Life and Theology*. Grand Rapids: Baker, 2003. Pages 410-77.

————. *Theology of the New Testament*. Grand Rapids: Baker, 2009. Pages 221-68.

Soards, Marion L. "Christology of the Pauline Epistles." Pages 88-109 in *Who Do You Say That I Am? Essays on Christology in Honor of Jack Dean Kingsbury*, ed. Mark Allan Powell and David R. Bauer. Louisville: Westminster John Knox, 1999.

Stuhlmacher, P. "On Pauline Christology." Pages 169-81 in *Reconciliation, Law, and Righteousness: Essays in Biblical Theology*. Philadelphia: Fortress, 1986.

Towner, Philip H. "Christology in the Letters to Timothy and Titus." Pages 220-44 in *Contours of Christology in the New Testament*, ed. Richard N. Longenecker. Grand Rapids: Eerdmans, 2005.

Tuckett, Christopher. *Christology and the New Testament: Jesus and His Earliest Followers.* Louisville: Westminster John Knox, 2001. Pages 41-89.

Witherington, Ben. *The Many Faces of the Christ: The Christologies of the New Testament and Beyond.* Companions to the New Testament. New York: Crossroad, 1998. Pages 103-26.

4. The Saving Grace of Jesus Christ

Introduction

In the previous chapter I discussed Pauline Christology in terms of Christ as the embodiment of God's saving grace. In doing so I highlighted the intimate relationship that exists between Paul's call and conversion on the one hand, and the implicit Christology of his letters on the other. Although Paul undoubtedly grew in his understanding of Christ, his call/conversion was the decisive moment when he understood that the crucified one was God's Son, the risen and exalted Lord.

The Pauline letters, however, are not christological treatises. Because of their pastoral nature, they are passionately concerned with the question of soteriology. What has God brought about through the death and resurrection of Christ? What are the "benefits" that Christ brings to those who believe in him? How does the event of Christ's death and resurrection save and redeem humanity? Having investigated Pauline Christology in the last chapter, in this chapter I turn to the soteriology of Paul's letters. This chapter proceeds in three steps. First, I will show that Paul's own experience of God's saving grace in Jesus Christ is the foundation for his soteriology. Thus, just as Paul's call is at the origin of his Christology, so it stands at the origin of his soteriology. Second, I will consider how the Pauline letters envision the human condition apart from Christ. This will allow us to see why it was necessary for God to send his Son into the world. After describing the human predicament prior to Christ, in the third part of this chapter I will discuss the metaphors that the Pauline letters employ to clarify the new situation in which redeemed humanity finds itself because of God's salvific work in Christ.

Paul's Experience of God's Saving Grace

Paul's preaching about God's work in Christ begins with a personal experience of God's saving grace in his own life. Before he preached the gospel, *he* had been called by God's grace. Before he became Christ's ambassador, summoning others to be reconciled to God, *he* had been reconciled to God. Although 1 Timothy is a letter whose Pauline authorship is disputed, its portrayal of Paul's conversion (1:12-17) provides a helpful example of what I mean. According to 1 Timothy, Paul had been "a blasphemer, a persecutor, and a man of violence" (v. 13). But through Christ Jesus, "who came into the world to save sinners" (v. 15), he received mercy so that the merciful way in which God treated him would provide an encouraging example to others who would come to believe in Christ. Having been rescued from the powers of sin and death that held sway over his pre-Christian life, then, Paul preaches the grace of Christ in light of his own experience of God's saving grace.[1]

Paul frequently refers to "grace," by which he means the divine favor and mercy that God extended to him. On several occasions he speaks of the grace that was given to him at his call and conversion (Rom 12:3; 15:15; 1 Cor 3:10; Eph 3:8). He is deeply aware that his apostleship is the outcome of God's grace (Rom 1:5).[2] He acknowledges that it is by the grace of God that he is what he is, and this grace has not been in vain (1 Cor 15:10). He was called through God's grace (Gal 1:15), and others recognized the grace of God that had been given to him (2:9). Having received this favor, Paul refuses to nullify God's grace by preaching justification on the basis of legal observance (v. 21). Accordingly, he conducts his life on the basis of God's grace rather than on the basis of earthly wisdom (2 Cor 1:12). Furthermore, he has learned that God's grace is sufficient, for "power is made perfect in weakness" (2 Cor 12:9). The later Pauline letters make similar

---

1. I emphasize that it was only in light of God's grace that Paul understood the dire predicament of his former situation. Prior to his conversion, he saw himself as zealous for the law and blameless in his observance of it. But in light of God's saving grace in Christ, he evaluated his former life in a way he previously could not. Although he thought he had attained righteousness through legal observance, he did not attain the saving righteousness that God manifested in Christ (Phil 3:6-9). As he will explain in Romans 7, the power of sin made it impossible for unredeemed humanity to do the just requirements of the law.

2. The words *charin kai apostolēn* in Rom 1:5 are best taken as hendiadys. They should be translated as "the grace of apostleship" rather than as "grace and apostleship."

statements about the grace given to Paul. In Ephesians, for example, Paul writes that "God's grace was given me for you" (3:2) by the working of God's power (v. 7), and in 1 Timothy he notes that "the grace of our Lord overflowed for me" (1 Tim 1:14).

This grace is the unmerited favor that God extended to Paul when he called him to be an apostle to the nations. It is this unmerited favor that Paul experienced when God reconciled him to himself. Having encountered the risen Christ, whom he formerly evaluated from "a human point of view" as a messianic pretender (2 Cor 5:16), Paul now understands that he had been fighting against God's purpose for Israel and the nations as revealed in Christ. He now realizes that through his zeal for the law he had become God's enemy inasmuch as he was excluding from the community of Israel those whom God was including through the death of his Son.[3] In a word, Paul needed to be reconciled to God. His statement in 2 Cor 5:18, then, is as much about himself as it is about every believer: "And all this is from God, who has reconciled us to himself through Christ and given us this ministry of reconciliation."[4] Before Paul was entrusted to preach that God was reconciling the world to himself in Christ, then, he had been reconciled to God. And before he proclaimed that "a person is justified by faith apart from the works of the law" (Rom 3:28), he had been justified by God's grace.

Deeply aware of this experience of God's unmerited grace in his own life, Paul regularly begins his letters with a greeting of "grace and peace" from God, whom believers now call "Father," and Jesus Christ, whom they confess as their "Lord." By this greeting, Paul extends to his readers the very grace and peace he experienced: the grace of God's unmerited favor

3. Michael J. Gorman (*Inhabiting the Cruciform God: Kenosis, Justification, and Theosis in Paul's Narrative Soteriology* [Grand Rapids: Eerdmans, 2009], 135) makes a similar point: "It seems likely that the pre-conversion Paul — like Phinehas, his unnamed but very real spiritual hero — believed his violent zeal would contribute to the purification of Israel and bring about his own justification before God."

4. Seyoon Kim (*Paul and the New Perspective: Second Thoughts on the Origin of Paul's Gospel* [Grand Rapids: Eerdmans, 2002], 236) writes: "2 Cor 5:11-21 is full of allusions to Paul's Damascus experience of conversion/call: what he is talking about in that passage is *what happened to him on the Damascus road*" (emphasis in the original). Cilliers Breytenbach ("Salvation of the Reconciled [with a Note on the Background of Paul's Metaphor of Reconciliation]," in *Salvation in the New Testament: Perspectives on Soteriology,* ed. Jan G. van der Watt [Leiden: Brill, 2005], 271-304, here 279) makes a similar point: "God reconciled Paul, the persecutor of the assembly, to him and entrusted him as his ambassador with the message of reconciliation."

and the peace of reconciliation that accompanies this favor. In addition to beginning his letters in this way, Paul concludes many of them with a simple statement: "The grace of our Lord Jesus Christ be with you" (Rom 16:20; 1 Cor 16:23; 1 Thess 5:28).[5] By bracketing his letters with these grace-wishes, the Apostle indicates that everything begins and ends with the unmerited favor and peace that God has bestowed on believers through Jesus Christ.

In addition to these opening and closing grace formulas, Paul refers to the grace that believers have experienced through their own call. In Romans, for example, he writes that since all have sinned and are deprived of God's glory, all "are now justified by his grace as a gift" (3:24). Having been justified by God's grace, those who believe in Christ have access to God's grace (5:2). Christ-believers are no longer under the regime of the law with its legal requirements, then, but under God's grace (6:14). All this has come about through the obedience of the eschatological Adam, Jesus Christ; for "where sin increased, grace abounded all the more" (5:20). Although the majority of Israel has not believed in Christ, Paul insists that there is a remnant, "chosen by grace," that has believed (11:5).

In Galatians Paul reminds his converts, who have been tempted to turn to a different gospel, that God called them "in the grace of Christ" (Gal 1:6), and he warns that if they seek to be justified on the basis of the law they will cut themselves off from Christ; they will have fallen from grace (5:4). Although Paul's teaching on justification does not play a central role in his Corinthian correspondence, grace does, especially in 2 Corinthians 8–9, where the Apostle presents his collection for the poor of Jerusalem as a manifestation of "grace." Paul tells the Corinthians of "the grace of God" that was given to the Macedonians to participate in this collection (8:1). He describes the collection in terms of grace, as "this generous undertaking" (*tēn charin tautēn,* vv. 6, 19). In exhorting the Corinthians to respond generously, he reminds them of the grace, "the generous act" *(tēn charin)* of their Lord Jesus, who became poor for their sake so that they might become rich (v. 9). Finally, after encouraging them to share their material resources with the church at Jerusalem, which has shared its spiritual resources with them, Paul informs the Corinthians that the Jerusalem believers long for them because of "the surpassing grace of God" that has been given to the Corinthians (9:14).

---

5. Other grace-wishes at the end of the letters take slightly different forms. See 2 Cor 13:13; Gal 6:18; Phil 4:23; Col 4:18; 2 Thess 3:18; 1 Tim 6:21; 2 Tim 4:22; Tit 3:15.

Grace continues to play an important role in the later Pauline letters, especially in Ephesians and 2 Timothy. In Ephesians, Paul reminds his audience of the "glorious grace that he [God] bestowed on us in the Beloved" (1:6), that is, in Jesus Christ. Redemption, he writes, comes from the riches of Christ's grace (1:7). Accordingly, Paul reminds the Ephesians that they have been saved by grace (2:5, 8). 2 Timothy makes a similar statement about the relationship between justification and grace. There Paul insists that believers were not saved and called by their works but according to the purpose and grace of God that was given to them in Christ (2 Tim 1:9). In these and other texts, Paul (or those writing in his name) has in view the unmerited favor of God that he and other believers have experienced in Jesus Christ. They were called and justified by a free and unmerited act of God in Christ that freely and graciously saved them rather than by something they had done.

Pauline soteriology is rooted in Christology, and we can understand what God has done for humanity in light of Christ. In the remainder of this chapter, I will focus on two points: the human situation *apart from Christ* and the human situation *in Christ*. The first point describes how Paul presents the dire predicament in which unredeemed humanity found itself apart from Christ, even though humanity was not fully aware of it. The second describes the new situation of redeemed humanity that has been brought about by God's saving grace in Christ. In effect, I will be considering Pauline anthropology (how Paul views the human situation) as well as Pauline soteriology (how Paul views the effects of what God has done in Christ).

Humanity apart from Christ

Before considering Pauline soteriology, we must ask how the Pauline letters describe the human situation apart from Christ. Why is humanity in need of salvation? Why did God send his Son into the world? Given the occasional nature of the letters, we will find several descriptions of the human situation apart from Christ *as required by the individual letters*. After I have examined the individual letters, I will synthesize the overarching themes that characterize the Pauline understanding of the human condition apart from Christ.

The Plight of Sinful Humanity

Paul's most extensive discussions and allusions to the human situation prior to Christ are in Romans, Galatians, Colossians, and Ephesians. Romans and Galatians are related to each other by their focus on justification by faith, and Colossians and Ephesians are related by their interest in the cosmic scope of God's work in Christ. While other letters refer to the situation of unredeemed humanity, they do not describe that situation to the extent these letters do.

Galatians The letter to the Galatians was occasioned by the arrival of Jewish Christ-believers who questioned the circumcision-free gospel that Paul had preached to the Galatians. In response to this crisis, the Apostle must persuade the Galatians that they need not have themselves circumcised nor adopt a Jewish way of life. To accomplish this, he develops three arguments. First, the Galatians can rely on the gospel Paul preached to them because he received it through a revelation of Jesus Christ when God revealed his Son to him. Second, the Galatians are Abraham's offspring because they have been baptized into Christ. Third, those justified on the basis of faith fulfill the law by the love commandment through the power of the Spirit that dwells in them.

Although Paul's primary objective is to dissuade Galatians from being circumcised and placing themselves under the law, there are several occasions when he alludes to their former situation as well as to the situation of his own people, Israel. For example, at the outset of the letter, he notes that Christ gave himself for their sins to set them free "from the present evil age" (1:4), thereby implying that the time prior to Christ was under the sway of evil from which humanity needed to be rescued. They were enslaved "to the elemental spirits of the world" (4:3), and they did not know God because they were enslaved to beings that were not gods, to "the weak and beggarly elemental spirits" (v. 9). Furthermore, since they did not enjoy the gift of the Spirit, they were not numbered among Abraham's offspring. Like slaves who needed to be set free (5:1, 13), they were under the power of the flesh with its desires (v. 17). Consequently, they produced the works of the flesh ("fornication, impurity, licentiousness, idolatry, sorcery, enmities, strife, jealousy, anger, quarrels, dissensions, factions, envy, drunkenness, carousing"), which excluded them from the kingdom of God (vv. 19-21). The present evil age from which Christ rescued them, then, was a period of enslavement to the desires of the flesh and false gods.

Although Paul's Galatian audience consisted of Gentiles, he also alludes to the situation of Israel prior to Christ. According to the salvation-historical scheme that Paul develops in Galatians 3, the period of the law was the time of Israel's religious minority. Israel was under the power of sin (3:22), "imprisoned and guarded under the law" (v. 23) until Christ appeared. During that period, the law functioned as Israel's "disciplinarian" (v. 24), indicating that Israel's transgressions were violations of God's law (v. 19). Furthermore, since the law threatened everyone who did not do its prescriptions with a curse, those who relied on doing the law were under its threatening curse (vv. 10, 13). Consequently, although Gentiles and Jews found themselves in different situations prior to Christ, from Paul's perspective both were in a period of religious minority, enslaved to powers beyond their control. It is not surprising, then, that when Paul summarizes "the truth of the gospel" (2:15-21), he says that Jews as well as Gentiles are justified on the basis of faith rather than on the basis of doing the works of the law (v. 16).

Romans Although scholars dispute the occasion of Romans, this letter provides a summary of the Pauline gospel in light of the saving righteousness that God manifested in the crucified Christ.[6] A longer and more irenic letter than Galatians, Romans provides Paul with an occasion to develop his understanding of the human situation under the power of sin. Consequently, whereas Galatians alludes to but never develops an understanding of the situation of unredeemed humanity, Romans presents a detailed description of the plight of Gentiles and Jews apart from God's saving righteousness in order to demonstrate the universal need for God's grace: all have sinned, therefore all are in need of God's grace. Four texts are especially important: 1:18–3:20 (Gentiles and Jews under the power of sin); 5:12-21 (Adam and Christ); 6:12-23 (slavery to sin); and 7:1-25 (the law frustrated by the power of sin).

Paul's most developed exposition of the human predicament apart from Christ is 1:18–3:20, a section in which he maintains that all "are under the power of sin" (3:9). Paul begins his argument by describing the situation of the Gentile world (1:18-32). Although the Gentiles knew something of God because the Creator revealed something of himself in creation, the

---

6. The debate surrounding the occasion of Romans has been chronicled by Karl P. Donfried, ed., *The Romans Debate* (revised and expanded ed.; Peabody: Hendrickson, 2003). See also A. Andrew Das, *Solving the Romans Debate* (Minneapolis: Fortress, 2007).

Gentile world did not honor God as God. Instead, it exchanged the glory of God for the image of mortal beings. Accordingly, the Gentiles became vain in their thinking and their minds were darkened. They exchanged the truth of God for a lie, serving the creature rather than the Creator. The fundamental sin of the Gentile world is idolatry, which is the root of every other sin. As a result of this, God's wrath is presently being revealed against the "ungodliness and wickedness" of the Gentile world that suppresses the truth about God through its idolatry (1:18). Having constructed a world that refuses to acknowledge the Creator, unredeemed humanity must live in a godless world of its own making.[7]

After portraying the Gentile world in terms of its rebellion against the Creator, in Romans 2 Paul turns his attention to the failure of the Jewish world. Although the Jewish world should have known better because it enjoyed the benefits of the law and circumcision, it found itself in a similar situation and did not observe the law that God graciously gave it. In 3:9 Paul explains the reason for the human predicament: "all are under the power of sin." The result is that no one is righteous in God's sight (v. 10); all have gone astray (v. 12). There is no distinction between Gentile and Jew, for "all have sinned" (v. 23).

Although Paul presents this pessimistic view of the human condition at the outset of Romans, it is not until 5:12-21 that he explains how this situation came about. Sin, which Paul personifies as a cosmic power, entered the world through Adam's transgression, and with it came a second power, death (v. 12a). As a result of Adam's transgression, all find themselves under the power of death as well as sin; for all have sinned (v. 12b). Although the outset of Paul's Adam-Christ comparison might give the impression that Adam's progeny merely imitated his transgression, what Paul writes in vv. 18-19 indicates that he draws a connection between Adam's transgression and the transgressions of his progeny:

> Therefore *just as* one man's trespass led to condemnation for all,
>   *so* one man's act of righteousness leads to justification and life for
>   all.

7. In his discussion of the Gentile predicament, Paul writes: "the wrath of God is revealed from heaven against all ungodliness and wickedness of those who by their wickedness suppress the truth" (1:18). The emphasis here is on the present manifestation of God's wrath/judgment, which expresses itself by delivering sinful humanity to its own devices, rather than on God's eschatological wrath/judgment. Thus the initial punishment for sin is that humanity must live in the sinful world it has constructed.

> For *just as* by the one man's disobedience the many were made sinners,
> *so* by the one man's obedience the many will be made righteous.

For Paul, Adam and Christ are corporate figures, the former the progenitor of sinful humanity, the latter the progenitor of redeemed humanity. Consequently, Adam's transgression was more than the pattern for future transgressions: it *made* Adam's progeny sinners. Likewise, Christ's obedience was more than a pattern for future acts of obedience: it *made* his progeny righteous. Paul's Adam-Christ comparison, then, is the key to understanding his description of the human condition in 1:18–3:20. All humans are under the power of sin because of Adam's transgression.

Although Paul describes the human predicament in the opening of Romans and the origin of sin and death in his Adam-Christ comparison, it is only in chs. 6 and 7 that he shows the insidious way in which the powers of sin and death rule over the unredeemed. In ch. 6 he must explain why the justified should no longer persist in sin, even though "where sin increased, grace abounded all the more" (5:20). In his response, Paul portrays sin as a cosmic power that rules over Adam's progeny. So long as humanity is "in Adam" it is under the power of sin. Employing the metaphor of slavery, Paul portrays those who are in Adam as obedient slaves of sin, which pays a wage of death (6:23), by which Paul means eternal separation from God. Prior to Christ, unredeemed humanity did not possess the inner power to overcome the domination of sin. The more it obeyed sin, the more it became sin's slave. Once in sin's service, the only benefit it received was death, which results in separation from God.

Paul's description of sin as a cosmic power that enslaves those who obey it enables him to discuss the law from a new vantage point in Romans 7.[8] Whereas in Galatians he presented the law as the period of humanity's religious minority, in Romans he puts it in a more positive light. He affirms that "the law is holy, and the commandment is holy and just and good" (7:12). The problem is not the law but the power of sin, which

---

8. Joseph A. Fitzmyer (*Paul and His Theology: A Brief Sketch* [2nd ed.; Englewood Cliffs: Prentice Hall, 1989], 78) notes that whereas in Galatians "Paul sets forth an extrinsic explanation, ascribing to the law of Moses a temporary role in salvation history," in Romans "Paul abandoned the extrinsic explanation and used a more intrinsic one, that is, a philosophical explanation of the human predicament. In Rom he shows that the difficulty is not with the law, but with humanity in its this-worldly condition of *sarx*, 'flesh,' alienated from God and hostile to him."

takes the occasion of the law to produce "covetousness" or "desire" in unredeemed humanity. For example, when the law says "You shall not covet" (7:7), sin asks "why not?" Making use of this insight, Paul describes the conflicted self of unredeemed humanity from the point of view of someone who has been redeemed (7:13-24).[9] The unredeemed person under the law does not understand his own actions since he does not do the good he wants but the evil he hates (v. 15). Whenever he wants to do what is good he finds that "evil lies close at hand" (v. 21). In his analysis of this predicament, Paul concludes that the problem is not the law, which is spiritual, but the condition of unredeemed humanity, which is carnal and enslaved to the power of sin (v. 14).[10] The real culprit is the power of sin that dwells in unredeemed humanity (v. 20). So long as humanity is under the power of sin it is in the realm of the flesh and cannot carry out the just requirements of the law, even when it knows and approves of God's commandments. Unredeemed humanity needs to be transferred to a sphere in which it can fulfill the just requirement of God's law.

To summarize, in Romans Paul presents his most detailed analysis of the human condition apart from Christ. Prior to Christ, Gentiles and Jews were under the domination of sin, a cosmic power that Adam introduced into the world by his singular act of disobedience. Because of this transgression, his progeny became enslaved to the power of sin, whose wage is death. Consequently, not even those who were under the law were able to observe the law.

Colossians The occasion for Colossians was the appearance of an esoteric teaching that Paul calls a "philosophy," which promised the Colossians a way to appease the cosmic powers that threatened their lives. In response to this seductive teaching, Paul reminds the Colossians of the cosmic scope of God's victory in Christ whereby God overcame these powers. Although Paul's primary purpose is to highlight the significance of God's work in Christ, on several occasions he adverts to the situation in which the

---

9. The identity of the "I" of Romans 7 is one of the most debated questions of Pauline exegesis. Is it autobiographical? Does it refer to a corporate "I"? If so, is it the "I" of redeemed or unredeemed humanity? I have adopted the solution proposed by Georg Werner Kümmel, *Römer 7 und das Bild des Menschen im Neuen Testament: Zwei Studien* (TB 53; Munich: Christian Kaiser Verlag, 1974): Paul is speaking of the situation of unredeemed humanity from the point of view of one who is redeemed.

10. By "carnal" I mean determined by the power of the flesh rather than by the power of God's Spirit.

Colossians found themselves prior to their faith in Christ. At the outset of the letter, for example, Paul indicates that the Colossians dwelled in a realm of darkness from which they could not release themselves: "He [God] has rescued us from the power of darkness and transferred us into the kingdom of his beloved Son" (1:13). He then reminds the Colossians that once they were "estranged and hostile in mind, doing evil deeds" (v. 21). Next, in explaining the significance of their baptism, he recalls their former way of life: they were "dead" because of their transgressions and their flesh (their old self) which had not yet been circumcised (2:13).[11] Employing the cosmic imagery of the teaching that he opposes, Paul reminds the Colossians of the "bond" or "record" with its "legal demands" (*cheirographon tois dogmasin*) that the cosmic rulers and authorities held against the Colossians (v. 14), thereby indicating that they were threatened by, and held hostage to, these cosmic powers.[12] Formerly, they submitted themselves to these "elemental spirits of the universe," and if they adopt this new teaching they will return to their former situation (v. 20). In his moral exhortation, Paul reminds the Colossians of "the old self" (*palaion anthrōpon*, 3:9) that was stripped away when they were baptized. That self was characterized by "fornication, impurity, passion, evil desire, and greed (which is idolatry)." Living in this way, they were destined for God's wrath (vv. 5-6).

The manner in which Paul portrays the situation in which the Colossians found themselves apart from Christ echoes themes we have met in Romans and Galatians: The Colossians were destined for God's wrath because their life was still determined by their old self. That is, they belonged to adamic humanity. Their transgressions were expressions of their hostility to and alienation from God. Accordingly, they needed to be transferred from one realm (darkness) to another (the kingdom of God's Son). The new element in Colossians, which is occasioned by the Colossian situation, is the manner in which Paul relates humanity's alienation from God to the cosmic rulers and authorities that held sway over humanity. Whereas Paul tends to present "sin" as a cosmic power in Romans and Galatians, in Colossians he employs the language of "the ele-

11. Here Paul employs circumcision metaphorically to refer to the stripping away of the old self, which occurs at baptism. This is evident from what he writes in 2:11: "In him also you were circumcised with a spiritual circumcision, by putting off the body of the flesh in the circumcision of Christ."

12. This metaphor of the "bond" or "record" appears to refer to transgressions of the Mosaic Law. If so, the sense is that the cosmic powers held these transgressions as a bond of indebtedness that humanity owed but could not repay.

mental spirits of the universe" (*stoicheiōn tou kosmou*, 2:20), which we have already met in Gal 4:3, 9.

Ephesians It is difficult to identify the precise occasion for Ephesians, which may have been written as a circular letter to Gentile believers in Asia Minor.[13] If it was a circular letter, its purpose would have been to remind Gentiles in Asia Minor of their new status in Christ. They have been reconciled to God and to the community of Israel. Thus their former situation was one of alienation from God and the people of Israel. Closely related to Colossians and several other Pauline letters, especially Romans, Ephesians functions as a summary of Paul's teaching for a new generation of Gentile believers.

After an elaborate benediction that summarizes the benefits God has brought about in Christ, Paul reminds his audience of its former situation:

> You were *dead through the trespasses and sins* in which you once lived, following the course of this world, following *the ruler of the power of the air,* the spirit that is now at work among those who are disobedient. All of us once lived among them in the passions of our flesh, *following the desires of flesh and senses,* and we were by nature *children of wrath,* like everyone else. (2:1-3)

Prior to Christ, then, the Ephesians were dead (in terms of their relationship to God) because of their trespasses and sins. They submitted to a malevolent power, which Paul calls "the ruler of the power of the air." Following the desires of their flesh, they were destined for God's wrath. In this description of the human predicament, Ephesians echoes themes found in Romans, Galatians, and Colossians such as trespasses, sins, and the desires of the flesh.

After this description, Paul introduces a new element. In addition to being alienated from God, the Gentiles were alienated from the community of Israel.

> So then, remember that at one time you Gentiles by birth, called "the uncircumcision" by those who are called "the circumcision" — a physi-

---

13. The text of Ephesians suggests that the letter may have been addressed to many congregations since "in Ephesus" (1:1) is absent from the best manuscript tradition. This suggests that the name of a particular congregation was introduced when the letter was read to it.

cal circumcision made in the flesh by human hands — remember that you were at that time *without Christ, being aliens from the common-wealth of Israel,* and strangers to the covenants of promise, having no hope and *without God in the world.* (2:11-12)

By saying that they were "without Christ" and "without God in the world," Paul relates their alienation from Israel to their alienation from God and Christ. He explains their alienation from Israel in terms of the law, which separated Gentiles from the people of Israel (vv. 14-15). Alienated from Israel, the Gentiles had no share in Israel's covenants and promises. They were without hope in the world because they were "without God" *(atheoi).* Later, when he exhorts these Gentile Christians to refrain from living as Gentiles do, he provides a further description of their former way of life: "They [the Gentiles] are darkened in their understanding, alienated from the life of God because of their ignorance and hardness of heart. They have lost all sensitivity and have abandoned themselves to licentiousness, greedy to practice every kind of impurity" (4:18-19). To summarize, Ephesians presents a comprehensive description of the situation in which the Gentiles found themselves apart from God: they were alienated from God and Christ, and they were alienated from the people of Israel.

Other Letters Other Pauline letters also advert to the human situation apart from Christ. For example, Paul's remarks in 1 Thess 1:9-10 indicate that before their conversion the Thessalonians were destined for God's wrath because they worshiped idols and did not know the true and living God. Furthermore, when Paul reminds them that God's will for them is their holiness, he suggests that prior to their election their lives were characterized by immorality (4:3, 7). A similar conclusion can be drawn from Paul's discussion of the moral disorders that infected some members of the Corinthian community (1 Corinthians 5–7). Reminding the Corinthians of their former life before they were washed, sanctified, and justified in Christ (6:9-11), he summons them to avoid immorality since they have become the dwelling place of God's Spirit (6:18-19). In both 1 Thessalonians and 1 Corinthians, then, Paul exhorts his Gentile converts to flee the immorality that characterizes the world outside the sanctified sphere of the church.

In addition to describing the unredeemed human condition in terms of immorality, Paul views humanity apart from Christ as bereft of hope. This is why the Thessalonians, who believe in the resurrection, must not grieve like their contemporaries who have no hope (1 Thess 4:13). In 1 Corinthians 15, Paul portrays death, which Adam introduced into the world (15:21), as the last and greatest enemy, which will only be destroyed at the general resurrection of the dead (v. 26). Although 1 Thessalonians and 1 Corinthians do not speculate about the cause of the human predicament, Paul gives some indication of the problem when he says that the world refused to acknowledge the power and wisdom of God revealed in the weakness and folly of the crucified Christ. Striving to know God through its own wisdom rather than though the wisdom of God, unredeemed humanity did not know God (1 Cor 1:21). And so the world became a sphere of immorality destined for God's wrath and eternal death.[14]

In 2 Corinthians Paul is concerned lest his converts return to the immorality that characterized their lives prior to Christ. He exhorts them to live as a sanctified community with clear boundaries that distinguish them from the surrounding world (6:14-18)[15] and warns those who have not repented of their immorality to do so before he arrives (12:20-21). The distinctive contribution of 2 Corinthians, however, is Paul's teaching about his new covenant ministry. Portraying the ministry of Moses as a ministry that led to death and condemnation (3:7, 9), he affirms that as glorious as that ministry was, it could not lead people to righteousness and life.[16] Consequently, although the Israelites gazed on the glory of the Mosaic ministry that was coming to an end, that ministry was not able to bring Israel to God's glory. Proclaiming that God has brought about a "new creation" in Christ (5:17) and that his own ministry is a ministry of reconciliation (5:18), Paul implies that the "old creation" was at enmity with, and in need of being reconciled to, God. Consequently, even though Paul's purpose in 2 Corinthians is to describe his new covenant ministry, what he says about his ministry implies the need for a righteousness and reconciliation that the old covenant could not effect.

Philippians provides us with a deeper understanding of the human

---

14. Although Paul does not explicitly make this connection, I have made it in light of what he writes in Romans 1: the refusal to acknowledge God results in idolatry and sin.

15. I am aware that some scholars view 2 Cor 6:14-18 as a non-Pauline interpolation. But in recent years, many scholars have defended the authenticity of this text. Moreover, since I am primarily concerned with the canonical form of the text rather than with a reconstructed form of the text, I have included this text in my discussion.

16. The Mosaic ministry could not bring about righteousness and life, according to Paul, because it was a ministry of the letter that dealt with a law written on stone tablets (the letter), whereas Paul's new covenant ministry is a ministry of the Spirit that inscribes the law on the hearts of those who believe.

predicament. In a statement about his pre-Christian life (3:4-11), Paul portrays himself as "blameless" as to righteousness under law (v. 6). But now, in light of his Damascus road experience, he considers his former gains as losses because of Christ (v. 7). What has happened? While the pre-Christian Paul could say that he had attained a legal righteousness, the Christian Paul understands that the righteousness he gained under the law was of no avail in light of the righteousness that comes from God through Christ. As in Romans 7, Paul looks back at his pre-Christian life from the vantage point of his Christian life and for the first time understands what his former situation was truly like.[17]

In the Pastorals Paul gives Timothy and Titus instructions for handing on what he entrusted to them so that they can combat false teaching with sound doctrine and, on several such occasions, averts to the need for salvation. In 1 Timothy, for example, he affirms that "Christ Jesus came into the world to save sinners — of whom I am the foremost" (1:15), thereby indicating the sinful situation in which humanity found itself prior to Christ. He says that Christ "gave himself a ransom for all" (2:6), thereby implying that humanity needed to be redeemed from something. In 2 Timothy, Paul describes the Savior, Christ Jesus, as the one "who abolished death and brought life and immortality to light through the gospel" (1:10), thereby echoing a major theme of Romans and 1 Corinthians, namely, apart from Christ, humanity was destined for death and separation from God. In Titus, Paul affirms that the grace of God has appeared, "training us to renounce impiety and worldly passions, and in the present age to live lives that are self-controlled, upright, and godly" (2:12), the implication being that, apart from this grace, humanity did not know how to live such a life. Thus the reason that Jesus Christ gave himself for us was "to redeem us from all iniquity and purify for himself a people of his own who are zealous for good deeds" (v. 14). Toward the end of his letter to Titus, Paul describes the life from which the redeemed have been saved: "For we ourselves were once foolish, disobedient, led astray, slaves to various passions and pleasures, passing our days in malice and envy, despicable, hating one

17. Whereas in Romans 7 Paul presents himself as one who knows the law but cannot do it, in Philippians 3 he portrays himself as one who did the law but now realizes that it was of no avail. While Paul does not resolve this tension, this tension provides us with two ways of looking at the pre-Christian condition. On the one hand, the unredeemed cannot do the good they want because they are frustrated by sin (Romans 7). On the other, the righteousness they attain by legal observance is not comparable to the righteousness that God freely gives (Philippians 3).

another" (3:3). According to the Pastorals, then, before God's saving grace appeared, humanity lived in sin and was destined for eternal death because it was untrained in the ways of righteousness.[18]

The diverse ways in which the Pauline letters describe the human condition can be attributed to the various circumstances that occasioned them. Despite these differences, there are some overarching themes to which I now turn.[19]

Dominant Themes

Alienation from God Although we must distinguish between the situations of Gentiles and Jews, the overall condition of unredeemed humanity can be summarized as alienation from God. Preferring its own wisdom to the wisdom of God, and refusing to acknowledge the Creator, who revealed something of himself in creation, the Gentile world worshiped beings that were not gods. As a result of their idolatrous worship, the Gentiles forfeited their moral compass and lived lives of immorality, godlessness, and wickedness. Moreover, since they blinded themselves to the truth of God, they did not know their true situation. Thinking they were living in the light, they were dwelling in the darkness. Consequently, they were destined to experience God's judgment against sin — the wrath of God. Although the Jewish world enjoyed the knowledge of God's law, and although this enabled it to know God's will, it too was alienated from the God who had graciously elected it. Thus, even though the Jewish people knew the law, they did not do the law. From the Pauline perspective, Jews

18. In his discussion of the soteriology of the Pastoral Epistles ("Christ Jesus Came into the World to Save Sinners," in *Salvation in the New Testament: Perspectives on Soteriology,* 331-58, here 356), Abraham J. Malherbe summarizes how the Pastorals view the human condition apart from Christ: "That condition reflects a pessimistic view of human beings who have not come to a knowledge of the truth and do not live according to the sound teaching of the church."

19. Every synthesis is artificial. On the one hand, themes of Romans tend to dominate the synthesis, as they do here. On the other, no one letter reflects the entire synthesis since the letters are occasional. My purpose is to present a theology of the Pauline letters. In doing so, I assume that Paul did not forget what he wrote in other letters, nor did those who wrote in his name. For example, although Paul's Adam Christology is found only in Romans and 1 Corinthians, I am supposing that it is not at odds with the theology developed in other letters and may even underlie the theology of those letters, even though it is not explicitly mentioned.

and Gentiles alike were liable to the coming wrath/judgment of God. Both needed to be reconciled to God.

Under the Power of Sin and Death In addition to being alienated from God, unredeemed humanity finds itself under the domination of sin. Adam introduced the power of sin into the world by his singular act of disobedience, and in doing so he constituted his progeny as sinners. Adam's descendants, in turn, ratified his sin and increased the presence and power of sin in this world by their own transgressions. Consequently, adamic humanity finds itself enslaved to and under the domination of sin that frustrates its attempt to do what is good. In addition to being under the power of sin, adamic humanity is under the power of death, which Adam's transgression introduced into the world. More than the physical destruction of the body, death results in eternal separation from God. Under the domination of sin, then, unredeemed humanity finds itself in need of redemption and liberation. Having sinned and transgressed the laws of the Creator, unredeemed humanity is in need of forgiveness. Destined for eternal death and separation from God, unredeemed humanity must be saved from the last and greatest enemy — death.

Under the Powers of This Age In addition to personifying the powers of sin and death, the Pauline letters refer to other cosmic powers that rule over and threaten the lives of unredeemed humanity. Sinful human beings are under a host of heavenly powers that rule over the lives of those who submit to them. For example, Paul speaks of the elemental powers, the *stoicheia* (Gal 4:3, 9), that the Galatians once served and to which the Colossians are tempted to submit (Col 2:8, 20).[20] In Rom 8:38-39 he lists a series of forces, some of which appear to be cosmic powers, that can no longer separate the justified from God. In 1 Cor 15:24 Paul says that before Christ hands over the kingdom to the Father, "every ruler and every authority and power" will be destroyed. In Eph 6:12 he warns the recipients of his letter that their struggle is against "the cosmic powers of this present

---

20. These elemental spirits could refer to malevolent angelic beings, the rudiments of religion, the elements of the world. James D. G. Dunn (*The Theology of Paul the Apostle* [Grand Rapids: Eerdmans, 1998], 108) writes: "The long debate about the reference of *stoicheia* should almost certainly be regarded as settled in favor of the elemental substances of which the cosmos was usually thought to be composed (earth, water, air, and fire). The point here is that these substances were also commonly divinized (mythologized or personified) as divine spirits or deities."

darkness, against the spiritual forces of evil in the heavenly places." Although not all of these powers were malevolent and not all were heavenly powers, many of them exerted a baleful influence over unredeemed humanity, which needed to be set free from the powers that controlled the old age of sin and death.

Under the Law Whereas Gentiles found themselves outside, and so ignorant of, God's law as revealed in Torah, the Jews were "under the law." Prior to his incorporation into Christ, Paul understood this situation as a legitimate boast rather than as a liability, and it was out of zeal for the law that he persecuted the followers of the crucified one. But when God revealed his Son to him, Paul found it necessary to reevaluate his prior understanding of the salvation-historical role of the law.

The revelation of the crucified one as the Son of God confronted Paul with the question of the law's role in God's salvific plan. In Galatians he frames the question in terms of God's promise to Abraham: If God's work in Christ is rooted in the promise that God made to Abraham, what was the purpose of the law? In Romans he frames the question in terms of God's righteousness: If the Gentiles have obtained the righteousness that Israel failed to attain through the law, has God rejected and been unfaithful to Israel? The problem Paul confronts can be stated in another way: If the law was not the solution to humanity's plight, was it the problem? As he responds to these and other questions, the Apostle must balance two competing themes.[21] On the one hand, he must affirm the goodness and holiness of the law, which is spiritual because it comes from God. On the other, he must maintain that it was never the purpose of the law to give righteousness and life, which come from Christ.

Paul insists that there is a unity to God's salvific plan that attains its goal in Christ.[22] He does not believe that the law failed in its purpose,

---

21. Udo Schnelle (*Theology of the New Testament* [Grand Rapids: Baker, 2009], 310) notes that Paul makes both positive and negative statements about the law. In doing so, Paul is trying to balance competing realities. On the one hand, the law is good because it is God's law; on the other the law is not the source of salvation.

22. In his chapter on Galatians, N. T. Wright (*Justification: God's Plan and Paul's Vision* [Downers Grove: InterVarsity, 2009], here 122-23) points to the single purpose of God's plan. He writes: "Paul is working, throughout this section [3:1–4:11], on the basis of the single-plan-of-God-through-Israel-for-the-world. . . . God has begun the great single purpose, to bless the world through choosing Abraham, calling him and making promises to him. . . . The problem is that the law *gets in the way of the promise to Abraham*, the single-plan-

thereby requiring God to make a midcourse correction. Rather, he affirms that the terminus of the law has always been Christ. Accordingly, in Galatians he presents Christ as the promised seed of Abraham to whom the inheritance was promised, and he views the role of the law as temporary and custodial until the promised offspring of Abraham (Christ) should make his appearance. God's plan always envisioned the salvation of Gentiles and Jews alike on the basis of the promise God made to Abraham and his offspring. Israel's failure to attain the righteousness to which the law pointed (but could not bring about) was its failure rather than a failure of God's plan; for by pursuing its own righteousness, Israel failed to see the righteousness that God revealed in Christ for both Gentile and Jew. The problem, according to Romans 7, was not the law but the power of sin, which made it impossible for those under the law to carry out its just requirements.

When Paul speaks of "being under the law," then, he is pointing to the period of Israel's spiritual minority prior to the appearance of its Messiah. At that time Israel knew God's will but could not do it because, like the rest of humanity, it was under the cosmic powers of sin and death. To be justified by God's saving grace, those under "the law" needed to be transferred to the realm of the Spirit.

The condition of unredeemed humanity can be summarized in terms of alienation and slavery: alienation from God, and slavery to sin, death, and the cosmic powers of this age. It was a time of religious minority, a time "under the law."

Humanity in Christ

The Pauline understanding of the human situation apart from Christ illustrates humanity's need for the salvation God brings in Christ. Alienated from God, under the domination of powers beyond its control, unredeemed humanity finds itself in a predicament from which it cannot free itself. Consequently, "God sent his Son, born of a woman, born under the law" (Gal 4:4), "in the likeness of sinful flesh" (Rom 8:3), to do what hu-

---

through-Israel-to-the-world, first by apparently choking the promise within the failure of Israel (Galatians 3:10-14), then by threatening to divide the promised single family into two (Galatians 2:15-18), then finally by locking everybody up in the prison house of sin (Galatians 3:21-22)."

manity could not do for itself. To explain the redemptive effect of God's work in Christ, Paul employs a number of metaphors. While some of these (justification, redemption, and reconciliation) have played a more prominent role in the history of Pauline interpretation than others, it would be a mistake to focus on them to the neglect of the others. Since God's redemptive work in Christ is a transcendent reality beyond the scope of any single metaphor, we need to view that work from as many vantage points as possible to understand the totality of God's work in Christ.

Fitzmyer lists ten benefits of Christ's death and resurrection: justification, salvation, reconciliation, expiation, redemption, freedom, sanctification, transformation, new creation, and glorification.[23] I have made use of his concepts, replacing expiation with forgiveness, and putting them into four categories: (1) Justified and Reconciled to God, (2) Redeemed, Freed, and Forgiven, (3) Sanctified, Transformed, a New Creation, (4) Waiting for Final Salvation and Glorification.

The first two categories highlight the objective reality of God's work in Christ. Through Christ's death and resurrection, humanity was justified and reconciled to God, redeemed, freed, and forgiven, apart from anything it did. The third category points to the new existence believers presently enjoy in Christ. Sanctified, they are a new creation that is in the process of being transformed. Finally, the fourth category looks to the future. Those who enjoy this new being wait in hope for the fullness of salvation that will occur when they are glorified at the general resurrection of the dead. These four categories present God's redemptive work through Christ in terms of the past, the present, and the future: what God has done in Christ, what God is doing in Christ, and what God will do in Christ.

Justified and Reconciled to God

As a result of Christ's saving death and resurrection, humanity finds itself in a new relationship to God that Paul describes as justification *(dikaiōsis)* and reconciliation *(katallagē)*. God has justified (that is to say, God has "acquitted" humanity, thereby declaring it "innocent"), not on the basis of anything humanity has done, but on the basis of what God has accomplished through the death and resurrection of his Son. By this act of justification, God anticipates the verdict of acquittal that will be pronounced at

---

23. Fitzmyer, *Paul and His Theology,* 59-71.

the last judgment. Inasmuch as God has graciously justified human beings, they have been reconciled to God. This has not occurred because humans have reconciled themselves to God but because God has reconciled them to himself, for it was not God who needed to be reconciled to humanity but humanity that needed to be reconciled to God. Although justification and reconciliation are different terms (the former a legal metaphor and the latter a social metaphor), both make a similar point: whether humanity knows it or not, it stands in a new relation to God. The appropriate response to such a gracious gift is "the obedience of faith" (Rom 1:5), which expresses itself in love (Gal 5:6).

Galatians and Romans Paul's letter to the Galatians is the earliest written account of his teaching on justification by faith.[24] Responding to missionaries who challenged his circumcision-free gospel, Paul affirms that a person is not justified by doing the works of the law but through faith. His most explicit statement of this occurs in his account of the incident at Antioch when Peter, Barnabas, and other Jewish Christ-believers withdrew from table fellowship with Gentile believers.

> We ourselves are Jews by birth and not Gentile sinners; yet we know that a person is justified not by the works of the law but through the faithfulness of [or, "faith in"] Jesus Christ. And we have come to believe in Christ Jesus, so that we might be justified by the faithfulness of [or, "faith in"] Christ, and not by doing the works of the law, because no one will be justified by the works of the law. But if, in our effort to be justified in Christ, we ourselves have been found to be sinners, is Christ then a servant of sin? Certainly not! But if I build up again the very things that I once tore down, then I demonstrate that I am a transgressor. For through the law I died to the law, so that I might live to God. I have been crucified with Christ; and it is no longer I who live, but it is Christ who lives in me. And the life I now live in the flesh I live by the faithfulness of [or "faith in"] the Son of God, who loved me and gave himself for me. I do not nullify the grace of God; for if justification comes through the law, then Christ died for nothing. (Gal 2:15-21)[25]

24. Although Galatians is Paul's earliest *written* statement about justification, we must reckon with the possibility that he formulated this teaching earlier and that it played a role in his preaching.

25. In this translation I have modified the NRSV by construing three genitives as sub-

In this statement, Paul juxtaposes "doing the works of the law" and "the faithfulness of Jesus Christ" or "faith in Jesus Christ." The first phrase refers to carrying out the prescriptions of the Mosaic Law, which Paul understands within the context of God's promise to Abraham. Employing a salvation-historical scheme that begins with God's promise to Abraham, Paul argues that the law had a temporary role in God's redemptive plan, in which it served as humanity's "disciplinarian" until the promised offspring (Christ) should appear. The "works of the law" of which Paul speaks, then, are not merely good deeds; they are the prescriptions of Torah that identify the Jewish people as God's covenant people. The literary context of this passage, the incident at Antioch, suggests that circumcision and the dietary prescriptions of the law play an especially important role in Paul's understanding of the works of the law in Galatians.[26] I have construed the second phrase, which is traditionally understood as "faith in Jesus Christ," as "the faithfulness of Jesus Christ," by which I mean the faithfulness that Christ manifested in his obedient death on the cross. This faithfulness is the reason why the justified believe *in* Christ. Paul's teaching on justification, then, can be stated in this way: *A person, whether Jew or Gentile, is not acquitted before God on the basis of doing the covenant prescriptions of the law, whether it be the ethical prescriptions of the Decalogue or circumcision and the dietary prescriptions of the law, which identify a person as a Jew. Rather, a person is justified before God on the basis of the faithful act of obedience that Christ manifested by his saving death on the cross, for which reason the justified believe in Christ.*

Paul came to his understanding of justification in light of what God had done in Christ. Working from solution (Christ's death) to plight (the need for righteousness), Paul reasons that if righteousness could have come through the law, then Christ's death was of no avail (2:21). Con-

---

ject genitives (the faithfulness of Jesus Christ, the faithfulness of Christ, and the faithfulness of the Son of God) rather than as objective genitives (faith in Jesus Christ, faith in Christ, faith in the Son of God). This reading, with which not all agree, highlights Christ's redemptive work without excluding faith in Christ. It affirms that a person is justified on the basis of Christ's faithfulness, which was exhibited by his obedient death on the cross. Because of Christ's faithful obedience, which leads to justification, the justified believe in Christ.

26. James Dunn views the work of the law in terms of those prescriptions that functioned as identity markers (circumcision, food laws, Sabbath observance). This is the view that I proposed in my commentary (*Galatians* [SP 9; Collegeville: Liturgical, 1992]); however, I am now inclined to think that Paul had the other prescriptions of the law in view as well as these.

vinced that Christ gave himself to rescue us from this present evil age (1:4), Paul concludes that Christ's death effected something that doing the works of the law could not. Consequently, when he discusses the law and the promise in Galatians 3, he notes that if a law had been given that was capable of giving life, then righteousness would have come through the law (3:21). In light of the new life that he enjoys in Christ (2:20), Paul concludes that the law could not give such righteousness, which he equates with life. Such life-giving righteousness comes from the Spirit. Those who are in Christ are already Abraham's offspring because they enjoy the promised gift of the Spirit (3:14). This is why Paul asks the Galatians whether they received the Spirit from doing the works of the law or from believing Paul's proclamation of the crucified Christ (vv. 1-6). Since the Galatians have an experience of the Spirit, which they received on the basis of faith rather than on the basis of doing the works of the Mosaic law, they are already justified because of the life-giving Spirit dwelling in them. What Paul says in Galatians 3 about the relationship between righteousness and the Spirit indicates that he views justification as more than a legal metaphor. The acquittal the justified enjoy results in the life-giving righteousness that comes from the presence of the Spirit. Paul describes this new situation when he says that he has been crucified with Christ: it is no longer he who lives but Christ who lives in him.[27] Consequently, he now lives on the basis of the faithfulness of the Son of God who loved him and gave himself for him (2:19-20). *Justification, then, results in life in Christ and the Spirit.* Already justified inasmuch as they live in Christ and the Spirit, the justified eagerly "wait for the hope of righteousness" (5:5), by which Paul means the final pronouncement of acquittal that will occur at the end of the ages.

---

27. Gorman (*Inhabiting the Cruciform God,* 101) describes justification, within Paul's logic, as co-crucifixion with Christ and as theosis, thereby overcoming the divide between justification and sanctification. He insightfully writes: "God's declaration of 'justified!' now is a 'performative utterance,' an effective word that does not return void but effects transformation. Thus God's declaration now of 'justified!' accompanies the divine crucifixion and resurrection of the believer and effects, by the Spirit, a real, existential process of transformation, which is nothing like a legal fiction." Thomas R. Schreiner (*Paul: Apostle of God's Glory in Christ: A Pauline Theology* [Downers Grove: InterVarsity, 2001], 189-217, here 206) also seeks to unite justification and sanctification. Adopting a forensic view of justification, however, he believes that this can be done without "smuggling in the idea of transformation." Although justification is a forensic metaphor, the effect of God's work in Christ includes some form of transformation, not in the sense that the justified suddenly become ethically good, but in the sense that they become a new creation in Christ and are being transformed into the image of Christ.

In Romans Paul presents his teaching on justification in relationship to "the righteousness of God," a concept that does not occur in Galatians. The righteousness of God is God's own uprightness, that is, God's saving justice, God's covenant loyalty.[28] God manifested this righteousness in the redemptive death of his Son. Paul describes the effects of God's saving righteousness in this way.

> *But now,* apart from law, *the righteousness of God* has been disclosed, and is attested by the law and the prophets, *the righteousness of God* through the faithfulness of Jesus Christ for all who believe. For there is no distinction, since all have sinned and fall short of the glory of God; they are now *justified by his grace as a gift,* through the redemption that is in Christ Jesus, whom God put forward as a sacrifice of atonement by his blood, effective through faith. He did this to show *his righteousness,* because in his divine forbearance he had passed over the sins previously committed; it was to prove at the present time that *he himself is righteous* and that *he justifies the one who has the faith of Jesus.*[29] (3:21-26)

In this statement, Paul presents his teaching on justification (that all are freely justified by God's grace) within the context of the saving righteousness that God manifested in Christ's death on the cross. Having argued that all have sinned and are under the power of sin (1:18–3:20), Paul employs the pregnant phrase "but now" to signal God's solution to the human plight (3:21). Because all have sinned and are in need of God's grace, God has *now* manifested his saving righteousness in Jesus Christ. As a result of this saving righteousness, all are justified by God's grace through the redemption that God has worked in Christ (v. 24).

Because God has done what humanity could not do for itself, Paul insists that human beings cannot boast before God about anything they have done. Summarizing his teaching on justification, Paul writes: "For we hold that a person is justified by faith apart from works prescribed by the law"

28. The term can also be construed as a genitive of origin: the righteousness that comes from God. But for reasons I have explained in my commentary (*Romans* [Paideia; Grand Rapids: Baker, 2010]), I have aligned myself with those who interpret the term in Rom 1:17 as a subjective genitive. In my view Rom 3:5; 3:21, 22; 10:3; and 2 Cor 5:21 should be read in the same way.

29. Here I have modified the NRSV by employing two subjective genitives: "the faithfulness of Jesus Christ" rather than "faith in Jesus Christ" and "the faith of Jesus" rather than "faith in Jesus."

(3:28).[30] To illustrate what he means by justification by faith, in Romans 4 Paul points to the example of Abraham, who was justified on the basis of his faith rather than on the basis of his works. Providing his audience with a christological exegesis of Gen 15:6 ("And he believed the LORD; and the LORD reckoned it to him as righteousness"), Paul argues that Abraham's faith in God's promise was credited to him as righteousness, even though Abraham had not yet been circumcised. At the end of Romans 4, Paul applies this exegesis to those who believe in Christ: "Now the words, 'it was reckoned to him,' were written not for his sake alone, but for ours also. *It will be reckoned to us who believe in him who raised Jesus our Lord from the dead, who was handed over to death for our trespasses and was raised for our justification*" (4:23-25). Just as the faith of Abraham was reckoned to him as righteousness, so will the faith of those who believe in God who raised Jesus from the dead. This is why Christ died "for our trespasses" and was raised "for our justification" *(dia tēn dikaiōsin hēmōn).*

In Romans 5 Paul relates justification and reconciliation to each other for the first time. He notes that since believers have been justified by faith they are at peace with God (5:1). God has done away with the enmity and hostility against God that once characterized their lives. The peace to which Paul refers is the result of God's work of justification and reconciliation, of which Paul speaks in vv. 9-11:

> Much more surely then, now that we have been *justified* by his blood,
>   *will we be saved* through him from the wrath of God.
> For if while we were enemies, we were *reconciled* to God through
>   the death of his Son, much more
>   surely, having been *reconciled, will we be saved* by his life.
> But more than that, we even boast in God through our
>   Lord Jesus Christ,
>   through whom we have now received *reconciliation.*

Since believers are *already justified* by the blood of Christ and reconciled to God through the death of his Son, they can be all the more confident that they *will be saved* from the eschatological wrath to come. Although Paul uses two metaphors to describe the present situation of believers, one that

---

30. Whereas in Galatians, circumcision and dietary prescriptions play a prominent role in Paul's understanding of "the works of the law," in Romans Paul has in view *all* the prescriptions of the law.

evokes a legal verdict of acquittal and another that evokes the restoration of a broken relationship, the two are intimately related to each other in this sense: *the justified are reconciled to God, and the reconciled have been justified by God.*[31]

The verb "justify" tends to recede to the background after 5:9, but the noun "righteousness" continues to play a prominent role in the rest of Romans.[32] In his Adam-Christ comparison, Paul notes that whereas death reigned through Adam's trespass, those who have received the gift of righteousness will rule in life through Jesus Christ (5:17). Consequently, whereas sin exercised its rule through death, grace exercises its rule through righteousness (5:21). Next, Paul reminds his readers that whereas they were slaves of sin, now they have become slaves of righteousness, which leads to sanctification (6:18-20). In these texts, Paul portrays righteousness in two ways. First, it is God's free gift, the result of justification. It is not something the justified have earned but a new status God has bestowed upon them.[33] Second, righteousness is the new master to whom the justified give their allegiance.

The anomaly that Gentiles who were not pursuing righteousness attained it, whereas Israel, which pursued a law of righteousness, did not attain to the goal of the law provides Paul with another occasion to present his teaching on righteousness (9:30-31). Arguing that Israel pursued the law on the basis of works rather than on the basis of faith, Paul quotes Isa 28:16 to show that Israel stumbled on the "stone" that is Christ, in whom God manifested his saving righteousness. Ignorant of God's righteousness revealed in Christ, Israel mistakenly pursued its own righteousness (Rom

31. Joseph A. Fitzmyer ("Reconciliation in Pauline Theology," in *To Advance the Gospel: New Testament Studies* [New York: Crossroad, 1981], 162-85, here 178) writes: "It [reconciliation] expresses an aspect of the Christ-event that justification does not, and it is really impossible to say which is more important."

32. Paul employs the verb in two other instances after 5:9. In 8:30, he uses "justify" along with a series of other verbs that summarize God's redemptive plan, including predestination, election, justification, and glorification: "And those whom he *predestined* he also *called;* and those whom he called he also *justified;* and those whom he justified he also *glorified.*" In 8:33 he employs the verb to assure the justified that nothing can separate them from God: "Who will bring any charge against God's elect? It is God who *justifies.*"

33. Wright (*Justification*, 121, 206) insists that righteousness denotes a status rather than a moral quality or virtue. While I agree with this, I would add that God's righteousness also transforms believers inasmuch as they become a new creation in Christ. To be sure, they are not ethically transformed, but they are transformed in such a way that the ethically good life becomes a possibility for them in a way it was not before.

10:3), as did the pre-Christian Paul (Phil 3:6). Unaware that Christ was the terminus of the law (Rom 10:4), Israel continued to pursue a righteousness based on the law after God had manifested his righteousness in the faithfulness of the crucified Christ.

The Pauline teaching on justification can be summarized in this way: Gentiles and Jews are justified on the basis of the saving grace God manifested when God revealed his righteousness in the crucified Christ. The faith of those who believe in God's saving righteousness is reckoned to them as righteousness, the gift of a new status and life that God graciously bestows on the justified.

Philippians and 2 Corinthians In his letter to the Philippians, Paul contrasts the righteousness that he attained on the basis of legal observance with the righteousness that comes from God through the faithfulness of Christ, a righteousness that depends on faith (3:9).[34] Noting that he formerly observed the law and could boast that he was blameless according to a righteousness based on the law (v. 6), Paul no longer accounts his former righteousness as of any value in light of the righteousness that comes from God. Consequently, the righteousness that he now seeks is a righteousness that comes from God on the basis of what God has done in Christ. It is a gift that provides believers with a new status before God, not because of what they have done but because of what God has done for them in Christ.

Paul makes a similar point when he writes: "For our sake he made him to be sin who knew no sin, so that in him we might become the righteousness of God" (2 Cor 5:21). Noting that Christ took humanity's place so that humanity could stand in Christ's place, Paul identifies Christ with "sin," not because Christ was sinful but because he fully entered into the condition of unredeemed humanity (see Rom 8:3, which makes a similar point). Because of this exchange, humanity has become the righteousness of God inasmuch as it participates in the righteousness of Christ.[35] Paul's statement in 1 Cor 1:30 makes a similar point: believers exist in Christ Jesus who has become for them "wisdom from God, and *righteousness* and sanctification and redemption." Whatever righteousness believers enjoy, then, is

34. Here I have interpreted the genitive as a subjective genitive, the faithfulness of Christ rather than faith in Christ.

35. Gal 3:13 is another example of such an interchange. By dying on the cross, Christ absorbed the curse that the law pronounced on one who "hung on a tree" (Deut 21:23) in order to ransom those under the curse that the law pronounces upon those who do not do all of its prescriptions (Gal 3:10).

Christ's righteousness, which is the righteousness of God. Given the centrality that righteousness plays in Paul's theology, it is not surprising that he describes his ministry as a ministry of the Spirit and of righteousness (2 Cor 3:9) that transforms believers into the image of Christ (v. 18), who is the image of God (4:4).

In addition to portraying his ministry in terms of righteousness and the Spirit, Paul speaks of the ministry of reconciliation that God granted to him when God reconciled Paul to himself (2 Cor 5:18).[36] In an important teaching about reconciliation (vv. 17-21), Paul notes that those who are in Christ are part of a new creation that God has brought about by reconciling the world to himself through Christ. Entrusted with this message of reconciliation, Paul appeals to others to "be reconciled to God" (v. 20). Although this appeal could suggest that humanity must reconcile itself to God, the wider context does not allow this interpretation: God has already reconciled humanity. Humanity's task is to accept the gift God offers in Christ.

Colossians and Ephesians Whereas justification plays a major role in Romans and Galatians, reconciliation enjoys a more central place in Colossians and Ephesians. We have already seen that in the Colossians hymn Paul describes the cosmic work of Christ in the realm of creation (1:15-18a) and in the realm of redemption (vv. 18b-20). Just as all things were created through Christ, so all things were reconciled through him by the blood of his cross. God's work of reconciliation through Christ occurred on the cross and was cosmic in scope. Relating Christ's cosmic work to the situation of the Colossians, Paul reminds them that whereas they were once alienated from God, now they have been reconciled through Christ's fleshly body by his death so that Christ might present them as holy, blameless, and irreproachable before God (v. 22). As in Romans 5, the cross is the locus of reconciliation, and, as in 2 Corinthians 5, this reconciliation changes the relationship of those who were formerly at enmity with God.

Ephesians 2 illustrates how Paul's teaching on justification and reconciliation is updated for a new generation of believers. In the first part of the chapter (vv. 1-10) Paul reminds the Ephesians that God delivered them from their former sinful predicament and raised and seated them with

---

36. Although Paul employs the plural here, I have interpreted this verse as a personal statement.

Christ in the heavens. Paul insists that this is the result of God's work, not their own:

> For *by grace you have been saved through faith,* and this is not your own doing; it is the gift of God — *not the result of works, so that no one may boast.* For we are what he has made us, created in Christ Jesus for good works, which God prepared beforehand to be our way of life. (vv. 8-10)

In this statement Ephesians updates Paul's teaching on justification by faith apart from doing the works of the Mosaic Law in two ways. First, whereas Romans and Galatians speak of being "justified" by faith, Ephesians refers to being "saved" through faith. Second, whereas Romans and Galatians use the expression "by doing the works of the law," Ephesians simply speaks of "works." By presenting Paul's teaching on justification in this way, Ephesians makes it accessible to a generation for whom doing the works of the Mosaic Law is no longer the issue. At a time when Gentiles were becoming a majority in the church, Ephesians reminds believers that they are not saved by their "works" (a broader category than "the works of the law") but by God's grace, faith being the means by which they appropriate this grace. Moreover, whatever good works they accomplish are works that God has already prepared in advance for them. Accordingly, while good works are important for their new life, everything begins and ends with God's grace.[37]

In the second part of the chapter (2:11-22), Paul reminds the Ephesians of their former alienation from Israel. At that time they were without Christ, strangers to the covenants and the promises, without hope in the world. But now they have been brought near to the commonwealth of Israel by the blood of Christ, who broke down the dividing wall (the law) that separated them from Israel, thereby creating a new humanity drawn from Gentiles and Jews alike. By doing this, Christ has made peace between Gentiles and Jews by reconciling both to God, in one body, through the cross.[38] In light of Christ's work of reconciliation, Paul can say, "you are no longer strangers and aliens, but you are citizens with the saints and also members of the household of God" (v. 19).

---

37. The teaching of Ephesians on justification is, in some ways, closer to the Reformation doctrine than the teaching of Galatians is since the focus is on "works" in general rather than on "the works of the law."

38. Here the body refers to Christ's own body, in which the new humanity is found.

In this remarkable chapter Ephesians updates Paul's teaching on justification and reconciliation for a new generation. On the one hand, it presents justification in a way that its meaning is no longer limited to the old debates about doing the works of the Mosaic Law; on the other, it highlights the social dimension of reconciliation whereby Gentiles and Jews are brought together in a new humanity, something we did not find in Romans 5 and 2 Corinthians 5.[39]

The Pastorals Like Ephesians, the Pastorals formulate Paul's teaching on justification in a way that frees it from the old debate about the need to do the works of the Mosaic Law. In 2 Timothy Paul refers to God "who *saved* us and called us with a holy calling, *not according to our works* but according to *his own purpose and grace*. This grace was given to us in Christ Jesus before the ages began" (1:9). Instead of framing this text in terms of being justified by faith rather than by doing the works of the Mosaic Law, Paul casts it in terms of being saved according to God's purpose and grace rather than by works. Thus he affirms that salvation is the outcome of grace rather than human striving.

Tit 3:4-7 presents a fuller development of Paul's teaching on justification:

> But when the goodness and loving kindness of God our Savior appeared, *he saved us,* not because of any *works of righteousness* that we had done, but according to his mercy, through the water of rebirth and renewal by the Holy Spirit. This Spirit he poured out on us richly through Jesus Christ our Savior, so that, *having been justified by his grace,* we might become heirs according to the hope of eternal life.

Here, Paul presents his teaching within the context of the appearance of the Savior God, which occurred in the first appearance of Christ. At that moment, God saved believers through baptism and the Spirit according to his mercy rather than on the basis of works of righteousness. The result is that believers have been justified by God's grace in the hope of eternal life. Although Titus echoes earlier Pauline language when it speaks of being justified by God's grace (compare Rom 3:24), it focuses on the appearance

---

39. The teaching of Ephesians on reconciliation makes a point similar to the point that Galatians and Romans make about justification: the purpose of God's work in Christ is to unite Gentiles and Jews.

of the Savior God in Christ rather than on the cross. The central message, however, remains intact: salvation/justification is God's work in Christ rather than humanity's work.

Redeemed, Freed, and Forgiven

The Pauline teaching on redemption *(apolytrōsis)*, freedom *(eleutheria)*, and forgiveness *(aphesis)* provides another way to view the benefits of Christ's saving death and resurrection. Drawn from Israel's Scriptures as well as from the social world in which the Pauline writings were conceived, the concepts of redemption and freedom suggest that humanity was in a situation of slavery and bondage from which it could not extricate itself.[40] The concept of forgiveness is more specific, presupposing that sins have been committed. Making use of these concepts to explain the benefits of Christ's death and resurrection, the Pauline letters present Christ as the one through whom God redeemed, freed, and forgave humanity.

Paul makes an important statement about redemption when he reminds the Corinthians of the message of the cross that he preached to them and its significance for their election. Recalling that God chose the foolish, the weak, and the lowly of the world so that no one can boast before God, Paul says that it is due to God that the Corinthians exist in Christ Jesus, who has become their wisdom, righteousness, sanctification, and "redemption" (*apolytrōsis*, 1 Cor 1:30). Inasmuch as Paul has been speaking about the crucified Christ throughout this section, he implies that this situation has come about because the Corinthians have been justified, sanctified, and redeemed by the death of the crucified Christ.

Paul alludes to Christ's redemptive work in two other contexts in 1 Corinthians. In the first, he exhorts the Corinthians to avoid sexual immorality since they belong to Christ (6:12-20). At the end of this exhortation, he writes: "For you were bought *(ēgorasthēte)* with a price; therefore glorify

---

40. On the background of this metaphor, see Fitzmyer, *Paul and His Theology*, 66-67, and D. François Tolmie, "Salvation as Redemption: The Use of 'Redemption' Metaphors in Pauline Literature," in *Salvation in the New Testament*, 247-69, here 253. Both authors note that it is difficult to identify the origins of the metaphor with certainty. Tolmie is inclined to find the conceptual background of the term in "the well-known phenomenon of slavery." Fitzmyer relates it to the OT idea of Yhwh as Israel's redeemer as well as to the cultural background of the sacral remission of slaves, which he relates to the vocabulary and background found in the LXX.

God in your body" (v. 20). In the second, after exhorting believers to remain in the state in which they were called (7:17-24), he concludes with a similar phrase: "You were bought *(ēgorasthēte)* with a price; do not become slaves of human masters" (v. 23). In both instances, Paul is referring to Christ's death. By saying that "Christ died for sins" (*Christos apethanen hyper tōn hamartiōn*, 15:3), he indicates that Christ's redemptive work involves the forgiveness of sins.[41] It is not surprising, then, that later Pauline letters identify redemption with forgiveness of sins or trespasses (Col 1:14; Eph 1:7), thereby indicating that, even if Paul is not their author, those who wrote in his name understood his teaching.

In Rom 3:21-26 Paul connects God's righteousness, justification, redemption, atonement/expiation, and forgiveness of sins. Affirming that God manifested his righteousness in the faithfulness of Jesus Christ,[42] Paul states that all are now justified by God's grace "through the redemption *(apolytrōseōs)* that is in Christ Jesus, whom God put forward as a sacrifice of atonement *(hilastērion)* by his blood, effective through faith. This he did to show his righteousness, because in his divine forbearance he had passed over sins previously committed; it was to prove at the present time that he himself is righteous and that he justifies the one who has the faith of Jesus" (vv. 24-26).[43] In this complex text Paul defines justification in terms of redemption by noting that God justified humanity *by the redemption that is in Christ Jesus.* Next, he explains this redemption by presenting Christ as a sacrifice of atonement, which brought about the forgiveness of sins that God, in his forbearance, had previously passed over, but which God has now dealt with through Christ's death, thereby showing that God is righteous.[44] If this interpretation is correct, Paul employs the metaphor of re-

---

41. In other texts that employ the formula "for" or "for us," Paul writes that Christ died for the godless (Rom 5:6), that he died for us (v. 8), that God handed over his own Son for us all (8:32), that one man died for all (2 Cor 5:14), that Christ was made sin for us (v. 21), that he handed himself over for our sins (Gal 1:4), that he became a curse for us (3:13), that Christ handed himself over for us as an offering to God (Eph 5:2), that it was the Lord Jesus Christ who died for us (1 Thess 5:9-10), and that he gave himself as a ransom for us (1 Tim 2:6).

42. Once more, I am interpreting the genitive as a subjective genitive.

43. Again, the subjective genitive ("the faith of Jesus") rather than the objective genitive ("faith in Jesus").

44. The phrase "sacrifice of atonement" translates *hilastērion*, which refers to the "mercy seat" or "lid" that covered the ark of the covenant, which the high priest smeared with blood each year on the Day of Atonement to make expiation or atonement for sins (Leviticus 16). According to Paul, Christ has become the new mercy seat, who expiates humanity's sins by his own blood.

demption to develop the metaphor of justification, and he uses the metaphor of atonement to fill out the metaphor of redemption. *Redemption, which is the means by which God justifies humanity, results in atonement for and forgiveness of sins.*

In Galatians, Paul relates redemption more closely to the law since he must persuade the Galatians not to seek their justification on the basis of legal observance. Consequently, he tells those who want to place themselves under the law, which threatens those who do not observe it with a curse (3:10), that "Christ redeemed us from the curse of the law" (3:13). Then, to show the Galatians that the period of the law was a preparatory period, he states that it was "to redeem those who were under the law" that God sent his own Son so that all might become God's adopted children (4:5). In this way Paul portrays the period of the law as the time of humanity's minority from which it needed to be redeemed in order to enter the period of its majority, the time of the Spirit.

Although Paul usually refers to redemption as something God has already brought about, there are a few instances when he speaks of the redemption for which believers wait and hope.[45] For example, the justified await the redemption of their bodies (Rom 8:23), which will occur at the general resurrection of the dead. At the present time, the Spirit is the first installment of the inheritance they have toward their redemption as God's possession (Eph 1:14). Consequently, they wait in hope for the day of redemption (4:30).

Whereas the Pauline concept of redemption highlights the deliverance believers have experienced (especially the forgiveness of their sins), which came about at the cost of Christ's saving death, the concept of freedom *(eleutheria)* focuses on the liberation believers enjoy because they are no longer under the powers of sin and death, or under the law. Consequently, while both concepts include notions of release, the notion of freedom highlights liberation from enslavement whereas redemption explains how this liberation came about.

In his letter to the Galatians Paul discusses freedom in terms of the law since he must dissuade them from being circumcised and placing themselves "under the law." To accomplish his goal, he interprets the story of

45. This is similar to what we noticed in our discussion of Paul's teaching on justification. Although Paul normally speaks of justification as something that has already occurred, he notes that believers "eagerly await the hope of righteousness," that is, the fullness of righteousness that will occur at the end of the ages.

Sarah and Hagar allegorically to show them that they belong to the line of the free woman, Sarah, rather than to the line of the slave woman, Hagar (4:21-31). In light of this allegory, Paul reminds the Galatians that it was for freedom that Christ set them free. Consequently, they should not submit themselves to another yoke of slavery by placing themselves under the law (5:1). Freedom from the law, however, does not mean they can do whatever they want. Having been called to freedom, they must use their freedom from the law as an occasion to serve each other through love (v. 13). The freedom Paul envisions in Galatians is rooted in the Spirit, who enables the justified to fulfill the love commandment. Paul's words in 2 Cor 3:17 are apropos here: "where the Spirit of the Lord is, there is freedom," the freedom to serve the Lord through the power of the Spirit.

Whereas in Galatians Paul discusses freedom from being under the law, in Romans he considers how God's work in Christ has freed the justified from the powers of sin and death, as well as from being under the law. After arguing that all are under the power of sin (Rom 3:9), in Romans 6 Paul affirms that "having been set free from sin," the justified "have become slaves of righteousness" (6:18). In ch. 8 he explains that "the law of the Spirit of life in Christ Jesus has set you free from the law of sin and death" (8:2). Employing "law" in the sense of principle, Paul means that it is the Spirit that has freed the justified from sin and death, which once ruled over their lives.[46] Expanding his horizon, Paul considers the present situation of creation, which has not been able to attain its purpose because of human sin. Personifying creation, he says that it waits with eager longing for the moment when the justified will be revealed as God's children. At that moment, creation "will be set free from its bondage to decay and will obtain the freedom of the glory of the children of God" (v. 21).

To summarize, whereas justification and reconciliation highlight the new status believers enjoy because of Christ's redemptive death, the concepts of redemption, liberation, and forgiveness underscore how Christ has released the justified from the powers that threatened and enslaved them.

---

46. Not all would agree that Paul employs law as "principle" here. Some would argue that he is speaking of the Mosaic law from two different perspectives: the law under the power of sin and death and the law empowered by God's grace.

Sanctified, Transformed, a New Creation

The metaphors of sanctification *(hagiasmos)*, transformation *(metamorphoō)*, and new creation *(kainē ktisis)* provide insights to the interior change that Christ's saving death and resurrection effects in the lives of those who belong to the community of the justified and reconciled. In making this statement, I am not suggesting that the previous metaphors only point to an external change with the result that there is a chasm between justification, reconciliation, and redemption on the one hand and sanctification and transformation on the other. Although they evoke different images, all these concepts point to the same reality: the benefits of Christ's saving death and resurrection. Inasmuch as they speak of the same reality, they are interconnected so that what Paul writes about redemption informs what he says about justification, and what he says about justification informs what he writes about reconciliation. In the same way, what Paul says about sanctification, transformation, and new creation provides us with a deeper insight to what he affirms about justification, reconciliation, and redemption. To be more explicit, these concepts indicate that in justifying, reconciling, and redeeming humanity in Christ, God sanctifies and transforms the justified, who belong to the new creation that God has created in Christ.

Those who have been justified and redeemed by Christ are not called "holy" because they have attained a particular degree of ethical holiness but because God, who is holy, has consecrated and set them apart for service. Accordingly, the holiness of which Paul speaks is not an ethical quality but a cultic notion deeply rooted in Israel's Scriptures. Understood from this vantage point, holiness means that believers have been set aside and dedicated for service to God, who is holy.

Before they were "in Christ," Paul's Gentile converts did not live in the sphere of God's holiness. Separated from Christ, they lived in a realm of immorality and impurity. But now, through Christ's death and resurrection, they have been "sanctified in Christ Jesus" (1 Cor 1:2). Alluding to their baptism, Paul affirms that the Corinthians have been washed, sanctified, and justified in the name of the Lord Jesus Christ (6:11). Consequently, just as Christ became their wisdom, righteousness, and redemption, so he has become their sanctification (1:30). That is, Christ has dedicated and consecrated them to God's service through his saving death and resurrection.

Because Christ has sanctified them, Paul calls those to whom he writes *hoi hagioi,* which can be translated as "the saints," "the holy ones," "the con-secrated ones," "the dedicated ones." The holiness in which they participate is the result of God's elective call (Rom 1:7), which unites them with all who "call on the name of the Lord Jesus Christ" (1 Cor 1:2). When addressing a Gentile audience, therefore, Paul writes, "you are citizens with the saints and also members of the household of God" (Eph 2:19). The holy kiss that the holy ones exchange, then, is a sign of the communion that exists among those consecrated to God (Rom 16:16; 1 Cor 16:20; 2 Cor 13:12; 1 Thess 5:26).

In his exhortation to the Thessalonians, Paul reminds them that God's will for them is their holiness (*ho hagiasmos hymōn,* 1 Thess 4:3), for God did not call them to impurity but to holiness (*hagiasmō,* v. 7). Because the Thessalonians participate in God's holiness, Paul prays that the Lord will strengthen their hearts "in holiness" so that they may be "blameless" be-fore God at the coming of the Lord (3:13; 5:23).

In Romans 6 Paul connects freedom, sanctification, and life. When unredeemed humanity obeyed sin, this obedience led to death. Having been freed from sin, the justified have become slaves of righteousness for the purpose of sanctification (v. 19), which leads to eternal life (v. 22). The relationship Paul establishes here can be summarized in this way: freedom from sin leads to righteousness, the goal of righteousness is sanctification, and sanctification leads to eternal life. In light of this, it should be apparent that, even though Paul derives his notion of holiness from Israel's cult, he does not limit his understanding of holiness to its cultic meaning. The sanctification the justified enjoy in Christ leads to eternal life because God communicates something of his holiness to them. Because they have been sanctified, the justified ought to live an ethically good life that corresponds to the holiness that has been communicated to them.[47]

Although the concept of transformation does not occur as frequently in Paul's letters as holiness does, it plays an important role in his soteri-ology. Contrasting his ministry with the ministry of Moses, who put a veil over his face "to keep the people of Israel from gazing at the end of the glory that was being set aside" (2 Cor 3:13), Paul states that the ministry of the new covenant enables believers to gaze directly on the glory of the Lord because the veil has been removed. As believers gaze on this glory, they "are being transformed (*metamorphoumetha*) into the same image

---

47. This last statement indicates that there is an ethical dimension to the Pauline no-tion of sanctification. Those who have been sanctified must flee immorality and live in such a way that they will be blameless on the day of the Lord's coming.

(eikona) from one degree of glory to another" (v. 18). Since the "image" to which Paul refers is Christ, who is "the image of God" (4:4), he means that believers are being transformed from one degree of glory to another into the image of Christ, who is the image of God. Paul recounts the transformation that is presently occurring in his own life in light of his apostolic sufferings. Although his outer nature is wasting away because of these sufferings, his inner nature is being renewed *(anakainoutai)* day by day, preparing him for the glory that is beyond all measure (vv. 16-17).

In Rom 12:2 Paul speaks of transformation in a hortatory setting. Employing the same verbs as in 2 Cor 3:18 and 4:16, he writes: "Do not be conformed to this world, but be transformed *(metamorphousthe)* by the renewing *(anakainōsei)* of your minds, so that you may discern what is the will of God — what is good and acceptable and perfect." Although the emphasis is on what the justified should do, the wider context of Romans indicates that it is God's work in Christ that makes it possible for the justified to be transformed by the renewal of their minds. The transformation that is presently taking place in them, then, is intimately related to God's work of justification, reconciliation, and redemption in Christ.

God's redemptive work in Christ has brought about a new creation so that "everything old has passed away; see, everything has become new!" (2 Cor 5:17). Paul employs a similar phrase at the end of Galatians. Having argued that the Galatians should not have themselves circumcised, he concludes this letter by saying that circumcision and uncircumcision are no longer of any concern, that what counts is the "new creation" that is the outcome of God's work in Christ (6:15). This new creation is life in Christ, whom Paul identifies in Romans 5 as the eschatological Adam. To be in the eschatological Adam is to belong to this new creation, where everything has been made new.

To summarize, God's redemptive work in Christ transforms those who live in the new creation God has brought forth in Christ. They share in God's holiness, which leads to eternal life; they are being transformed from glory to glory into the very image of Christ, who is the image of God.

Waiting for Final Salvation and Glorification

Although believers *already* experience the benefits of Christ's death and resurrection inasmuch as they have been justified, redeemed, reconciled, and sanctified, they have *not yet* attained the final salvation that will occur when they will be glorified according to the pattern of their risen Lord at the general resurrection of the dead. This is why Paul writes: "But our citizenship is in heaven, and it is from there that we are expecting a Savior, the Lord Jesus Christ. He will transform *(metaschēmatisei)* the body of our humiliation that it may be conformed to the body of his glory, by the power that also enables him to make all things subject to himself" (Phil 3:20-21).[48] Although Ephesians affirms that believers *have been saved* by God's grace (2:5, 8), and although Titus states that God saved us according to his mercy (3:5), the Pauline notion of salvation *(sōtēria)* is more complex than this.[49] Believers *are being saved* by the message of the cross (1 Cor 1:18; 15:2; 2 Cor 2:15) and *will be saved* at the general resurrection of the dead. It is more accurate to say, then, that believers have been saved *in hope* (Rom 8:24), their hope for the general resurrection of the dead, when they will be glorified with Christ (v. 17).

The gospel is the good news of salvation (Eph 1:13). Therefore, Paul is not ashamed of it, for, when the gospel is proclaimed, the power of God is at work for the purpose of salvation for all who believe (Rom 1:16). Accordingly, those who confess that Jesus is Lord and believe that God raised him from the dead will be saved (10:9). In an important statement about the relationship between justification, reconciliation, and salvation, Paul writes that, since believers were justified and reconciled to God when they were still alienated from God, they can be all the more confident that they *will be saved* now that they have been justified and reconciled (5:9-10). Although this fullness of salvation is yet to occur, believers can be confident that God has not destined them for wrath but for salvation through Jesus Christ (1 Thess 5:9). Drawing a relationship between election, salvation, and sanctification, Paul tells the Thessalonians that "God *chose* you as the first fruits for *salvation* through *sanctification* by the Spirit and through belief in the truth" (2 Thess 2:13). Although the fullness will not come until the eschaton, Paul reminds the Romans that it "is nearer to us now than when we first became believers" (Rom 13:11), and he exhorts the Corinthians to be reconciled to God because "now is the day of salvation" (2 Cor 6:2).

48. Although this text is an example of the Pauline notion of transformation, I did not treat it in the previous section since it speaks of the future transformation that believers will enjoy rather than the transformation they presently experience.

49. Even though Ephesians and Titus use the past tense ("saved"), both letters anticipate a final consummation of God's salvation that has not yet occurred. They are not saying that the *fullness* of salvation has occurred but that believers can be assured that they have been saved.

In Romans, Paul explains that the fullness of salvation that the gospel brings is the glorification that believers will enjoy when they will be glorified with *(syndoxasthōmen)* Christ at the general resurrection of the dead (8:17).[50] Prior to its justification and reconciliation, humanity sinned and fell short of God's glory (3:23). Deprived of God's glory, it was deprived of communion and life with God.[51] The justified, however, have now obtained access to God's grace so that they can boast of their "hope of sharing the glory of God" (5:2). Filled with the Spirit that testifies that they are God's children, the justified have become "heirs of God and joint heirs with Christ — if, in fact, we suffer with him so that we may also be glorified with him" (8:17). The present sufferings the justified endure, then, are as nothing compared to the glory that will be revealed to them (v. 18) when their bodies will be redeemed at the general resurrection of the dead (v. 23). Summarizing the full scope of God's plan, Paul notes that those whom God foreknew God also predestined to be conformed to the image of his Son (v. 29) through their own resurrection from the dead. Paul then relates election, justification, and glorification to each other by affirming that those whom God predestined, God called. Those whom God called, God justified, and those whom God justified, God glorified (v. 30). As we have already seen in our discussion of transformation, Paul believes that God's gift of glorification in Christ is already at work in the lives of believers who are being transformed into the image of the Son "from one degree of glory to another" by the Spirit (2 Cor 3:18). The afflictions believers presently endure, then, are preparing them "for an eternal weight of glory beyond all measure" (4:17), which they will experience when they are clothed with their heavenly dwelling, the resurrection body (5:2). Colossians affirms that when Christ is revealed, believers "will be revealed with him in glory" (3:4), and Ephesians speaks of the "glorious inheritance" that awaits believers (1:18).[52]

50. In saying this, Paul is not implying that Christ has not been glorified. Rather, believers will be glorified *with* Christ because they will enjoy the glorious resurrection body that he *already* possesses.

51. The sense here is that humanity lost the glory that God originally intended for it when God created humanity in his image and likeness. This is why humanity must be conformed to the image of Christ if it is to be glorified.

52. Although neither of these texts explicitly refers to the general resurrection, the fact that Colossians and Ephesians affirm that believers have been raised with Christ (Eph 2:6; Col 2:12; 3:1) indicates that what will be revealed is what has already happened in Christ: their resurrection from the dead.

Coherence and Meaning in Pauline Soteriology

Although the Pauline letters employ several metaphors and concepts to describe the benefits of Christ's saving death and resurrection, they point to the same reality from different vantage points and so are intimately related to each other. Their interrelationship can be summarized in this way. Through Christ's saving death and resurrection, God *justified and reconciled* humanity. This new situation came about through the *redemption* that occurred on the cross, where sins were *forgiven* and humanity was *freed* from the powers of sin and death, and released from being under the law. Justified, reconciled, redeemed, forgiven, and freed, believers are *sanctified* because God has communicated his holiness to them. As a *new creation* in Christ, the justified are presently being *transformed*, from one state of glory to another, into the image of God's Son. This transformation will be complete when they are *glorified* with Christ at the general resurrection of the dead. At that moment, they will experience the fullness of *salvation* because death, the last enemy, will have been destroyed. Isolated from each other, these metaphors and concepts are incomplete. Related to each other and interpreted in light of each other, they provide us with an insight into the benefits God bestows in Christ.

Having surveyed the saving grace that God has bestowed in Christ, we must now ask where and how believers live in God's saving grace.

FOR FURTHER READING

Breytenbach, Cilliers. "The 'For Us' Phrases in Soteriology: Considering Their Background and Use," Pages 163-85 in van der Watt, *Salvation in the New Testament*.

———. "Salvation of the Reconciled (with a Note on the Background of Paul's Metaphor of Reconciliation)." Pages 271-86 in van der Watt, *Salvation in the New Testament*.

Brondos, David A. *Paul on the Cross: Reconstructing the Apostle's Story of Redemption.* Fortress: Minneapolis, 2006.

Dunn, James D. G. *The Theology of Paul the Apostle.* Grand Rapids: Eerdmans, 1988. Pages 317-459.

du Toit, Andrie B. "Forensic Metaphors in Romans and Their Soteriological Significance." Pages 213-46 in van der Watt, *Salvation in the New Testament*.

Fitzmyer, Joseph A. *Paul and His Theology: A Brief Sketch.* 2nd ed. Englewood Cliffs: Prentice Hall, 1989. Pages 55-84.

———. "Reconciliation in Pauline Theology." Pages 162-85 in *To Advance the Gospel: New Testament Studies.* New York: Crossroad, 1981.

Gathercole, S. J. "Justified by Faith, Justified by His Blood: The Evidence of Romans 3:21–4:25." Pages 147-84 in *Justification and Variegated Nomism: A Fresh Appraisal of Paul and Second Temple Judaism. The Paradoxes of Paul,* vol. 2, ed. D. A. Carson, Peter T. O'Brien, and Mark A. Seifrid. Grand Rapids: Baker Academic, 2004.

Gorman, Michael J. *Inhabiting the Cruciform God: Kenosis, Justification, and Theosis in Paul's Narrative Soteriology.* Grand Rapids: Eerdmans, 2009.

Gräbe, Petrius J. "Salvation in Colossians and Ephesians." Pages 287-304 in van der Watt, *Salvation in the New Testament.*

Hahn, Ferdinand. *Theologie des Neuen Testaments* 1: *Die Vielfalt des Neuen Testaments.* Theologiegeschichte des Urchristentums. Tübingen: Mohr Siebeck, 2002. Pages 242-67.

Harrison, James R. "Paul, Theologian of Electing Grace." Pages 77-108 in *Paul and His Theology,* ed. Stanley E. Porter. Leiden: Brill, 2006.

Hultgren, Arland J. *Christ and His Benefits: Christology and Redemption in the New Testament.* Philadelphia: Fortress, 1987. Pages 47-57, 91-112.

Joubert, Stephen J. "ΧΑΡΙΣ in Paul: An Investigation into the Apostle's 'Performative' Application of the Language of *Grace* within the Framework of His Theological Reflection on the Event/Process of Salvation." Pages 187-211 in van der Watt, *Salvation in the New Testament.*

Lee, Sang M. *The Cosmic Drama of Salvation: A Study of Paul's Undisputed Writings from Anthropological and Cosmological Perspectives.* Tübingen: Mohr Siebeck, 2010.

Malherbe, Abraham J. "'Christ Jesus Came into the World to Save Sinners': Soteriology in the Pastoral Epistles." Pages 331-58 in van der Watt, *Salvation in the New Testament.*

Martin, Ralph P. *Reconciliation: A Study of Paul's Theology.* New Foundations Theological Library. Atlanta: John Knox, 1981.

Porter, Stanley E. "Paul's Concept of Reconciliation: Twice More." Pages 131-52 in *Paul and His Theology,* ed. Stanley E. Porter. Leiden: Brill, 2006.

Ridderbos, Herman. *Paul: An Outline of His Theology.* Grand Rapids: Eerdmans, 1975. Pages 91-252.

Schnelle, Udo. *Apostle Paul: His Life and Theology.* Grand Rapids: Baker Academic, 2005. Pages 478-85, 494-545.

Schreiner, Thomas R. *Paul: Apostle of God's Glory in Christ.* Downers Grove: InterVarsity, 2001. Pages 189-249.

Tolmie, D. François. "Salvation as Redemption: The Use of 'Redemption' Metaphors in Pauline Literature." Pages 247-69 in van der Watt, *Salvation in the New Testament.*

van der Watt, Jan G., ed. *Salvation in the New Testament: Perspectives on Soteriology.* NovTSup 121. Leiden: Brill, 2001.

Villiers, Pieter G. R. "Safe in the Family of God: Soteriological Perspectives in 1 Thessalonians." Pages 306-30 in van der Watt, *Salvation in the New Testament.*

Winling, Raymond. *La Bonne Nouvelle du salut en Jésus-Christ. Sotériologie du Nouveau Testament. Essai de théologie biblique.* Paris: Cerf, 2007. Pages 169-301.

Wright, N. T. *Justification: God's Plan and Paul's Vision.* Downers Grove: Intervarsity, 2009.

5. Living in the Community of God's Saving Grace

Introduction

In the previous chapter I investigated Pauline soteriology in light of the saving grace that God manifested in Jesus Christ. In doing so, I began with Paul's experience of this saving grace before highlighting the differences between the human condition apart from and in this saving grace. I noted that even though Paul employs a variety of metaphors to describe what God accomplished in Christ, all of them witness to a common reality: the benefits of God's saving grace whereby humanity has been justified, reconciled, sanctified, and transformed. The new situation of those who are in Christ, then, results in newness of life that believers already experience because they belong to God's new creation. To be sure, the justified and reconciled are not yet finally glorified, but something has occurred that enables them to live in the newness of life that comes from God's Spirit. Such people have been incorporated into the eschatological people of God, the church, which is the body of Christ. They continue to live in the world, but now they form a sanctified community in which they can live in newness of life. My consideration of Pauline Christology and soteriology, therefore, leads to a reflection on the church and, in the next chapter, a study of the moral life of the justified.

Paul addressed his letters to particular churches, or, in the case of Philemon and the Pastorals, to people intimately related to and responsible for the life of the church. In most instances, he wrote in his capacity as the father and founder of the community.[1] While Paul wrote on a variety

---

1. This is certainly true for his letters to the Corinthians, Galatians, Philippians, and Thessalonians. Paul did not, however, establish the communities at Rome and Colossae.

of topics in response to the needs, questions, problems, and crises that arose in these communities, his overriding concern was to remind believers of their new being in Christ (the indicative of salvation) and the implications of this existence for how they ought to live their lives in Christ (the moral imperative). Consequently, although these letters employ a variety of rhetorical forms, all of them are concerned with building up the believing community that Paul identifies as the church, the body of Christ, the temple of God, the household of God. And, although they address a variety of practical issues and deal with a spectrum of theological topics, they regularly remind their recipients of what it means to belong to the church. An underlying theme of all the letters then is *the relationship between faith in Christ and life in the church.* In saying this, I am not implying that ecclesiology is more important than Christology or that the letters are theological treatises. But I am suggesting that the relationship between belonging to Christ and living in the community of the church is a central theme of the Pauline letters. In the material that follows, I consider the church as the people of God and the body of Christ before dealing with the ministry of the church and the church's relationship to Israel.

The People of God

According to the Acts of the Apostles, Paul was baptized by Ananias shortly after the risen Lord appeared to him (Acts 9:10-19a). He then associated himself with the very people whom he had sought to persecute in Damascus (vv. 19b-22) before trying to join the disciples in Jerusalem (vv. 23-30), and eventually associating himself with the church at Antioch (11:25-26). Although many scholars question the historical accuracy of Luke's account, there is general agreement that Paul's call/conversion resulted in a movement from one community of believers to another.[2] Whereas formerly he

---

While he spent a great deal of time at Ephesus (Acts 19), he may not have been the author of the letter to the Ephesians, which appears to be a circular letter rather than a letter to that community.

2. Alan F. Segal (*Paul the Convert: The Apostolate and Apostasy of Saul the Pharisee* [New Haven: Yale University Press, 1990], 117) makes this point: "In Paul's case the change was from Pharisaism, in which Paul received his education, to a particular kind of gentile community of God-fearers, living without the law, and the change was powered by Paul's absorption into the spirit. The influence of the gentile community on Paul's understanding of the content of his religious vision is crucial to explaining his religious vision. Paul did

identified himself with those who were zealous for the law, now he identifies himself with a community of believers zealous for Christ, a community he once persecuted. Before he reflected on the meaning of baptism, then, Paul was baptized; and before he reflected on the nature of the church, he was nurtured in the community of those who believed in Christ. Consequently, just as there is an intimate relationship between Paul's call/conversion and his understanding of the benefits of Christ, so there is an intimate relationship between his call/conversion and his understanding of the church. Having been explicitly called to preach the gospel to the nations, Paul understood (in a way that many did not) the inclusive nature of the new community that God was creating in Christ. It was Paul's Damascus road experience, then, that brought him into the community of the church and provided him with an initial insight into its inclusive nature.

Although Paul employs a variety of images to describe the community of those who believe in Christ (the temple of God, a field), the most frequent way in which he refers to it is as the "church" *(ekklēsia),* by which he means the gathering or assembly of those who have been called, elected, and sanctified in Christ.[3] In doing so, he and those who used this term before him echo the Septuagint, which employs *ekklēsia* to translate the Hebrew *qāhāl,* a term designating the "congregation" or "assembly" of Israel. For example, the book of Deuteronomy says: "Then Moses recited the words of this song, to the very end, in the hearing of the whole *assembly* of Israel" (31:30). Likewise, the book of Judges notes: "The chiefs of all the people, of all the tribes of Israel, presented themselves in the *assembly* of God" (20:2).[4] In both of these texts and others the "assembly" refers to a solemn gathering of the people of Israel in their capacity as God's chosen people.[5] In the Acts of the Apostles, Stephen employs the word in this

---

change religious communities. The effect of that change was volatile and unpredictable, apparently even to Paul, because it took him many years to understand what was demanded of him and his converts."

3. For a summary of how the Pauline letters use *ekklēsia,* see the article by K. L. Schmidt, *"kaleō,"* TDNT 3:501-36, and Lucien Cerfaux, *The Church in the Theology of Saint Paul* (New York: Herder and Herder, 1959), 187-206.

4. In Deut 31:30 the Greek phrase is *pasēs ekklēsias Israēl,* and in Judg 20:2 it is *en tę̄ ekklēsią tou laou tou theou.*

5. In addition to this religious usage in the LXX, *ekklēsia* was employed in the Greek world to designate the assembly of freed men who gathered to vote. Schmidt (*TDNT* 3:513) highlights the etymology of the word and its significance: "The citizens are the *ekklētoi,* i.e., those who are summoned and called together by the herald. This teaches us something concerning the biblical and Christian usage, namely, that God in Christ calls men out of the world."

sense when he says to his accusers: "He [Moses] is the one who was in the congregation *(ekklēsia)* in the wilderness with the angel who spoke to him at Mount Sinai, and with our ancestors; and he received living oracles to give to us" (7:38).

Although *ekklēsia* occurs more frequently in the Pauline letters than in any other part of the NT,[6] Paul was not the first to designate the community of those who believe in Christ as an *ekklēsia*. The use of *ekklēsia* in Acts suggests that the Christian community applied this term at a rather early stage to the Jerusalem community (5:11; 8:1, 3; 11:22; 12:1, 5) and then to other communities (11:26; 13:1; 14:23, 27; 15:3, 22; 20:17).[7] Consequently, prior to Paul others had already designated the communities of those who believed in Christ as churches.

The frequency with which *ekklēsia* appears in the individual Pauline letters is revealing. It occurs sixty-one times in the Pauline corpus: forty-three times in the non-disputed letters and eighteen times in the disputed correspondence. In the non-disputed correspondence nearly seventy-five percent of the occurrences are in 1 and 2 Corinthians. In the disputed correspondence, more than fifty percent of them occur in Colossians and Ephesians. Thus, 1 and 2 Corinthians, Ephesians, and Colossians are the letters in which Paul employs the term most frequently.[8] While there are important references to the church in other letters, the most explicit references occur in these four letters.[9]

6. *Ekklēsia* occurs 3 times in the Gospels, 23 times in Acts, 61 times in Paul (43 in the non-disputed letters, 18 in the disputed), 2 times in Hebrews, 3 times in 3 John, once in James, and 20 times in Revelation.

7. Although the Acts of the Apostles postdates most of the Pauline letters, it preserves earlier traditions about the church. After studying the material, Lucien Cerfaux (*The Church in the Theology of Saint Paul,* 114-15) concludes the title Church of God "belonged originally to the earliest Christian community. From Jerusalem, it would have passed on to the churches of Judaea. Saint Paul then applies it explicitly to the Corinthian community, whereas the suggestion was only implicit in his words to the Thessalonians: 'You have imitated the churches of God in Judaea in Christ Jesus.' These words implied, however, that all the Christian churches were also churches of God."

8. The number of times *ekklēsia* appears in each of the Pauline letters is as follows: Romans (5), 1 Corinthians (21), 2 Corinthians (9), Galatians (3), Ephesians (9), Philippians (2), Colossians (4), 1 Thessalonians (2), 2 Thessalonians (2), 1 Timothy (3), Philemon (1). It does not appear in 2 Timothy or Titus.

9. It is important to remember that Paul can make important ecclesiological statements even when he is not explicitly referring to the church. For example, the purpose of his discussion about Abraham in Galatians 3–4 is to show that his Gentile Galatian converts have full membership in the eschatological people of God, even though they are not circumcised.

There is an important difference, however, in the way that the Corinthian correspondence on the one hand, and Colossians and Ephesians on the other, employ *ekklēsia*. Whereas 1 and 2 Corinthians use *ekklēsia* when referring to the local congregation, Colossians and Ephesians employ the term in reference to the church spread throughout the world, which they identify as the body of Christ.[10] Accordingly, I begin by summarizing two ways in which Paul employs *ekklēsia* in the non-disputed letters (the church as a local assembly and the local assembly as the church of God) before considering its use in Colossians and Ephesians.

The Church as a Local Assembly

First, when Paul employs *ekklēsia* in the non-disputed letters, he has in view a local assembly in a particular geographical area that gathers, often in the setting of someone's home, for worship, prayer, praise, and instruction. Accordingly, he frequently identifies where a particular church is found: in Corinth, in Galatia, in Philippi, in Thessalonica, in Macedonia. Since the Pauline churches gathered in homes, he sometimes names the person in whose home the church assembles. For example, Phoebe hosts the church in Cenchreae (Rom 16:1). Prisca and Aquila host a gathering of the church in their home in Rome (v. 5), as do several other people.[11] The

---

Likewise, although the word "church" never occurs in Romans 9–11, what Paul writes in these chapters is important for his understanding of the eschatological people of God (the church), which God is calling forth from the Gentiles as well as from the Jews. Inasmuch as the Pauline letters were addressed to communities of believers, then, they have implications for the Pauline understanding of the church, even when they do not use the term.

10. Although I will argue that *ekklēsia* refers exclusively to the local church in the non-disputed Pauline letters, others maintain that there are passages, apart from Ephesians and Colossians, that refer to the church as a whole. For example, Herman Ridderbos (*Paul: An Outline of His Theology* [Grand Rapids: Eerdmans, 1975], 328) writes: "There are then outside of Ephesians and Colossians passages of which it is usually judged that Paul speaks of the *ekklēsia* as a whole, whether as the 'church of God' (1 Cor. 10:32; 11:22; 15:9; Gal. 1:13; 1 Tim. 3:15), or simply as the 'church' (1 Cor. 12:28; Phil. 3:6)."

11. Romans is an interesting case study since there is no greeting to "the church in Rome" in the letter opening. In the letter closing, however, it appears that in addition to the church in the home of Prisca and Aquila there were gatherings of the church in the family of Aristobulus (16:10) and the family of Narcissus (v. 11) and that the two groups of people listed in vv. 14 and 15 represent the leadership of two more house churches. If this is so, the Christians at Rome belonged to several different house churches rather than to a single community.

church in Corinth meets in Gaius's home, where Paul is lodging and from which he writes Romans (v. 23), and Philemon is the host of a community that is probably situated in Colossae (Phlm 2).[12]

On several occasions, Paul speaks of the church gathering or assembling. For example, in 1 Cor 11:18, he writes: "when you come together as a church" *(synerchomenōn hymōn en ekklēsia)*. Here the Greek phrase indicates that the *ekklēsia* comes into being when it gathers for worship, prayer, praise, and instruction. Thus, although it may appear that Paul is referring to the church as a building in 1 Cor 14:23, 28, 35, he has in view the gathering of the community as the *ekklēsia* rather than a building.

Since Paul identifies each local assembly as an *ekklēsia*, he also speaks of the churches as well as of the church. For example, he tells the Romans that all the churches of Christ greet them (16:16). He reminds the Corinthians of what he teaches in all the churches (1 Cor 7:17), and he speaks of "all the churches of the saints" (14:33). Likewise, he refers to the churches of Galatia (Gal 1:2), the churches of Asia (1 Cor 16:19), the churches of Macedonia (2 Cor 8:1), the churches of Judea (Gal 1:22), all the churches (2 Cor 8:18), and other churches (11:8). These and other references to "the churches" highlight the local aspect of the church. This church of God, which originated in Jerusalem, now exists in several places. This, however, does not mean that these local assemblies are unrelated to each other. The fact that Paul reminds his readers of what he teaches in *all* the churches and that he sends greetings from *all* the churches to another church indicates that he views the churches as related to each other, even though he never explains how they are related.[13]

---

12. This is not stated in the letter to Philemon, but it can be inferred from Col 4:9, where Paul identifies Onesimus (the slave in the letter to Philemon) as "one of you," that is, as coming from or belonging to Colossae.

13. George Barker Stevens (*The Theology of the New Testament* [2nd ed.; International Theological Library; Edinburgh: Clark, 1918], 467) presents Paul as the point of unity between the many different Gentile congregations that he founded or was familiar with. He writes: "The apostle Paul, for example, was a kind of overseer to all the Gentile churches. He concerned himself with their welfare; he wrote them letters, even if he had not personally founded them, as in the case of the Roman and Colossian churches, he visited them when he was able. Through him one Church learned about the progress and devotion of others. Mutual interest was fostered. The apostle was a kind of medium of communication and bond of connection between these widely scattered churches."

The Local Assembly as the Church of God

Second, Paul views every local assembly of the church as a manifestation of "the church of God." This expression, which is closely related to the use of *ekklēsia* in the Septuagint and *qāhāl* in the Hebrew text, identifies the church as the eschatological people of God who have been called into existence through the death and resurrection of God's Son. On two occasions, Paul explicitly says that he persecuted the church of God (1 Cor 15:9; Gal 1:13).[14] Since the church that Paul first persecuted was the Jerusalem community, this suggests that "the church of God" originally referred to the Jerusalem community, which understood itself as the eschatological people of God. After his conversion, however, when he established communities of Gentile believers in the Mediterranean basin, Paul applied this honorific designation to his Gentile congregations, thereby granting them the same dignity as the originating church of God in Jerusalem.

An example of how Paul applies the designation "the church of God" to one of his communities is found in 1 Cor 1:2: "To the *church of God* that is in Corinth, to those who are *sanctified* in Christ Jesus, *called* to be saints, together with all those who in every place call on the name of our Lord Jesus Christ, both their Lord and ours" (see 2 Cor 1:1 for a similar greeting). By greeting the Corinthians in this way, Paul reminds them that their local assembly enjoys a status similar to that of the church of Jerusalem. It has been called into being by God's grace by which they have been *sanctified* in Christ Jesus and *called* to be holy in union with all those who call on the name of Jesus Christ and confess him as Lord.

The way in which Paul identifies those who belong to the church of God, a people sanctified in Christ Jesus and so called to be holy, plays a central role in his understanding of the church. Because its members have been sanctified in Christ, the church is a sanctified sphere that must expel all that is immoral from its midst. Accordingly, Paul reminds the Thessalonians that God's will for them is their sanctification, and he exhorts them to abstain from immorality (1 Thess 4:3). Because the church is a sanctified community, he calls upon the Corinthians to expel a particularly immoral individual (1 Cor 5:5). Since they have been washed, sanctified, and justified in the name of the Lord and in the Spirit of God, they must flee immorality (6:11, 18). Having been sanctified in Christ, those who

---

14. In Phil 3:6 he simply says that he persecuted "the church," which could be interpreted as the universal church, but more likely refers to the church at Jerusalem.

belong to the church are "called to be saints" *(klētois hagiois)*, by which Paul means they have been consecrated and set aside for service to God. Paul, then, identifies those who belong to the *ekklēsia* as "the saints" or "the holy ones" *(hoi hagioi)* because they have been dedicated and set apart for service to God, which requires them to live morally good lives.

Although there are occasions in 1 Corinthians when it may appear that Paul employs "the church of God" as though it were a designation for the entire church spread throughout the world (10:32; 11:22), the wider context of these passages indicates that he has the local assembly of Corinth in view. This is also apparent from his use of the plural ("the churches of God") in 1 Cor 11:16; 1 Thess 2:14; 2 Thess 1:4. Each congregation is the church of God inasmuch as God called it into existence. Consequently, although the non-disputed Pauline letters do not appear to employ "the church" or "the church of God" to designate the entire church throughout the world, the manner in which Paul identifies each of the churches as the church of God indicates that God's saving grace in Jesus Christ is at the origin of each congregation.[15]

Whereas in the non-disputed letters *ekklēsia* refers to the local assembly, in Colossians and Ephesians it refers to *the* church that exists throughout the world. Addressed to a specific community, Colossians still employs *ekklēsia* in a local sense when it speaks of the church that gathers in the house of Nympha (4:15) and the church of the Laodiceans (v. 16). But in its two other uses of the term, which I will discuss in greater detail in the next section, Colossians identifies the church as a cosmic reality because it is the body of the cosmic Christ (1:18, 24). Ephesians, which appears to have been a circular letter addressed to Gentile congregations in Asia Minor rather than to any specific congregation, develops this ecclesiology further.[16] In this letter, *ekklēsia* no longer refers to the local congregation but to *the* church over which Christ is the head (1:22; 5:23). Employing the relationship between Christ and the church to explain the meaning of the marital

15. See the expression "the church of the Thessalonians in God the Father and the Lord Jesus Christ," which only occurs in 1 Thess 1:1 and 2 Thess 1:1. In this expression, which is similar to but not exactly the same as "the church of God," Paul explicitly grounds the existence of the church at Thessalonica in God and Christ.

16. Although the letter is traditionally called the letter to the Ephesians, the words "in Ephesus" (1:1) are absent from the best manuscripts. Accordingly, the opening verse of the letter reads, "Paul, an apostle of Christ Jesus by the will of God, to the saints who are also faithful in Christ Jesus." This reading suggests that Ephesians may have been a circular letter and that each congregation introduced its name when the letter was read.

relationship between man and woman, Paul portrays the church as subject to Christ (5:24) who loves and nourishes her (vv. 25, 29). While Ephesians is clearly aware that there are local congregations that can be called churches, its focus is on *the* church to which these local congregations belong.

To summarize, the Pauline letters employ *ekklēsia* in two ways. In the non-disputed letters, especially in the Corinthian correspondence, it refers to the local congregation, which is God's sanctified and chosen people, the eschatological people of God. In Colossians and Ephesians the emphasis shifts to the church spread throughout the world. To understand how this comes about we must turn to the Pauline understanding of the church as the body of Christ.

The Body of Christ

Paul's most important contribution to the early church's self-understanding is his use of the metaphor "the body of Christ." Whereas he inherited the language of *ekklēsia* from others, he appears to have introduced the metaphor of the body to describe the church. This metaphor occurs in 1 Corinthians, Romans, Colossians, and Ephesians. But whereas in 1 Corinthians and Romans Paul uses it to highlight the diverse gifts that the members of the community have received for the benefit of all, Colossians and Ephesians apply the metaphor to the entire church whose "head" is Christ. Thus, just as *ekklēsia* refers to the local congregation in the non-disputed Pauline letters and then to the entire church in Colossians and Ephesians, so the body metaphor is applied to the local congregation in 1 Corinthians and Romans and to the whole church in Colossians and Ephesians. It is the use of this metaphor, I suggest, that explains why Colossians and Ephesians use *ekklēsia* in reference to the whole church rather than to the local congregation.

The Body and Its Members

Before analyzing how Paul employs the metaphor of the body for the church in 1 Corinthians, we must examine three texts in which he refers to the body in order to dissuade his audience from engaging in immorality, idolatry, and factions. The first of these occurs in 1 Cor 6:12-20, a passage in which the Apostle explicitly mentions the human body seven times. Writing to those who have been recently baptized into Christ, he reminds them that their bodies are not intended for sexual immorality "but for the Lord, and the Lord for the body" (v. 13). He then notes that their bodies are "members of Christ" (v. 15). Therefore, it is incongruous to take the members of Christ (their bodies) and make them members of a prostitute. One who engages in sexual immorality with another becomes one body with that person whereas one who is united with the Lord becomes "one spirit" with the Lord (v. 17). Although there is no explicit reference to the church here, Paul's remark that the "bodies" of the Corinthians are "members" of Christ indicates that they have been incorporated into Christ, presumably at their baptism.

Second, a similar argument occurs in 10:14-22 in a discussion of idolatry. Paul exhorts the Corinthians to refrain from participating in banquets in which they partake of food sacrificed to idols, since they cannot be in communion with demons and with Christ simultaneously. Those who participate in such worship are "partners" (v. 20) with demons,[17] whereas the eucharistic cup is a sharing in the blood of Christ and the eucharistic bread "a sharing in the body of Christ" (v. 16). There is "one bread," and even though the Corinthians are many, they form "one body" since they partake "of the one bread" (v. 17). In this passage, Paul employs "body" twice: first in reference to the eucharistic body of Christ (v. 16) and second in reference to the Corinthians who form one body by their participation in the Eucharist (v. 17). As in the previous passage, there is no explicit mention of the church, but it is evident that the community becomes one body when it assembles to participate in the Eucharist.

Third, in response to the divisions that have occurred in the eucharistic assembly, Paul reminds the Corinthians of the eucharistic tradition he handed on to them (11:17-34). After recalling this tradition, he warns them that anyone who eats and drinks the Eucharist "without discerning *the body*" (v. 29) condemns himself. Although it may appear that "the body" refers to the eucharistic body of the Lord, the context suggests that Paul has in view the body of the church. By celebrating the Eucharist in a way that discriminates against others, the Corinthians fail to discern that they form one body in Christ.

In these three passages Paul tells the Corinthians that their bodies are members of Christ (6:15), that they are one body by their participation in

---

17. The word that Paul employs here, *koinōnous,* is significant since it highlights a sharing or participation in a common reality. Those who participate in such worship, then, are participants with demons in a common reality.

the eucharistic body of Christ (10:16-17), and that they will condemn themselves if they fail to recognize "the body" they form when they assemble as the church to celebrate the Eucharist (11:29). It is in light of these texts that Paul portrays the church as the body of Christ in 12:12-31.

Once more Paul is responding to a particular problem within the community: a dispute about which spiritual gifts are the most important. To address this dispute he makes use of a well-known metaphor: society is like a body in which each member plays a role.[18] Although some members may appear to be more important than others, each plays a pivotal role. No member is unimportant, and each is necessary for the proper functioning of the body.

The manner in which Paul begins his use of this metaphor indicates that he is employing it in a new way: "For just as the *body* is one and has many members, and all the members of the *body*, though many, are one *body*, so it is with Christ. For in the one Spirit we were all baptized into one *body* — Jews or Greeks, slaves or free — and we were all made to drink of one Spirit" (12:12-13). Whereas the first three uses of "body" in these verses refer to the human body, the fourth has in view the body into which the Corinthians were baptized, namely, the body of their crucified and risen Lord.

By the phrase "so it is with Christ," Paul indicates that he is drawing a relationship between the human body and Christ's body. In 12:14-26 he develops this metaphor further, referring to the human "body" thirteen times. After drawing out the metaphor of the body, he concludes: "*Now you are the body of Christ* and individually members of it" (v. 27).[19] Here it is important to note that Paul is not presenting a simile. He is not saying that the Corinthians are *like* the body of Christ: they *are* the body of Christ.

But what does Paul mean by "the body of Christ"? To this point in the letter, the body of Christ has referred to the crucified and risen body into which the Corinthians were baptized. But in the next verse, he draws a relationship between the body of Christ and the church: "And God has ap-

---

18. For example, see the fable of M. Agrippa in Livy 2.32. For an overview of how the body metaphor was used in the ancient world, see Michelle V. Lee, *Paul, the Stoics, and the Body of Christ* (SNTSMS 137; Cambridge: Cambridge University Press, 2006), 29-45, which provides several examples from ancient texts.

19. The Greek *(hymeis de este sōma Christou kai melē ek merous)* is not as smooth as the translation implies. A more literal translation would be "You are (or you form) the body of Christ, and a member from members," the sense being that the community constitutes the body of Christ, each member related to the other.

pointed *in the church* first apostles, second prophets, third teachers; then deeds of power, then gifts of healing, forms of assistance, forms of leadership, various kinds of tongues" (12:28). By saying that God has appointed different ministries in the church (v. 28), immediately after drawing out the metaphor of the body (vv. 14-26) and then telling the Corinthians that they *are* the body of Christ (v. 27), Paul indicates that he is establishing an intimate relationship between the body of Christ and the church of God in Corinth.

To summarize, in 1 Corinthians the body of Christ is the body of the crucified and risen Lord into which believers have been baptized. Inasmuch as they are one body in Christ, the church is the body of Christ, in which each member plays a role according to the gift the Spirit has bestowed on him or her.

In Romans, Paul mentions the body of Christ twice. First, in 7:4 he says that believers died to the law "though the body of Christ." To understand what he means, it is important to recall what he wrote in 6:3: namely, those who were baptized into Christ Jesus were baptized into his death. Inasmuch as baptism into Christ is a baptism into his death, it is a baptism into his crucified and risen body. Consequently, when Paul affirms that believers died to the law *through the body of Christ,* he is alluding to their baptism into Christ's death. They have died to the law *through the body of Christ* by their baptismal association with Christ's death.

Second, in Rom 12:4-5 Paul employs "the body of Christ" in a more ecclesial sense. Drawing a comparison similar to the one he made in 1 Cor 12:12, he writes:

> For as
> in one body we have many members,
>   and not all the members have the same function,
> so
> we, who are many, are one body in Christ,
>   and individually we are members one of another.

Here Paul draws an analogy between a human body that has many members (all of which possess different functions) and the body of Christ, which has many members, all of which are related to each other. As in 7:4 Paul has the body of the crucified and risen Lord in view. But whereas in 7:4 the focus is sacramental, here it is ecclesial, as is apparent from the different spiritual gifts that he lists in 12:6-8.

Despite the similarity between Romans 12 and 1 Corinthians 12, there is an important difference. Whereas in 1 Corinthians Paul has in view the Corinthian community, which he has already identified as the church of God that is in Corinth, in Romans he has not referred to the recipients of this letter as the church or the church of God. Indeed, *ekklēsia* does not appear until 16:1, where it becomes apparent that the recipients of this letter belong to a number of diverse and perhaps competing house churches.[20] In reminding the Romans that they are one body in Christ, then, Paul employs the body metaphor in a slightly different way than he does in 1 Corinthians. Whereas in 1 Corinthians he applied it to the local congregation at Corinth, here he applies it to several house churches in Rome. In doing so, he suggests that these several congregations are united in the body of Christ.

The Body in Relation to Its Head

Whereas the body of Christ refers to the local congregation in 1 Corinthians and Romans, in Colossians and Ephesians it designates the entire church that exists throughout the world. Moreover, whereas 1 Corinthians and Romans employ the metaphor of the body to explain the relationship between the members of the church, Colossians and Ephesians use it to clarify the relationship of the church to Christ.

The ecclesiology of Colossians provides a bridge between the ecclesiology of 1 Corinthians and Romans and that of Ephesians. On the one hand, although Paul does not speak of "the church at Colossae,"[21] it is clear that he is addressing the congregation at Colossae to whom Epaphras taught the gospel (1:7). Moreover, at the end of the letter he extends greetings to Nympha and the church in her house and asks that the letter be read in the church of the Laodiceans (4:15-16). On the other hand, when

---

20. As noted above, there appear to have been several house churches at Rome. Peter Lampe ("The Roman Christians of Romans 16," in *The Romans Debate*, ed. Karl P. Donfried [rev. ed.; Peabody: Hendrickson, 1991], 216-30, here 229) provides an overview of the situation at Rome. He writes: "With separate pockets of Christians in the city of Rome being prevalent through the first two centuries and even beyond them, Romans 16 must be read in this light. Indicating the divided nature of Roman Christianity, Paul does not call it *ekklēsia* anywhere in Romans, not even in 1:7, where we would expect it according to the other Pauline letters."

21. In his greeting to the Colossians, Paul greets "the saints and faithful brothers and sisters in Christ in Colossae" (1:2) rather than the church in Colossae.

Paul uses the metaphor of the body to refer to the church in 1:18 and 1:24 he has something more in view than the local congregation. The church is the "body" whose "head" is Christ (v. 18), and by his own suffering Paul is completing what is lacking in "Christ's afflictions" for the sake of this body, which is the church (v. 24).[22] In these texts, the church is greater than the local congregation at Colossae. It is the church that exists throughout the world, of which Paul has become a minister in accordance with the stewardship he has received from God (v. 25). It is cosmic in scope inasmuch as its head is the one in, through, and for whom all things were created and reconciled to God (vv. 15-20).

When Paul refers to the body of Christ in Colossians, then, he no longer discusses the distinctive role that each member plays within the local congregation as he does in 1 Corinthians 12 and Romans 12. Instead, he employs the metaphors of the "head" and the "body" to highlight the relationship between the church and Christ. Christ is the head of the church, which is his body. As the head of the body, he is the one "from whom the whole body, nourished and held together by its ligaments and sinews, grows with a growth that is from God" (2:19).

Because they belong to the body of Christ, believers exist in Christ. They live their lives in him; they are rooted and built up in him (2:6-7). Moreover, since the fullness of deity dwells in him, they have been filled with divine life (vv. 9-10). This understanding of the body of Christ allows Colossians to affirm that believers have not only been buried with Christ in baptism, *they have been raised with him* (2:12; 3:1).[23] For inas-

---

22. The expression "the afflictions of Christ" (*tōn thlipseōn tou Christou*, Col 1:24), refers to the suffering or afflictions that the church must endure on behalf of Christ rather than to Christ's own sufferings. Consequently, Paul is speaking of the suffering and afflictions that he endures for the sake of the Christ on behalf of the church rather than something lacking in Christ's sufferings on the cross.

23. Paul's remarks about baptism in Colossians go beyond what he writes in Romans. In Romans he speaks of baptism in terms of being baptized into Christ's death (6:3), affirming that in their baptism believers were buried with Christ so that they might walk "in newness of life" (v. 4). He assures his audience that if they have been united with Christ in death, they will be united with him in a resurrection like his (v. 5); but he does not say what Colossians affirms: believers have been raised up with Christ (2:12; 3:1). This may be an indication that Colossians was written by a Pauline disciple who takes his teacher's thought a step further, or it may be the result of Paul's deeper understanding of the body of Christ. For, if the church is the body of Christ and if Christ is its head, then those who belong to the body already participate, in some way, in what has already happened to the head of the body: with him they have been raised up.

much as they are the body of Christ, they share in the resurrection of their head.[24]

By focusing on the relationship between Christ (the head) and the church (his body) rather than on the diverse roles of the members within the body, Colossians highlights the unity and universality of the church; for just as there can be only one head who is Christ, so there can only be one body, the church, which exists throughout the world.

The line of thought that Paul inaugurates in Colossians comes to full expression in Ephesians. In this letter, which is the summit of Pauline ecclesiology, there is little attention paid to the particular church. Ephesians is expansive in its praise of what God has accomplished for the church through Christ. Reminding its audience of the power that God displayed in Christ when God raised him from the dead and seated him at his right hand, above every earthly and heavenly power, Paul affirms that God put all things under Christ's feet and gave him as head over all things to the church, which is his body. This church is the fullness of Christ who is filling all things (1:20-23). On the basis of this body of Christ ecclesiology, Ephesians says that God has raised believers up with Christ and seated them in the heavens with Christ.[25]

Ephesians employs this body metaphor to explain the new relationship that exists between Gentiles and Jews, who are now reconciled to each other in Christ. Christ has created a new humanity in himself by reconciling Gentiles and Jews to God "in one body through the cross, thus putting to death that hostility through it" (2:16). The mystery that has been revealed to Paul is that "the Gentiles have become fellow heirs, members of the same body (syssōma), and sharers in the promise in Christ Jesus through the gospel" (3:6). Although Paul does not explicitly identify the body with the church here, what he writes in 1:22-23 and 2:16 indicates that the body in which Gentiles and Jews are fellow members is the body of Christ who suffered for them, which is now present to them as the church.

There is only one body, just as there is only one Spirit, one Lord, one faith, one baptism, and one God and Father (4:4-6). To equip the saints to

24. Colossians tempers its notion of having been raised up with Christ by noting that, at the present time, the believer's life in Christ is hidden and will only be revealed when Christ is revealed (3:4).

25. Here, Ephesians goes further than Colossians by speaking of being seated with Christ as well as being raised up with him. Thus there is a trajectory from Romans (baptism as sharing in Christ's death) to Colossians (baptism as dying and being raised up with Christ) to Ephesians (baptism as dying, being raised up, and being enthroned with Christ).

build up this body, which is the body of Christ, God gave apostles, prophets, evangelists, pastors, and teachers (4:11-12). By practicing the truth in love, believers grow into Christ, who is the head of the church, from whom the whole body grows and is built up in love (4:15-16).[26]

The most distinctive aspect of the ecclesiology in Ephesians is the analogy Paul draws between husband and wife on the one hand and the church and Christ on the other. The analogy begins with Paul noting that just as the husband is the head of his wife, so Christ is the head of the church, with Christ himself as the savior of the body, which is the church (5:23). He then concludes that just as the church is subject to Christ, so wives should be subject to their husbands (v. 24). Continuing the analogy, Paul exhorts husbands to love their wives just as Christ loved the church and handed himself over for the church (v. 25) to sanctify it so that he might present the church to himself as a spotless bride (vv. 26-27).[27] Husbands, then, should love their wives as they love their own bodies, just as Christ loved his body, the church (vv. 28-30). At the end of this analogy, Paul quotes from Gen 2:24, a text that occurs in the second creation story to explain why a man leaves his parents to be joined to a wife (5:31). But whereas in Genesis the text explains the mystery of marriage, Paul applies it to the mystery of Christ and the church (v. 33). The relationship between Christ and the church is analogous to the relationship between husband and wife. Just as husband and wife become one flesh in marriage, so Christ and the church are one. Thus the metaphor of the body of Christ reaches its climax in Ephesians. The church is not like a body in which people play different roles; it *is* the body of the crucified and risen Lord.

If we ask how Colossians and Ephesians came to focus on *the* church rather than the local churches, the answer is found in their theology of the body of Christ. Whereas 1 Corinthians and Romans employ this metaphor to explain the relationship among believers in the local congregation, Colossians and Ephesians focus on the relationship between Christ and his body, the church. In doing so, they conclude that just as there is one body, so there is one church throughout the world that is more than the sum of

26. In these verses, Paul speaks about the proper functioning of each part of the body, but in a slightly different way than in 1 Corinthians 12 and Romans 12. By speaking the truth in love, believers grow into the head of the body, who is Christ. Each part of the body, working properly, promotes the growth of the entire body by building itself up in love.

27. In 2 Cor 11:2 Paul also alludes to the image of the church as the bride of Christ when he writes that he has a divine jealousy for the Corinthians because he promised them in marriage to one husband (Christ), to whom he must present them as a chaste virgin.

the many local congregations in the world. While each of these local assemblies is the church in a particular locale, each belongs to the body of Christ, which is the church.

Ministry and Ministers

Any consideration of the church must include a discussion of its ministry: How does the church order itself so that its members can minister to each other and to the world? Given the various ways in which the Pauline letters present the church, it is not surprising that they portray ministry in different ways. For example, whereas 1 Corinthians and Romans discuss ministry in terms of the diverse gifts that the Spirit bestows on all the members of Christ's body, 1 Timothy and Titus speak of ministry in terms of leadership roles within the church (the household of God), which require certain qualifications. Accordingly, there is a tension within the Pauline corpus in regard to ministry. On the one hand, there are letters that present ministry in terms of the spiritual gifts that have been bestowed upon all of the members of the community for building up the church. On the other hand, there are letters that emphasize the offices that are conferred upon qualified members of the community for the purpose of supervising and ordering the community. Although these two visions of ministry are not mutually exclusive and can coexist in the church, there is a tension between ministry understood as charism and ministry understood as office.[28] Whereas the former highlights the responsibility of *all* to build up the community, the latter singles out *certain individuals* as having a particular responsibility for the community.

Gifts of the Spirit

Paul's most extensive consideration of ministry (apart from his reflections on his own ministry) occurs in 1 Corinthians 12–14, chapters in which he

28. For the background to the German debate about charism and office, see James D. G. Dunn (*The Theology of Paul the Apostle* [Grand Rapids: Eerdmans, 1998], 565-71). He notes that whereas Rudolph Sohm argued that early Christianity was organized charismatically, Adolf von Harnack (while agreeing with much that Sohm said) maintained that it was also organized socially and corporately. The debate, then, is whether charism and office are mutually exclusive or whether they can coexist within the church.

must persuade the Corinthians to use their diverse spiritual gifts to build up the church rather than to edify themselves. At the outset of this discussion he emphasizes that although there are different "gifts" *(charismatōn),* "services" *(diakoniōn),* and "activities" *(energēmatōn),* it is the same Spirit, the same Lord, and the same God who is at work in all of them (12:4-6). He then lists nine gifts that the Spirit bestows on believers to build up the community: wisdom, knowledge, faith, healing, miracles, prophecy, discernment of spirits, tongues, and interpretation of tongues (vv. 8-10). After explaining how every member of the body plays a vital role, Paul concludes that all the members of the church exercise an essential role in accordance with the gift or gifts that the Spirit has given them. Highlighting three gifts that are foundational for the life of the church, he notes that some are apostles, some are prophets, and some are teachers.[29] He then lists a series of other gifts: deeds of power, healing, assistance, leadership, and tongues (v. 28). The fact that Paul does *not* reproduce the same list here as in vv. 8-10 indicates that neither list is exhaustive. The Spirit produces diverse gifts within the community as needed, and each member of the community has received at least one of these gifts for the purpose of building up the church. Through these gifts of the Spirit *everyone* is engaged in the work of ministry. To the extent that all are active in ministry, the body functions as it ought. To the extent that only a few exercise their gifts, the body is ill.[30] The work of ministry, then, is the work of the entire church.

In Rom 12:4-8 Paul presents a similar view of ministry. Noting that believers form one body with many parts, each part having its own function, he lists seven roles that believers play within the body: prophecy, ministry, teaching, exhortation, generosity, leading, being compassionate. Here again, he presents a slightly different list of gifts, thereby indicating that the Spirit bestows gifts on the body as needed.[31] As in 1 Corinthians, the

29. Paul places apostles, prophets, and teachers at the head of his list, numbering them first, second, and third, but he does not number the other gifts. The apostle announces the gospel and establishes the community. The prophet helps the community to discern and interpret God's will. And the teacher instructs the community in the gospel that it has received. Paul enjoyed all three of these gifts, as well as many, if not all, of the others that he lists.

30. Dunn (*The Theology of Paul the Apostle,* 560) writes: "In short, when ministry is limited to the few the result is a grotesque parody of the body, a body eighty or ninety percent paralyzed, with only the few organs functioning, and functioning to little effect, since the effectiveness of the body depends on its diversity functioning in unity."

31. Although there is no explicit mention of the Spirit here, Paul speaks of "gifts" (Rom 12:6), thereby indicating that he has the Spirit in view.

work of ministry engages the entire church. To be sure, in Romans 16 Paul signals out certain persons as having labored especially diligently for the gospel, but the work of ministry is not limited to them: it belongs to all.[32]

In Ephesians there is a slight change of emphasis in the Pauline understanding of ministry. Whereas 1 Corinthians and Romans highlight the "gifts" *(charismata)* that the Spirit bestows on all the members of the church, Ephesians speaks of the "gifts" *(domata)* that the ascended Christ gives to the church: apostles, prophets, evangelists, pastors, and teachers (4:11). While this list includes some of the gifts of the Spirit mentioned above (apostles, prophets, teachers), it also includes gifts not previously noted (pastors and teachers). Other gifts, however, such as healing, mighty works, tongues, and interpretation of tongues are absent. Instead, Ephesians focuses on the gifts that "some" people exercise in order "to equip the saints for the work of ministry, for building up the body of Christ" (v. 12). Ministry remains the work of the entire church, but certain people play a more prominent role in making it possible.

The new emphasis in Ephesians derives from the manner in which Ephesians envisions the body of Christ. Whereas in 1 Corinthians and Romans, Paul employs the metaphor of the body to illustrate how *every* member plays a role in the body, Ephesians uses this metaphor to highlight the relationship between Christ and his church. Consequently, rather than list the gifts that all the members exercise in the church, Ephesians highlights the gifts that Christ gives to *some* for the purpose of enabling others to carry out the work of ministry. Although Ephesians is on the way to understanding ministry in terms of office, it has not forgotten that ministry is the work of the whole church.

Ministry as Office

Ministry plays a prominent role in 1 Timothy and Titus.[33] But whereas 1 Corinthians, Romans, and Ephesians highlight the variety of *gifts* that the Spirit and Christ bestow on the church, 1 Timothy and Titus emphasize the

---

32. Paul identifies Phoebe as a minister of the church at Cenchreae (16:1) and Priscilla, Aquila, and Urbanus (vv. 3, 9) as his coworkers. He calls Andronicus and Junia apostles (v. 7), and he says that Mary (v. 6), Tryphaena, Tryphosa, and Persis (v. 12) have worked hard for the gospel.

33. For a helpful study of ministry in the Pastoral Epistles, see Joseph A. Fitzmyer, "The Structured Ministry of the Church in the Pastoral Epistles," *CBQ* 66 (2004): 582-96.

need for Timothy and Titus to designate qualified individuals who will be able to combat false teaching with the sound teaching Paul has handed on to them. These people, in turn, must do the same, thereby establishing a succession of office and teaching that can be traced back to the gospel that Paul entrusted to Timothy and Titus (2 Tim 2:2). Although Paul does not explicitly command Timothy or Titus to lay hands on these people, the fact that he reminds Timothy of the "gift" he received "through prophecy with *the laying on of hands* by the council of elders" (1 Tim 4:14) suggests that the imposition of hands played a role in designating certain individuals as overseers, presbyters, and deacons.[34]

1 Timothy envisions a threefold ministry of "bishop" or "overseer" *(episkopē),* "minister" or "deacon" *(diakonos),* and "elder" or "presbyter" *(presbyteros),* as well as something akin to an order of widows.[35] Most of the qualifications for the first office highlight the need for the overseer to be a man of upright moral character who is capable of teaching and managing his household since he must manage the household of God, which is the church (3:1-7). The qualifications for deacons also insist on the need for impeccable moral character and the ability to manage one's children and household (vv. 8-13). But there is no mention of teaching, which suggests that this was not the role of the deacon. Although Paul does not mention any qualifications for the elder, he indicates that they exercise a role of leadership in the community and that some of them preach and teach as well (5:17). The precise relationship between the overseer and elder, however, is not clear.[36] The order of widows consists of women over sixty whom the church supports because they have no other means of support and have proven themselves by their service to the church (vv. 3-16).

Whereas there appears to be an emerging threefold ministry of overseer, deacon, and elder in 1 Timothy, the letter of Titus does not mention deacons and presents the office of elder (1:5) and overseer (v. 7) as one and the same. Those who hold this office must exhibit outstanding moral char-

34. Two points should be noted here. First, whereas in 1 Tim 4:14 Paul speaks of the council of elders laying hands on Timothy, in 2 Tim 1:6 he speaks of himself imposing hands on Timothy. Second, in both instances Paul reminds Timothy of the gift he has received. In doing this he indicates that Timothy's ministry is a gift from God.

35. Although the NRSV uses "bishop," I prefer "overseer," a term that is not burdened with contemporary notions of what a bishop is.

36. It does not appear that there is one overseer surrounded by a council of presbyters as described in the letters of Ignatius of Antioch at the beginning of the second century.

acter and have a firm understanding of the gospel so that they can preach sound doctrine and refute those who oppose it (vv. 5-9).

Although 1 Timothy and Titus have begun to view ministry in terms of specific offices to which certain qualified people are appointed by the laying on of hands, the manner in which Paul describes Timothy's appointment to ministry indicates that he has not forgotten that ministry is a gift. Timothy is not to neglect the "gift" that was conferred upon him (1 Tim 4:14) and is to rekindle the "gift" he received when Paul laid hands on him (2 Tim 1:6). Furthermore, the fact that certain people are appointed to the ministry of oversight and teaching does not exclude the ministry of others, as Paul's remarks about the service that widows provide indicates (1 Tim 5:10). However, there is a movement in the Pastorals from the charismatic ministry of 1 Corinthians and Romans to the ordained ministry of 1 Timothy and Titus that has important implications for the contemporary church. Churches that emphasize ordained ministry need to recover the charismatic dimension of ministry, which is the dominant form of ministry in the Pauline corpus, whereas those that enjoy a charismatic ministry must recover the importance of ministerial office that begins to emerge in 1 Timothy and Titus.

Although Paul does not develop a concept of ministerial office in the non-disputed letters, he does mention people who hold leadership roles in various congregations to which he writes. He tells the Thessalonians to "respect those who labor among you, and have charge *(proistamenous)* of you in the Lord and admonish you" (1 Thess 5:12). He reminds the Corinthians how the household of Stephanas "devoted themselves to the service of the saints" and urges them to put themselves "at the service of such people, and of everyone who works and toils with them" (1 Cor 16:15-16). He instructs the Galatians that "those who are taught the word must share in all good things with their teacher" (Gal 6:6). Among the gifts he lists in Rom 12:8 is "the leader" (*ho proistamenos,* the same word that describes the work of the overseers, deacons, and elders in 1 Tim 3:4, 5, 12; 5:17). Finally, Paul begins his letter to the Philippians by greeting those in Philippi "with the bishops and deacons" (1:1). These and other texts indicate that while the Pauline churches enjoyed a charismatic ministry, there were people who exercised leadership roles within the community. Their role would have been to enhance the ministry of others, an ideal for which the contemporary church should strive.

Israel and the Church

The central role that the church plays in the Pauline writings raises the question of the relationship between Israel and the church. Is there continuity between the two, or is the church a new entity that replaces Israel? Although Paul deals with this question, he does not address it in precisely the way I have framed it, namely, the relationship between "Israel" and "the church." Writing mostly to Gentile believers before "the parting of the ways," Paul was primarily concerned about the relationship between Gentile and Jewish Christ-believers.[37] Thus he argued that his uncircumcised Gentile converts enjoyed an equal status within the eschatological people of God since all are justified on the basis of God's grace through faith rather than on the basis of doing the works of the Mosaic law. Paul's question, then, is not quite the same question I have posed. In 1 and 2 Corinthians, Galatians, Romans, and Ephesians, however, he provides us with some insight into how he understood the relationship between the historic people of Israel and the eschatological community of the church, which he identifies as the body of Christ.

Israel according to the Flesh

In 1 Cor 10:1-13 Paul employs the example of Israel's failure in the wilderness to warn the Corinthian community not to fall into idolatry as Israel did. To make his point, he draws a comparison between Israel and the Corinthian community. First, he implies that the Corinthians are related to Israel by identifying the members of the wilderness community as "our ancestors" (v. 1), even though the Corinthians are Gentiles. Second, he reinforces this relationship by portraying Israel in the wilderness as a sacramental community that enjoyed something akin to baptism and the Eucharist inasmuch as the Israelites were baptized into Moses (by passing

---

37. This expression "the parting of the ways" is the title of an important monograph by James Dunn (*The Parting of the Ways between Christianity and Judaism and Their Significance for the Character of Christianity* [Philadelphia: Trinity, 1991], 248). He notes: "So long as Christianity and Judaism were still part of an unbroken continuous spectrum. . . . It was possible to speak and think of a renewed and expanded Israel in continuity with the old, with the Christian claim as one of several competing claims within the first century." But when the parting of the ways occurs, the identity of the people of God becomes more urgent. Whereas Paul wrote before this parting of the ways, we live after it.

through the Red Sea), ate the same spiritual food (the manna from heaven), and drank the same spiritual drink from the rock that followed them, Christ (vv. 3-4). While the point of Paul's comparison is to warn the Corinthians that what happened to "Israel according to the flesh" (NAB; *Israēl kata sarka,* v. 18) can happen to their sacramental community, the relationship Paul draws between Israel and the Corinthians indicates that the wilderness congregation of Israel is a type of the *ekklēsia* at Corinth.

Drawing a comparison between his ministry and the ministry of Moses, in 2 Corinthians 3 Paul contrasts the manner in which Israel and those who believe in Christ read the old covenant, by which Paul means Israel's scriptures (3:14). He affirms that he has been made the minister of a new covenant empowered by God's Spirit, which gives life (v. 6). For whereas the ministry of Moses resulted in condemnation for those who did not carry out the letter of the law, Paul's ministry of the Spirit produces righteousness. As glorious as Moses' ministry was, its glory (which was coming to an end) paled in comparison to the glory of the new covenant that Paul exercises (vv. 7-11). Consequently, whereas Moses wore a veil over his face to prevent the Israelites from gazing on the reflected glory of God that shone on his face and was now coming to an end, Paul boldly proclaims his gospel so that believers can contemplate, with their faces unveiled, the glory of the Lord and be transformed from glory to glory into the image of Christ who is the image of God (vv. 12-18). Reflecting on the present situation of unbelieving Israel and playing on the word "veil," Paul notes that the veil that prevented the Israelites from seeing the glory on Moses' face remains over contemporary Israel whenever it reads the old covenant (v. 14).

Although Paul does not explicitly contrast Israel and the church in this passage, he indicates that whereas the *ekklēsia* of those who believe in Christ are the beneficiaries of a new covenant ministry empowered by the Spirit, Israel of old was not. According to Paul, unbelieving Israel belongs to the old covenant determined by the letter of the law, whereas the *ekklēsia* is the eschatological community of a new covenant empowered by the Spirit.

The Israel of God

In Galatians, Paul argues that there is no need for his Gentile converts to have themselves circumcised and to adopt a Jewish way of life; for all who have been baptized into Christ are Abraham's offspring and heirs according to the promise that God made to Abraham. Since all are one in Christ, the former divisions between Jew and Gentile are of no importance (3:26-29). Paul arrives at this conclusion by developing a salvation-historical scheme that makes the covenant at Sinai subservient to the promise God made to Abraham (vv. 6-25).

In the first part of his argument Paul maintains that God had always intended to justify the Gentiles on the basis of faith, and he reinterprets the promise in terms of the Spirit (3:6-9, 14). Thus the uncircumcised Galatians, who have already received the Spirit (vv. 1-5), are already justified. In the second part of his argument, Paul maintains that Christ is Abraham's singular offspring, the one whom God had in view when he made the promise to Abraham. The law that was given at Sinai, then, had only a temporary role until the promised offspring appeared (vv. 15-25). Consequently, those who belong to Abraham's singular offspring, the Christ, are Abraham's offspring, even if they are not circumcised. The implication of this argument for Paul's ecclesiology is that God's people are defined in terms of belonging to Christ rather than in terms of circumcision and legal observance.

Paul develops a similar argument in his allegorical interpretation of Abraham's two sons, Ishmael, who was born of the slave woman Hagar, and Isaac, who was born of the free woman Sarah (4:24-31). He explains that these two women represent two covenants: the covenant given at Sinai and a covenant that is not explicitly named here — the new covenant. Paul associates the first with the present Jerusalem that is still in bondage and the second with the Jerusalem above that is free. He employs this analogy to defend the circumcision-free gospel that he has preached among the Galatians. His converts belong to the line of Isaac, the Jerusalem that is free, whereas those who are trying to impose circumcision and legal observance on them are aligned with the present Jerusalem that is in bondage. Although Paul does not explicitly contrast Israel and the church here, his argument implies that the eschatological people of God are no longer limited to those whose lives are defined by legal observance.

Paul alludes to his understanding of the people of God in an enigmatic phrase that occurs at the end of Galatians: "For neither circumcision nor uncircumcision is anything; but a new creation is everything! As for those who will follow this rule — peace be upon them, and mercy, and upon *the Israel of God*" (6:15-16). Although the precise meaning of "the Israel of God" is elusive, the argument of Galatians suggests that it refers to the people God has created *from both the Gentiles and the Jews*.[38] This people is no longer limited to the Jewish people, nor does it exclude them. Rather, it embraces all who live by the "rule" or "canon" that Paul has presented in this letter: that a person is justified on the basis of faith rather than on the basis of doing the works of the law.

The Remnant of Israel

Paul's most extensive discussion of Israel occurs in Romans 9–11.[39] In these chapters he responds to three questions: Has the word of God failed (9:1-29)? Why didn't Israel attain the righteousness it so zealously pursued (9:30–10:21)? Has God rejected Israel (11:1-36)? In answer to the first, Paul provides numerous examples from Israel's history to show that God has always worked on the basis of promise and election to create and sustain Israel. Applying this insight to the present time, he points to those whom God has called forth, "not only from the Jews but from the Gentiles" (9:24), as an indication of God's continuing elective purpose. Although not all Israel has responded to God's call, a remnant has. This remnant belongs to the eschatological people of God whom God has called forth from the Gentiles as well as the Jews, and it is this remnant that guarantees the continuity between historic Israel and this new people.

In response to the second question, Paul argues that Israel did not attain the righteousness it sought because it failed to recognize God's saving righteousness manifested in Christ. Pursuing its own righteousness rather than God's righteousness, Israel did not recognize that Christ was the terminus of the law (10:4). Although Israel has heard the gospel, the vast majority of Israel has not responded to it. Consequently, God

---

38. "The Israel of God" has been interpreted in various ways: historic Israel, a portion of Israel within Israel, the whole of Israel that will be saved at the end, those Jewish Christians who do not try to persuade Gentiles to adopt a Jewish way of life, the church consisting of Gentiles and Jews, Jewish and Gentile believers who conduct themselves according to the rule of the new creation that Paul has developed in Galatians. Given the argument of Galatians, "the Israel of God" most likely refers to those Gentiles and Jews that live according to the gospel. Such a community is in continuity and discontinuity with historic Israel.

39. For a full discussion of the ecclesiology of these chapters, see Pablo A. Gadenz, *Called from the Jews and from the Gentiles* (WUNT 267; Tübingen: Mohr Siebeck, 2009). Gadenz's exegesis of Romans 9–11 shows that Paul does not view "the church" as taking the place of, or supplanting, historic Israel.

has made himself known to the Gentiles, who previously did not know the God of Israel, while Israel has remained stubborn and disobedient (10:18-21).

Although Paul's line of argument might lead one to expect that he will answer the third question positively ("yes, God has rejected his people!"), Paul insists that God has *not* rejected the people whom he foreknew (11:2). Pointing to himself and recalling the story of Elijah, he insists that there is a remnant of Israel, chosen by grace (v. 5). Then, explicitly addressing Gentile believers (v. 13), he reminds them that they have been grafted into the olive tree of Israel. It is not they who support the root of this tree but the root that supports them.[40] Although branches (those Jewish people who did not believe) were cut off from the tree because of unbelief, God is powerful to graft them in again (vv. 23-24).

[handwritten margin note: GREAT ANALOGY]

[handwritten note: BASIS OF EVANGELICAL SUPPORT FOR ISRAELI STATE.]

Paul concludes by revealing a mystery. At the present time a hardening has come on a portion of Israel until the full number of Gentiles enters the eschatological people of God; and so *all Israel will be saved* (vv. 25-26). By this statement, Paul indicates that God has not rejected that portion of Israel that has not believed. At a time and in a way known to God alone, all Israel will be saved and, we can presume, be united with the eschatological people of God that has been drawn from Gentiles as well as Jews.

Paul never refers to "the church" in Romans 9–11, in part, because his primary concern is the fate and destiny of the people to which he still belongs: Israel. He wants to show that even though the majority of Israel has failed to accept the gospel, the word of God has not failed. To the contrary, Israel's disobedience is part of a greater plan whereby the Gentiles will enter the eschatological people of God. Then all Israel will be saved. What this *implies* about the relation of Israel and the church can be stated in this way. The church is the eschatological people of God drawn from the remnant of Israel and from the Gentiles. But the church is not *a new Israel*, nor has it replaced historic Israel. Although it has not believed in the gospel, Israel continues to exist as Israel, whereas the church exists as the eschatological people of God. According to Paul's eschatological vision, however, all Israel will be saved. When this happens, Israel and the church will converge.

---

40. Here, the root of this olive tree is the patriarchs. If the patriarchs are the root, then the branches refer to Israel. See Gadenz, *Called from the Jews and the Gentiles*, 263.

The Mystery of Christ

Unlike Romans, where Paul expresses his profound anguish and concern for his people, Ephesians does not deal with the plight of Israel. Instead, Ephesians celebrates the reconciliation between Gentile and Jew that the death of Christ has effected. For Ephesians the "mystery of Christ" (3:4) is that "the Gentiles have become fellow heirs *(synklēronoma)* members of the same body *(syssōma)*, and sharers *(symmetocha)* in the promise in Christ Jesus through the gospel" (v. 6).

Previous to their incorporation into this body, which is the church, the uncircumcised Gentiles were without Christ, alienated from the community of Israel *(politeias tou Israēl)*, strangers to the covenants with their promises, deprived of hope, living in the world apart from the God of Israel (2:12). Stated simply, they did not belong to the people of Israel. But *now* they are fellow citizens *(sympolitai)* and members of the household of God *(oikeioi tou theou,* v. 19). All this has happened through Christ, who made both groups (Gentiles and Jews) one by his death on the cross. Abolishing the law with its commandments, which divided Gentiles and Jews from each other, Christ has created a new humanity *(kainon anthrōpon,* v. 15) in himself composed of Gentiles and Jews by "reconciling both groups to God in one body through the cross" (v. 16).

Ephesians does not speculate about the future of historic Israel, nor does it say anything about that portion of Israel that has not believed in Christ. Written to Gentiles who belong to the body of Christ, which is the church, it is more intent on reminding Gentiles of the privileges they now enjoy because they belong to the new humanity that exists in Christ. The church is not the new Israel or the successor to Israel but a new humanity, the body of Christ, in which Gentile and Jew are reconciled to each other. Gentiles and Jews outside this body have not yet experienced this reconciliation.

As I noted at the outset of this discussion, Paul does not address the question of the relationship between Israel and the church in the way we frame it today, two thousand years after the parting of the ways. His discussion of Gentiles and Jews, however, sheds important light on this relationship that can be summarized in this way: The church understands itself as the eschatological people of God that has been drawn from the Gentiles as well as from the Jewish people. Thus it is both different from and in continuity with Israel. It is different from Israel inasmuch as it includes Gentiles as well as Jews; it is in continuity with Israel inasmuch as a remnant of Israel is an essential component of its origin. As the eschatological people of God, the church is not so much the new Israel as it is the Israel of God: the eschatological people of God that exists because of God's grace and elective love. Historic Israel continues to exist and, according to Romans, will be saved. When this occurs, Israel and the church will converge.

Coherence and Meaning in Pauline Ecclesiology

Although there are differences in the way the Pauline letters develop their understanding of the church, there are also overarching themes that give the ecclesiology of these letters a certain coherence. First, the church is the eschatological people of God, whom God has drawn from Gentiles as well as from historic Israel. As the eschatological people of God, the church is closely related to Israel, but it is not a new Israel, nor does it supplant historic Israel, which remains God's people. Second, the community of believers understands itself as the eschatological people of God and is so intimately related to the one who sanctified it by his saving death and resurrection that it can be called Christ's body. While 1 Corinthians and Romans on the one hand, and Colossians and Ephesians on the other, employ this metaphor differently, they agree that the church is the saving community of God's grace in which believers dwell in Christ; it is the presence of his crucified and risen body to the world. Third, although the Pauline letters present the church's ministry in different ways, they agree that ministry is integral to the life of the church. 1 Corinthians and Romans discuss ministry in terms of the gifts of the Spirit, Ephesians speaks of the gifts that the ascended Christ gave to his church, and the Pastorals speak of something akin to an ordained ministry, which remains a gift from God. All these letters, however, agree that the church cannot live or function properly without a vibrant ministry.

Having considered the church as the community of God's saving grace, the place where the justified live, our next task is to ask how the redeemed live *according* to God's saving grace within this eschatological community of the church.

For Further Reading

Aletti, Jean-Noël. "La eclesiologia de las llamadas deuteropaulinas. Preguntas y propuestas." *EstBíb* 68 (2010): 53-71.

————. "Le statut de L'Église dans les lettres pauliniennes. Réflexions sur quelques paradoxes." *Bib* 83 (2002): 153-74.

————. "Les difficultés ecclésiologiques de la lettre aux Éphésians." *Bib* 85 (2004): 457-74.

————. *Essai sur l'ecclésiologie des lettres de saint-Paul.* *EBib* nouvelle série 60. Paris: Gabalda, 2009.

Banks, Robert. *Paul's Idea of Community.* Revised ed.; Peabody: Hendrickson, 1994.

Beker, J. Christiaan. *Paul the Apostle: The Triumph of God in Life and Thought.* Philadelphia: Fortress, 1980. Pages 202-47.

Bockmuehl, Markus, and Michael B. Thompson. *A Vision for the Church: Studies in Early Christian Ecclesiology.* Edinburgh: Clark, 1997.

Cerfaux, Lucien. *The Church in the Theology of St. Paul.* New York: Herder and Herder, 1959.

Collins, Raymond F. *The Many Faces of the Church: A Study in New Testament Ecclesiology.* New York: Crossroad, 2003.

Cwiekowski, Frederick J. *The Beginnings of the Church.* Mahwah: Paulist, 1988.

Doohan, Helen. *Paul's Vision of Church.* GNS 32. Wilmington: Glazier, 1989.

Dunn, James D. G. *The Theology of Paul the Apostle.* Grand Rapids: Eerdmans, 1998. Pages 533-98.

Fitzmyer, Joseph A. "The Structured Ministry of the Church in the Pastoral Epistles." *CBQ* 66 (2004): 582-96.

Harrington, Daniel J. *The Church according to the New Testament: What the Wisdom and Witness of Early Christianity Teach Us Today.* Chicago: Sheed and Ward, 2001.

Kee, Howard Clark. *Who Are the People of God? Early Christian Models of Community.* New Haven: Yale University Press, 1995.

Kertelge, Karl. *Gemeinde und Amt im Neuen Testament.* Biblische Handbibliothek 10. Munich: Kösel, 1972.

Meeks, Wayne. *The First Urban Christians: The Social World of the Apostle Paul.* New Haven: Yale University Press, 1983.

Minear, Paul S. *Images of the Church in the New Testament.* NTL. Louisville: Westminster John Knox, 2004.

O'Brien, P. T. "Church." Pages 123-31 in *Dictionary of Paul and His Letters,* ed. Gerald F. Hawthorne, Ralph P. Martin, and Daniel G. Reid. Downers Grove: InterVarsity, 1993.

Schnackenburg, Rudolf. *The Church in the New Testament.* New York: Herder and Herder, 1965.

Schnelle, Udo. *Apostle Paul: His Life and Theology.* Grand Rapids: Baker, 2003. Pages 559-76.

Schweizer, Eduard. *Church Order in the New Testament.* SBT 32. London: SCM, 1961.

Yorke, Gosnell. *The Church as the Body of Christ in the Pauline Corpus: A Re-Examination.* Lanham: University Press of America, 1991.

6. Living according to God's Saving Grace

Introduction

Although my previous chapter dealt with Pauline ecclesiology, it is related to the topic of Pauline ethics since the church is the sanctified sphere where believers live in the newness of life that God has made possible by the death and resurrection of his Son. This is why the Pauline letters regularly remind their recipients of their election and sanctification in Christ. This is why they exhort their auditors to build up the church in love. And this is why it is important for those who live within the sanctified sphere of God's eschatological people to avoid anything that is immoral and unclean. Those who have been incorporated into Christ have been empowered to live a new life, not merely as individuals, but as a sanctified community of believers. Consequently, there is an intimate relationship between Pauline ecclesiology and Pauline ethics that can be stated in this way: The sanctified community of the church is the sphere in which believers live their new life in Christ.

While Pauline ethics presents us with a new understanding of how to live the morally good life, it stands in continuity with the ethical heritage of Israel. The pre-Christian Paul, after all, was not an immoral man. Despite the self-description of him that we find in 1 Tim 1:13 (a blasphemer, a persecutor, a violent man), Paul could boast that he had been blameless as to righteousness under the law (Phil 3:6). Indeed, it was precisely because he was so zealously law-observant that he persecuted the first Christians, whom he judged to have violated the law. It was only when the risen Lord appeared to him that he began to understand the misguided nature of his zeal. It was only in light of that Christophany that he began to make moral judgments in the light of Christ rather than in the light of Torah.

What, then, is the difference in the ethical thinking and moral conduct of the Christian Paul when compared with the pre-Christian Paul? What are the points of continuity and discontinuity? How can we summarize Pauline ethics?

We can assume that the Christian Paul lived in accordance with the moral traditions that previously guided his life. For example, he would not have transgressed the Decalogue, nor would he have violated the dietary prescriptions of Torah when eating with Jews.[1] In this regard, there was little difference between his past and present moral conduct. But in addition to continuity, there was also discontinuity. For example, Paul reassessed his former understanding of the relationship between Gentiles and Jews in light of what God had done in Christ, and, having experienced the power of God's Spirit in his life, he now evaluated his conduct in terms of the Spirit and the love commandment rather than in terms of Torah. Put another way, Paul began to conduct his life in light of what God had done in Christ rather than in terms of legal observance. Whereas formerly it was the law that guided and instructed him, now it was the example of Christ's love and the power of the Spirit dwelling in him that served as his moral compass, enabling him to live in a way that accorded with the newness of life that he experienced in Christ.

The newness of Paul's moral teaching is found in the newness of life he experienced in Christ rather than in a new ethical system. While Paul's moral convictions about right and wrong remained essentially the same, something changed. Whereas formerly he lived by legal observance, now he lived by the power of the Spirit, imitating the pattern of Christ's self-emptying love. In the remainder of this chapter, I will examine Pauline

1. Paul makes two remarks that are helpful in this regard. First, in 1 Cor 7:19 he writes: "Circumcision is nothing, and uncircumcision is nothing; but obeying the commandments of God is everything." By this remark, he points to the enduring importance of obeying God's commandments, whether or not one is circumcised. In Rom 13:9-10 Paul affirms that the commandments are "summed up" in the commandment to love your neighbor as yourself. Second, in 1 Cor 9:21-22 Paul describes his behavior among Gentiles and Jews in this way: "To those outside the law I became as one outside the law (though I am not free from God's law but am under Christ's law) so that I might win those outside the law. To the weak I became weak, so that I might win the weak. I have become all things to all people, that I might by all means save some." This remark suggests that although Paul may have overlooked certain dietary prescriptions when sharing table fellowship with Gentile believers, he lived as an observant Jew when sharing fellowship with Jews.

ethics under the following headings: "A Soteriological Ethic," "A Spirit-empowered Ethic," "A Sacramental Ethic," "A Love Ethic," and "An Eschatological Ethic."

A Soteriological Ethic

I refer to Paul's moral teaching, as found in the thirteen letters attributed to him, as a soteriological ethic because it presupposes God's redemptive work in Christ. It is on the basis of what God has done in Christ (the indicative of salvation) that Paul exhorts believers to live in a particular manner (the moral imperative).[2] Accordingly, he does not merely tell people what they ought to do: he explains why they can and ought to live in a particular way. They can and ought to live a morally good life for a variety of reasons: for example, they have been justified, they have been reconciled to God, they have been sanctified, they are a new creation in Christ, they have died to sin, they have risen to new life, the power of God's Spirit dwells in them, and God's grace has trained them to live godly and upright lives.

This relationship between what God has done in Christ and how believers ought to live is not merely a matter of motivation — although it certainly includes this. Nor is it merely an exhortation to imitation — although it certainly includes this. Ultimately, it is the assurance that believers *can* live such a life because they have been *empowered* to do so. Formerly such an exhortation would have been in vain because those who are now redeemed were under the powers of sin and death. But now, freed from those enslaving forces, it is possible for the redeemed to live in a new way. They no longer live in the realm of the flesh, they live in the realm of God's Spirit, and so they live in newness of life. Paul witnesses to this new life, which is at work in his own life, when he writes: "it is no longer I who

---

2. On the relationship between the indicative and imperative in Paul's writings, see Rudolf Bultmann, "The Problem of Ethics in Paul," and Michael Parsons, "Being Precedes Act: Indicative and Imperative in Paul's Writing," in Brian S. Rosner, ed., *Understanding Paul's Ethics: Twentieth Century Approaches* (Grand Rapids: Eerdmans, 1997), 195-216 and 217-47 respectively. For a summary of the issue, see T. J. Deidun, *New Covenant Morality in Paul* (AnBib 89; Rome: Biblical Institute Press, 1981), 239-43, here 243. He concludes his study: "The christian [*sic*] imperative demands only free acceptance of a gift that is made independently of it. The Christian is *under obligation* not to resist the inward action of God's Spirit which already *impels* him to free obedience. He must 'abound' in holiness and love — that is, he must *let God be God* in the core of his liberty."

live, but it is Christ who lives in me. And the life I now live in the flesh I live by faith in the Son of God, who loved me and gave himself for me" (Gal 2:20). It is precisely because Christ lives in Paul, and because Paul lives in Christ, that Paul is able to do all things (Phil 4:13).

This relationship between what God has done in Christ (the indicative) and what believers ought to do (the imperative) is built into the structure of several Pauline letters whose moral paraenesis presupposes what Paul affirms about God's saving work in Christ. Romans, Galatians, Colossians, and Ephesians (two non-disputed and two disputed letters) are good examples of this structure. In the first eleven chapters of Romans, Paul explains how God revealed his saving righteousness in Christ so that all — Gentile and Jew alike — are justified by grace on the basis of faith in Christ. Having shown his Roman audience that they have been justified and reconciled to God and are no longer under the powers of sin, death, and the law, Paul embarks on an extended paraenesis that begins in this way: "I appeal to you therefore, brothers and sisters, by the mercies of God, to present your bodies as a living sacrifice, holy and acceptable to God, which is your spiritual worship. Do not be conformed to this world, but be transformed by the renewing of your minds, so that you may discern what is the will of God — what is good and acceptable and perfect" (12:1-2). On the basis of what God has already done ("the mercies of God"), Paul exhorts the Romans to do something they could not do when they lived apart from Christ: to present themselves as a living sacrifice to God. Their moral life, he implies, is an act of worship made possible by what God has done in Christ. The paraenesis that follows, then, is not merely a moral exhortation but a description of the moral life that God's redemptive work in Christ has made possible.

Galatians provides another example of how Paul relates his moral paraenesis to the gospel he proclaims. In the opening chapters of this letter, he presents a powerful argument for his gospel of justification on the basis of faith rather than on the basis of legal observance. Arguing that his Gentile converts are justified because they have received the gift of the Spirit (3:1-5) and that they are descendants of Abraham because they have been baptized into his singular descendant, the Christ (vv. 27-29), Paul provides his converts with a moral exhortation in which he summons them to live by the Spirit rather than gratify the desires of the flesh (5:13–6:10). As in Romans, Paul's exhortation is intimately related to the gospel he preaches. Having reminded the Galatians that they have been justified on the basis of faith, which results in the gift of the Spirit, Paul exhorts them to live by the gift of the Spirit they have received. His ethical teaching, then, is not merely a list of imperatives; it is the logical outcome of the gospel he preaches.

A similar pattern of gospel underlying paraenesis occurs in Colossians and Ephesians. In the first part of Colossians, Paul provides his readers with a powerful christological argument to persuade them that "the fullness of deity" dwells in Christ (2:9) in whom they were baptized (v. 12). Consequently, there is no need for them to worship the "elemental spirits" (v. 20). Having made this christological argument, in the second part of the letter Paul presents an extended moral exhortation based on the sacramental and christological argument of the first part of the letter: "So if you have been raised with Christ, seek the things that are above, where Christ is, seated at the right hand of God. Set your minds on things that are above, not on things that are on earth, for you have died, and your life is hidden with Christ in God" (3:1-3). It is precisely because believers have been raised up with Christ that they can live the kind of life that Paul describes in 3:1–4:6. For Paul, the moral life is a life made possible by God's work in Christ.

Ephesians, which has intriguing affinities with the theology of Colossians, works in the same way. In the first part of the letter (chs. 1–3), Paul celebrates God's redemptive work in Christ whereby Gentiles and Jews have been brought together in the one body of Christ (2:16). After celebrating God's redemptive plan in Christ, he presents an extended moral exhortation (4:1–6:20). At the outset of this exhortation (4:1-16), he relates what he is about to say to what he has already said. Believers are to maintain the unity that God's plan has brought about by growing into Christ who is the head of the body, the church. He then relates everything that follows to the goal of maintaining the unity of the body. Since it is God who has brought about this unity, the maintenance of unity is a task made possible by the gift of God in Christ.

Although the structures of the other letters do not exhibit the same division between the exposition of the gospel and its moral exhortation, they continue the pattern of relating the morally good life to what God has done in Christ. In 1 Corinthians, for example, moral exhortation occurs throughout the letter. Paul exhorts the Corinthians to refrain from falling into factions (1:10–4:21), to shun immorality and not to take each other to court (5:1–6:20), to avoid scandalizing the weak (8:1–11:1), and to stop disputing about the gifts of the Spirit (12:1–14:40). In every instance, these exhortations are intimately related to Paul's gospel: the Corinthians are to refrain from factions because they were baptized into the name of Christ, they are to avoid immorality because they belong to a sanctified community, they are not to take each other to court because they are destined to judge the world, they are not to scandalize the weak because Christ died for them, and they are not to argue about the gifts of the Spirit because these gifts are intended to build up the community.

In 1 Thessalonians Paul reminds his audience that God's will is their sanctification (4:3) and that God has called them to holiness rather than to impurity (4:7). He affirms that there is no need for him to write about the mutual love they ought to have for each other since they have been "taught by God" (v. 9). The nature of the moral life that Paul exhorts Thessalonians to live, then, is rooted in God's will for their sanctification. Through the gospel that they have heard, they have been taught by God.

In Philippians Paul exhorts his auditors to conduct themselves in a manner worthy of the gospel he preached to them so that they will be one spirit and one mind as they struggle for the sake of the gospel (1:27). He calls on them to do nothing out of selfish ambition but to regard others as more important than themselves (2:3). To enable them to attain this goal, he employs the hymn-like passage in 2:6-11 that describes how the one who was in the form of God emptied himself and took the form of a slave. By calling the Philippians to imitate the self-emptying of Christ, Paul draws out the intimate relationship between the gospel he preaches and his moral exhortation. To live in a manner worthy of the gospel is to imitate the one who emptied himself to the point of dying on the cross. Paul then exhorts the Philippians to work out their salvation in fear and trembling, reminding them that it is God who is at work in them, enabling them to carry out his purpose for them (vv. 12-13). The relationship between the indicative and imperative, then, can be summarized in two ways: (1) the pattern of Christ's life is the pattern for the believer's life; (2) God is at work within believers so that they can work out their salvation.

Paul's letter to Titus provides a final example of the relationship between salvation and moral exhortation. Toward the end of that letter, after instructing Titus how to teach and instruct others, Paul writes:

> For the grace of God has appeared, bringing salvation to all, training us to renounce impiety and worldly passions, and in the present age to live lives that are self-controlled, upright, and godly, while we wait for the blessed hope and the manifestation of the glory of our great God and Savior, Jesus Christ. He it is who gave himself for us that he might redeem us from all iniquity and purify for himself a people of his own who are zealous for good deeds. (2:11-14)

In this statement Paul makes two points about the relationship of the moral imperative to the indicative of salvation. First, he affirms that God's grace, which appeared in Christ, "trains" *(paideuousa)* believers to live in a way that accords with the teaching that Paul is handing on to Titus and that Titus must hand on to others. Second, he notes that Christ's purpose in redeeming humanity was to "purify" *(katharisē)* for himself a people zealous for good deeds. In the first instance, Paul indicates that believers must be trained to live the morally good life by God's grace. In the second, he indicates that people must be purified by Christ's redemptive death so that they can do good deeds. Consequently, while much of the moral teaching of Titus and the other Pastoral Epistles may appear to be similar to the moral teaching in the writings of the Hellenistic philosophers, this passage indicates that it is God's grace and Christ's death that enable believers to live such a life.[3]

To summarize, the Pauline ethic is grounded in the saving grace of God revealed in Jesus Christ. It is this saving grace that provides believers with (1) the motivation, (2) the example, and (3) the power to live the morally good life.

A Spirit-Empowered Ethic

The Spirit is the link between the indicative of salvation and the moral imperative. Those who enjoy the gift of the Spirit have been transferred from the realm of the flesh to the realm of God's Spirit. This Spirit, which is made available to believers through the death and resurrection of Jesus Christ, empowers them to carry out the moral imperative of the ethical life. To be sure, the Spirit does not relieve believers of their moral responsibility, nor does it magically guarantee their good behavior. Believers remain moral agents responsible for their actions. This is why Paul writes that those who belong to Christ "have crucified the flesh with its passions

---

3. Abraham Malherbe ("'Christ Jesus Came into the World to Save Sinners': Soteriology in the Pastoral Epistles," in *Salvation in the New Testament: Perspectives on Soteriology,* ed. Jan G. van der Watt [Leiden: Brill, 2005], 331-58, here 346) notes this when he explains how the author of 2 Timothy understands *euseb(e)ia* in relation to salvation: "He does give it his own nuances, only some of which have been noted above. The major thing for him is that *eusebia* is possible only if the sound teaching is strictly adhered to. According to Titus 2:11-12, it is God's saving grace that educates his people to live *eusebōs* in the present age."

and desires" (Gal 5:24).[4] But if one accepts the Pauline analysis of the human condition apart from Christ, it is clear that one cannot live in a way pleasing to God apart from the inner dynamism that comes from the Spirit. Given the importance of the Spirit in Pauline thought, in this section I will examine the role that the Spirit plays in Pauline ethics. After a few remarks about Paul's teaching in his Thessalonian and Corinthian correspondence, I will focus my attention on Galatians and Romans before concluding with some comments on the Spirit in Ephesians.

At the outset of 1 Thessalonians Paul draws a connection between the (1) election of the Thessalonians, (2) their moral life, and (3) the gift of the Spirit. First, he commends them for the quality of their moral life, which is revealed in their *work of faith,* their *labor of love,* and the *steadfastness of their hope* (1:2-3).[5] Next, he expresses his confidence in their election, which was confirmed by their acceptance of the gospel that came to them in the power of the Holy Spirit (vv. 4-5). Finally, he notes that they imitated the pattern of Paul's life when they received the gospel, despite afflictions, with the joy that comes from the Holy Spirit. As a result, they have become a model for others to imitate (vv. 6-7).

Paul returns to this relationship between election, the Spirit, and the moral life in the moral exhortation of 4:1-12. God's will for the Thessalonians is their sanctification (v. 3). Accordingly, God has called them to holiness, which is made possible by the Spirit that God has given to them (vv. 7-8). Aware that the Thessalonians have received this Spirit, Paul acknowledges that they have been taught by God to love one another (v. 9).[6]

---

4. This vivid metaphor indicates that believers have died to sin. It is slightly different from the metaphor that Paul uses in Rom 6:2-3, where he says that the justified have died to sin through their baptism into Christ's death. By saying that those in Christ have crucified their flesh with its passions and desires, Paul suggests that they entered into the suffering that accompanies dying to an old way of life. Although Paul presents this as something that happened once, one suspects that he understands the need for an ongoing process of crucifying the flesh with its passions and desires.

5. The expressions "work of faith," "labor of love," and "steadfastness of hope" highlight the quality of the faith, love, and hope of the Thessalonians. Their faith and love have expressed themselves in work and labor for the gospel, and their hope has been steadfast despite the afflictions they have suffered for the gospel. Abraham J. Malherbe (*The Letters to the Thessalonians: A New Translation with Introduction and Commentary* [AB 32B; New York: Doubleday, 2000], 108) writes: "The three terms thus describe the preaching of the gospel in an ascending order of intensity, culminating in *hypomonē.*"

6. This is the first occurrence in Greek literature of *theodidaktoi* ("taught by God"). While it could be an allusion to Jer 31:33-34, given the reference to the Spirit in 1 Thess 4:8,

Paul draws a similar relationship between the moral life, election, and the Spirit in 2 Thessalonians. There he gives thanks for the Thessalonians "because God *chose* you as the first fruits for salvation *through sanctification by the Spirit* and through belief in the truth. For this purpose *he called you* through our proclamation of the good news, so that you may obtain the glory of our Lord Jesus Christ" (2:13-14). The moral life, according to this passage, begins with God's elective call whose goal is the salvation of those who will believe. In the period between the call of the elect and their final salvation, the Spirit sanctifies them in order to prepare them for this salvation. The manner in which Paul discusses the moral life in his Thessalonian correspondence, then, reveals that there is a relationship between the ethical life of the believer on the one hand and God's elective call and the gift of the Spirit on the other. This relationship can be summarized in this way: *The elect are called to live the morally good life that the Spirit makes possible.* It is little wonder, then, that Paul exhorts the Thessalonians "not to quench the Spirit" (1 Thess 5:19).

The relationship between election, the Spirit, and the moral life continues in Paul's Corinthian correspondence. Facing divisions and factions within the community, Paul reminds the Corinthians of their call (1 Cor 1:26-31). Then, after noting that the wisdom and power of God were manifested in the weakness and folly of the cross (2:6-16), he explains why they have failed to appropriate this wisdom. Whereas he teaches in words taught by the Spirit, "interpreting spiritual things to those who are spiritual" (v. 13), their conflicts reveal their moral immaturity. They enjoy the gifts of the Spirit, but they have not embraced the wisdom of the Spirit. And because they have not fully appropriated this new life in the Spirit, they are "people of the flesh" (3:3).[7] Accordingly, although the Corinthians are God's elect and possess many spiritual gifts, their ethical conduct be-

---

Malherbe (*Letters*, 244) understands this term in light of the teaching the Thessalonians have received through the proclamation of the gospel, which they received as God's word. He writes: "Given Paul's earlier emphasis that he had spoken God's word to them (2:2, 4, 8, 9) and that the Thessalonians had received his teaching as God's word (2:13), the latter is the most probable meaning."

7. The Greek word that Paul employs here is *sarkikoi*, which the NRSV translates as "people of the flesh" and the NAB as "fleshly people." Given the contrast that Paul establishes in 1 Cor 3:1 between "spiritual people" and "people of the flesh," the former being mature (2:6) and the latter "infants in Christ," the *sarkikoi* are immature Christians who have failed to understand the meaning of the gospel and, more importantly, have failed to put it into practice.

trays a spiritual immaturity. Paul's experience with the Corinthians indicates that although the Spirit enables believers to live a morally good life, the Spirit does not compel them to do so. One must follow the Spirit's lead — a theme Paul will develop in Romans and Galatians.

Paul's discussion of immorality in 1 Corinthians 5–6 reflects a similar problem. Alluding to their baptism, Paul reminds the Corinthians that they were washed, sanctified, and justified "in the name of the Lord Jesus Christ and in the Spirit of our God" (1 Cor 6:11). Despite this, some of them continue to engage in immorality as if everything were permitted now that they have received the gift of the Spirit. In doing so, the Corinthians have failed to understand that their bodies are members of Christ and temples of God's Spirit (6:15, 19), for which reason they must avoid sexual immorality. Once more Paul describes the moral life in terms of election and the Spirit. But whereas the Thessalonian correspondence illustrates the successful outcome of this triad, the Corinthian correspondence provides an example of how even the elect can fail to live a morally good life when they forget that the Spirit is their moral compass as well as the source of their spiritual gifts.

In Romans and Galatians, Paul introduces a new dimension to his ethical teaching about the role of the Spirit in the moral life: the conflict between the Spirit and the flesh. He argues that a person is justified on the basis of what God has done in Christ rather than by doing the works of the law. Because of this, he exhorts the justified to live according to the Spirit they have received rather than according to the flesh. Employing "flesh" as a metaphor for what is merely human and mortal, Paul portrays the moral life as a choice between a life determined and empowered by God's Spirit and a life enslaved to the desires of the flesh. Believers must choose between living according to the flesh and living according to the Spirit. If they choose the former, they will be unable to please God; if they choose the latter, the Spirit will enable them to fulfill God's law.

Paul relates his teaching on justification to the moral life in the following way in Galatians. First, he assures his converts that they are justified because they received the gift of the Spirit when they believed in the gospel of the crucified Christ (3:1-6).[8] The experience of the Spirit is the evidence

---

8. In these verses Paul reminds the Galatians of the gift of the Spirit, which they have already experienced. They did not receive this Spirit from doing the works of the law but from faith in the gospel of the crucified Christ that Paul preached to them. The gift of the Spirit, Paul insists, is the gift of justification. It is the blessing of Abraham that has been extended to the Gentiles (Gal 3:14).

that they have been justified. Second, having established that the Galatians are justified on the basis of faith rather than on the basis of doing the works of the law, in the final chapters of Galatians Paul shows his converts that even though they are not under the law they can live a morally good life by living according to the Spirit.

Paul's moral exhortation begins with a reminder of their election: they were called to freedom (5:13a). Their freedom from the law, however, will be compromised if they allow it to become a staging ground from which the flesh carries out its desires (v. 13b).[9] Accordingly, Paul instructs the Galatians to live by the Spirit so that they will not carry out the desires of the flesh, noting that the flesh and the Spirit are so diametrically opposed to each other that one cannot simultaneously obey both (vv. 16-17). If the Spirit becomes their moral compass, there will be no room for the desires of the flesh. Next, Paul establishes a contrast between being led by the Spirit and being under the law, indicating that those who are led by the Spirit are not under the law (v. 18). Having been called to freedom from the law, they are led by the dynamic power of God's Spirit that enables them to live in a way pleasing to God.

Drawing a contrast between the many "works" of the flesh and the singular "fruit" of the Spirit,[10] Paul shows that whereas living according to the flesh results in every kind of moral disorder, a life guided by the Spirit results in the singular "fruit" that the Spirit produces in the justified: "love, joy, peace, patience, kindness, generosity, faithfulness, gentleness, and self-control" (vv. 22-23). The moral life of the justified, then, is not something believers accomplish by their good deeds but the "fruit" that the Spirit produces in them. But lest one think that the Spirit produces its fruit without regard to what the justified do, Paul notes that "those who belong to Christ Jesus have crucified the flesh with its passions and desires" (v. 24). This metaphor, which echoes Paul's words in 2:19 ("I have been crucified with

9. According to BDAG, the Greek word that Paul employs here, *aphormē* ("opportunity") means "a base or circumstance from which other action becomes possible, such as the starting-point or base of operations for an expedition." The sense of Paul's warning, then, is that the freedom from being under the law, which the justified enjoy in Christ, must not become the "staging ground" from which the power of the flesh can mount a new campaign against the justified.

10. In contrast to the singular fruit of the Spirit that expresses itself in nine ways, Paul presents the multiple "works" of the flesh (17 in all). Whereas the list of the "works of the flesh" gives a sense of the chaos and division that the works of flesh bring, the list of "the fruit of the Spirit" gives a sense of the unity and harmony that the Spirit produces in the justified.

Christ"), highlights the constant struggle the moral life entails: the justified must die to the desires of the flesh each day.

To summarize, the ethics of Galatians highlights the role of the Spirit
in the moral life. In this ethic, the Spirit is the moral compass that enables
the justified to know what is pleasing to God. More importantly, the Spirit
enables them to live in a way pleasing to God.

The pneumatological ethic that Paul develops in Galatians finds its
fullest expression in Romans. But whereas Galatians presents its teaching
in the letter's paraenesis, Romans expounds its teaching in Romans 8, a
chapter that occurs within the great central section of the letter, where Paul
describes the new life of the justified (Romans 5–8). By discussing the
moral life here, Paul highlights the intimate connection between the indicative of salvation and the moral imperative.

Romans 8 is Paul's response to the cry of unredeemed humanity,
which is expressed at the end of Romans 7.[11] The unredeemed may know
God's law, but the power of sin frustrates their doing it. Consequently, at
the end of ch. 7, unredeemed humanity cries out: "Wretched man that I
am! Who will rescue me from this body of death?" (v. 24). In ch. 8, Paul an-
swers this question.

Paul announces his thesis at the outset of the chapter: The justified
have been liberated from the cosmic powers of sin and death by "the law of
the Spirit of life," by which Paul means the principle or the power of God's
Spirit (8:2). While the law could tell humanity what was right and wrong,
it could not free it from the powers of sin and death. Therefore, God did
what the law could not do by sending his own Son into the realm of the
flesh to defeat sin on its own battlefield (v. 3). As a result of what God has
done in Christ, Paul affirms that the just requirement of the law is fulfilled
in those "who walk not according to the flesh but according to the Spirit"

---

11. The identity of the "I" in Romans 7 is one of the most disputed issues in the interpretation of Romans. Although Augustine, Aquinas, and Barth understood the "I" as the cry
of the Christian who has been wounded by the effects of sin *(concupiscentia)*, the study of
Georg Werner Kümmel (*Römer 7 und das Bild des Menschen im Neuen Testament. Zwei
Studien* [Theologische Bücherei 53; Munich: Kaiser Verlag, 1974]) has convinced many that
the "I" refers to the unredeemed person as viewed from the point of view of one who is redeemed. Thus there is an autobiographical dimension to this passage inasmuch as Paul
views his past life from the perspective of his new life in Christ. From that perspective, this is
how his life really was, even if he was not fully aware of it. What he writes here, however, applies to the whole of unredeemed humanity when viewed from the perspective of redeemed
humanity.

(v. 4). The upshot of this dense section is this: the justified can now live in a way pleasing to God because of God's redemptive work in Christ, which has been communicated to them through the power of the Spirit.

Having explained how humanity has been freed from the power of sin and death, in 8:5-11 Paul contrasts two ways of life: a life determined by allegiance to the flesh and a life determined by allegiance to the Spirit. Those whose lives are determined by the flesh allow the outlook of the flesh to determine their own outlook.[12] Paul describes this outlook in terms of death and hostility to God. Because all flesh is mortal, it leads to death. Because the flesh is opposed to the Spirit, it is hostile to God. And because the flesh is hostile to God, those whose outlook is determined by it cannot please God. In contrast to the outlook of the flesh, the outlook of the Spirit is life and peace; it submits to God's law and pleases God. Paul then reminds his auditors that they are no longer in the flesh if the Spirit of God dwells in them (v. 9). In affirming that they are no longer in the flesh, Paul means they are no longer in the realm of the flesh since they have been transferred from the realm of the old Adam to the realm of the eschatological Adam (5:12-21). Accordingly, while they still remain creatures of flesh and blood, they belong to the realm of the Spirit rather than to the realm of the flesh.

The upshot of Paul's discussion is that believers are no longer obligated to live according to the flesh, which leads to eternal death and separation from God (8:12-13). For the first time, there is the possibility of being led by the Spirit, which makes them sons and daughters of God, and fellow heirs with Christ (v. 14-17). As in Galatians, Paul portrays the moral life as a choice between living according to the flesh and living according to the Spirit. Whereas the flesh enslaves its adherents and leads them to disobedience and death, the Spirit frees its adherents and leads them to obedience and life.

Although the Spirit does not play the dominant role in the ethical teaching of the disputed Pauline letters that it does in the writings noted above, its powerful presence is invoked in Ephesians. In the first part of

12. The Greek word that Paul employs in Rom 8:6, 7 in relation to both flesh and Spirit is *phronēma*. Whereas the NRSV translates it as "the mind of the flesh" and "the mind of the Spirit," the NET translates it as "the outlook of the flesh" and "the outlook of the Spirit." This translation provides a richer description of the two kinds of life that Paul is contrasting, each of which has a particular way of viewing life. Whereas the flesh approaches life in terms of hostility to God, which leads to death, the Spirit approaches life in terms of peace with God, which leads to life.

that letter, Paul reminds his auditors how their past situation has been transformed in accordance with God's redemptive plan in Christ. Formerly, they were as good as dead because of their trespasses and sins. Like everyone else, they followed "the spirit that is now at work among those who are disobedient" (2:1-2). At that time, they were without Christ, alienated from the commonwealth of Israel, without hope, without God. But now they "have access in one Spirit to the Father" (v. 18). They have been sealed *(esphragisthēte)* with "the promised Holy Spirit" (1:13) that identifies them as God's own people. This Spirit is the pledge, the first installment *(arrabōn)* toward their future inheritance (v. 14). Accordingly, Paul prays that their inner being may be strengthened "with power through the Spirit" (3:16).

In the second part of Ephesians, Paul begins his moral exhortation by calling on his auditors to live in a way worthy of their election (4:1). To explain what he means, he writes, "with all humility and gentleness, with patience, bearing with one another in love, *making every effort to maintain the unity of the Spirit in the bond of peace*" (vv. 2-3). The goal of these "virtues" is to preserve the unity that the Spirit makes possible. This unity of life and purpose must guide the moral life of the believer since there is one body, one Spirit, one hope, one Lord, one faith, one baptism, one God and Father. In vv. 17-25 Paul provides the Ephesians with examples of the kind of behavior they must avoid lest they "grieve the Holy Spirit of God" with which they were marked "with a seal for the day of redemption" (v. 30). Those who live in a way contrary to the gospel they have embraced will offend the very Spirit that sealed them as God's elect.

Paul reminds his auditors that once they belonged to darkness but now, in the Lord, they dwell in light. Accordingly they should live as children of light (5:8). Calling upon them to understand the Lord's will for them, he exhorts them to be filled with the Spirit rather than inebriated with wine (v. 18), the implication being that if they allow the Spirit to fill their lives they will live as children of light rather than as children of darkness. Paul then describes the moral life as a spiritual battle in which the elect must combat the "cosmic powers of this present darkness" and "the spiritual forces of evil in the heavenly places" (6:12). To survive this battle they must clothe themselves with God's armor: "the belt of truth," "the breastplate of righteousness," "the shield of faith," "the helmet of salvation, and *the sword of the Spirit,* which is the word of God" (vv. 14-17).

The manner in which Ephesians presents the relationship between the Spirit and the moral life of the believer can be summarized in this way: the elect *ought* to live a morally good life because the Spirit has sealed and claimed them for God, and they *can* live such a life because the Spirit gives them access to God and strengthens their inner being. Although Ephesians does not develop its pneumatological ethic with the intensity that Romans and Galatians do, it presents the Spirit as the link between the indicative of salvation and the moral imperative.

A Sacramental Ethic

The Pauline understanding of baptism and Eucharist provides another link between the indicative of salvation and the moral imperative. Participation in these sacraments brings believers into the sphere of God's saving grace in Christ, where they are empowered to live a life that corresponds to the newness of life they enjoy in Christ. For example, those who are baptized into Christ are baptized into his death and thus die to the power of sin over their lives so that they can live in newness of life. Similarly those who participate in the Eucharist enjoy a communion with the risen Lord that excludes being in communion with other lords. In this section I will examine how the Pauline understanding of baptism and Eucharist is related to the moral imperative.

Paul's remarks about baptism and Eucharist are occasional in nature. He presupposes that those to whom he writes have been baptized into Christ and participate in the Eucharist. But on several occasions, he finds it necessary to remind his auditors of the deeper meaning and ethical significance of the sacraments they celebrate. This occurs several times in 1 Corinthians where Paul must deal with a series of community issues, all of which have moral implications. For example, at the outset of the letter, which describes how the Corinthians are boasting in the one who baptized them, Paul insists that he baptized only a few of them (1:11-17). He reminds them that they were not baptized into his name or the name of the one who baptized them but into the name of the one who was crucified for them. The moral implication of Paul's initial remarks, then, is that baptism should be a source of unity rather than division. People are not baptized into the minister of baptism but into Christ.

In 1 Corinthians 6 Paul alludes to baptism in the context of a discussion about immorality to remind the Corinthians that the wicked will not enter into the kingdom of God (v. 9). After providing the Corinthians with a list of the kinds of people that fall into this category, he writes: "And this is what some of you used to be. But you were washed, you were sanctified, you were justified in the name of the Lord Jesus Christ and in the Spirit of our God" (v. 11). Although he does not explicitly mention baptism, the language of being washed, sanctified, and justified alludes to their baptism. Thus Paul draws yet another relationship between baptism and the moral life that can be stated in this way: those who have been baptized are to avoid immorality since their baptism was the moment when they were washed of their sins, sanctified, and justified so that they could live a new life.

Although the Corinthians had been baptized and participated in the Eucharist, Paul's remarks about the experience of Israel in the wilderness indicate that some of them viewed baptism and Eucharist as rituals that magically protected them from sinning. Accordingly, he reminds them that Israel enjoyed something akin to baptism and Eucharist during its sojourn in the wilderness and still fell into idolatry (10:1-13). On the basis of Israel's experience, he warns the Corinthians that they cannot drink both the cup of the Lord (participate in the Eucharist) and the cup of demons (participate in idolatrous worship) since one excludes the other (v. 21). The communion that each cup establishes with its lord requires total allegiance to that lord.[13] Whereas some of the Corinthians mistakenly think of the sacraments as magical prophylactics, Paul reminds them that baptism and participation in the Eucharist involve a moral commitment on their part. Baptism is an act whereby the justified are baptized into the body of Christ, and the Eucharist is a ritual whereby they drink of the Spirit (12:13). Accordingly, those who participate in these sacraments must no longer live as they did before they were washed, sanctified, and justified. As Paul will explain in Romans 6, they are free to live in a new way.

Whereas in 1 Corinthians Paul speaks of baptism as an action by which believers were washed, sanctified, and justified in the name of Christ and so entered into the body of Christ, in Romans 6 he introduces his distinctive understanding of baptism: the justified have been baptized into Christ's death.[14] As with the other texts we have studied, Paul's re-

---

13. The key words in Paul's discussion of the Eucharist in 1 Cor 10:14-22 are *koinōnia* (twice in v. 16), which refers to communion or participation in a common reality, and *koinōnoi* (v. 18) and *koinōnous* (v. 20), which refer to those who are communicants in a common reality. Communion *(koinōnia)* with Christ is so profound that one cannot be a communicant *(koinonos)* in another reality such as the worship of idols. Each communion excludes the other.

14. Rudolf Bultmann (*Theology of the New Testament* [New York: Charles Scribner's

marks about baptism are part of a larger argument developed in Romans 6. For if it is true, as he argues in 5:12-21, that God's saving grace is more powerful than the destructive power of sin unleashed by Adam's disobedience, why not conclude that the justified should continue to sin so that God's grace will increase all the more (6:1)?

To counter this misrepresentation of his gospel, Paul introduces his understanding of baptism. Posing two rhetorical questions from which he draws his conclusion, he asks: "*How can we* who died to sin go on living in it? *Do you not know* that all of us who have been baptized into Christ Jesus were baptized into his death? *Therefore* we have been buried with him by baptism into death, *so that, just as Christ* was raised from the dead by the glory of the Father, *so we too* might walk in newness of life" (6:2-4). Here, I note two points. First, in 1 Corinthians Paul described baptism in terms of being baptized into the name of Christ and into his body. But here he portrays it as a sacramental participation in the historical death of Jesus whereby the baptized die to the power of sin that ruled over their lives. Second, we might have expected Paul to write as follows: "so that just as Christ was raised from the dead by the glory of the Father, *so we too might be raised from the dead by the glory of the Father.*" But instead of pointing to the resurrection of the baptized, he highlights the ethical implications of their baptism into Christ's death: "*so we too might walk in newness of life.*" In this concise statement, Paul presents baptism as the link between the indicative of salvation and the moral imperative.

Believers should not continue to sin because they are no longer under the power of sin. When they were under its power, sin ruled over their lives and frustrated their every attempt to do God's law. But when they were baptized into Christ, they were baptized into the historical event of his death whereby he overcame the power of death. Consequently, through their baptism into Christ's death, they died to the power of sin over their lives. Now, for the first time, they are free *not* to sin. Baptism, then, does not merely provide the justified with a motive for not sinning: it liberates them from the power of sin. In baptism the old adamic self is crucified

---

Sons, 1951], 1:140) thinks that Paul inherited this understanding of baptism from the Hellenistic church. He writes: "*Baptism imparts participation in the death and resurrection of Christ.* This interpretation undoubtedly originated in the Hellenistic Church, which understood this traditional initiation-sacrament on analogy with the initiation-sacraments of the mystery religions" (emphasis in the original). In my view, Bultmann too quickly presupposes a dependence on the mystery religions. Given Paul's consistent emphasis on the centrality of Christ's death, it is more likely that Paul introduced this understanding of baptism.

with Christ with the result that the sin-dominated body of that old humanity is destroyed and the justified are freed from the power of sin.[15] Those who have died to sin in baptism, then, are no longer under its power (6:6-7). Although this freedom does not mean that it is impossible for them to sin, it is inconceivable to Paul that the justified would want to continue to sin. Therefore he exhorts them, "consider yourselves dead to sin and alive to God in Christ Jesus" (v. 11).[16]

Like Romans, Colossians draws a relationship between baptism and death to an old way of life. Responding to an erroneous teaching that failed to comprehend the centrality of Christ in God's redemptive plan, Paul reminds the Colossians that the "fullness of divinity dwells bodily" in Christ and that they share in this fullness through their life in Christ (2:9-10). To explain how this came about, he describes their baptism as a "spiritual circumcision." At baptism their old self, which was dominated by the power of the flesh, was stripped away (v. 11). Having been buried with Christ through their baptism, they have been raised with him from the dead (v. 12). Formerly they were as good as dead because of their transgressions and uncircumcised flesh, but now they live with Christ who has forgiven their transgressions by destroying the bond of indebtedness (their sins) that was held against them (vv. 13-15). With this understanding of baptism, Paul begins his moral exhortation: "So if you have been raised with Christ,

15. Here, "body" *(sōma)* refers to the whole person as an embodied self. "The body of sin," then, is the human person under the power of sin. For a discussion of Paul's use of "body," see Bultmann, *Theology of the New Testament*, 1:192-203. On p. 195 he writes: "*Man, his person as a whole,* can be denoted by *soma*. . . . *Man is called soma in respect to his being able to make himself the object of his own action or to experience himself as the subject to whom something happens*" (emphasis in the original).

16. Throughout Romans 6, Paul argues that the justified are no longer under the power of sin since they have died to sin through their baptism into Christ. But this does not mean that the justified are incapable of sinning. Although it was probably incomprehensible to Paul that the justified would sin, he is painfully aware of the presence of sin among his converts. By writing "consider yourselves dead to sin and alive to God in Christ Jesus" (v. 11), Paul exhorts his recipients to look at the new reality that has entered their lives through baptism: they are dead to sin. While this new reality does not guarantee they will never again sin, it assures them that they are no longer under the compulsion to sin. Thus, although sinlessness may not be a reality, it has become a possibility. Udo Schnelle (*Apostle Paul: His Life and Theology* [Grand Rapids: Baker, 2003], 575) describes this new situation even more strongly: "For the church, sin is a reality that belongs to the past, and 6:14a states expressly, 'For sin will have not dominion over you.' . . . Baptized believers know themselves to have been essentially separated from the world, for they live in the realm of Christ's power and thus in the church as a realm free from sin."

seek the things that are above, where Christ is, seated at the right hand of God" (3:1). In this way, he grounds his moral exhortation in his baptismal theology: the Colossians *can* live the morally good life that Paul presents because their old carnal self was stripped away at baptism.

A comparison of how Romans and Colossians view baptism is interesting. In Romans Paul speaks of believers being (1) baptized into Christ's death, (2) buried with him through baptism, and (3) crucified so that the body of sin might be destroyed. In Colossians he refers to baptism in terms of a spiritual circumcision that stripped away the body of flesh. This happened when believers were buried in baptism with Christ and "raised with him in the power of God" (2:12). Although the two letters employ different imagery, they both relate baptism to the death of Christ in order to explain that believers have been freed to live a morally good life. The major difference between them is the manner in which they relate baptism to Christ's resurrection. Whereas Romans says that the baptized *will be raised* because they have associated themselves with Christ's death, Colossians speaks of the baptized as *raised up* in Christ "through faith in the power of God who raised him from the dead" (2:12). This emphasis on the present in Colossians is the outcome of a fuller understanding of the body of Christ that can be expressed in this way: inasmuch as Christ, the head of the body, has been raised up, those who belong to the body are raised up with him in faith.

Ephesians relates baptism and the moral life to each other in two ways. First, it exhorts believers to live in a manner worthy of their call/election by making every effort to maintain the unity of the Spirit (4:1-3). To support this exhortation, Paul lists seven points of unity (vv. 4-5). Taking baptism as a starting point, we can summarize the relationship between these points of unity: By baptism believers were incorporated into the *one body,* which is the church; they received the *one Spirit;* they were called to *one hope;* they confess *one Lord, one faith, one God and Father.* Paul's moral exhortation is a call to the unity expressed in these seven points of unity, which is made possible by living in one body, one Spirit, one hope, one Lord, one faith, one baptism, one God and Father.

The second way in which Ephesians relates the moral life and baptism occurs in Paul's marriage exhortation, which compares the relationship between husband and wife to the relationship between Christ and the church. Exhorting husbands to love their wives as Christ loved the church, Paul reminds them how Christ gave himself up for the church so that he might sanctify the church by cleansing her "with the washing of water by the word" (5:26). Although there is no explicit mention of baptism here, the language Paul employs alludes to baptism. The purpose of Christ's death was to cleanse believers from sin so that Christ might present the church to himself as "holy and without blemish" (v. 27). Although Paul is not explicitly developing a baptismal theology in this text, what he writes sheds light on the relationship between baptism and the moral life: believers have been called to live in a new way because, through their baptism, Christ has cleansed and prepared them for himself.

The letter to Titus develops this baptismal imagery further. After providing Titus with practical advice for exhorting and reprimanding believers at Crete, Paul concludes this brief letter with a hymn-like passage that summarizes his gospel:

> But when the goodness and loving kindness of God our Savior appeared, he saved us, not because of any works of righteousness that we had done, but according to his mercy, *through the water of rebirth and renewal by the Holy Spirit.* This Spirit he poured out on us richly through Jesus Christ our Savior, so that, having been justified by his grace, we might become heirs according to the hope of eternal life. (3:4-7)

In this concise statement, Paul begins with the epiphany of God that occurred in the appearance of Christ. Focusing on this epiphany rather than on the cross and resurrection, he affirms that believers have been *saved* by God's mercy rather than on the basis of anything they have done. Instead of saying that they have been saved through Christ's death, Paul affirms that they were saved "through the water of rebirth and renewal by the Holy Spirit," an allusion to their baptism, by which the Spirit was poured upon them so that they might be *justified* by grace. Baptism, then, is the means by which the saving effects of Christ's redemption are mediated to believers. By this allusion to baptism, Paul reminds his auditors that their baptism was the moment of their rebirth and renewal (3:5).[17] Those who have been baptized have undergone a transformation that makes the moral life

---

17. The two words that are used here, "rebirth" *(palingenesias)* and "renewal" *(anakainōseōs)*, occur rather infrequently in the NT. P. Trummer (*EDNT*, 3:8) notes that the former, which also occurs in Matt 19:28, belongs to the same "conceptual field" as "new person," "new creation," and "restoration." According to J. Baumgarten (*EDNT*, 2:232) the latter, which also occurs in Rom 12:2, "accents the existential reality of the salvation and *renewal* through the Holy Spirit that has taken place in baptism." Taken together, both words provide a rich description of the renewal that occurs through baptism.

possible, a point that Paul intimated when he wrote that Christ "gave himself for us that he might redeem us from all iniquity and purify for himself a people of his own who are zealous for good deeds" (2:14). Like Romans, Colossians, and Ephesians, the letter to Titus shows that the moral life is possible because of the rebirth and renewal that has come about as a result of God's work in Christ. Like the Spirit, baptism is the link between the indicative of salvation and the moral imperative.

A Love Ethic

Given the centrality that love plays in Jesus' ethical teaching, it is not surprising that it holds a prominent place in Paul's letters as well. For Paul love is the essence of the law. In light of what God has done in Christ, Paul grounds his understanding of love in God's own love and in the example of Christ's self-sacrificing love. Just as Jesus summoned his disciples to love God, their neighbors, and even their enemies, so Paul exhorts his converts to do the same. This he does in light of God's love for them and the self-sacrificing love of Christ, which provides the paradigm for Christian living. Paul's love ethic can be summarized in five points.

First, the Pauline understanding of love is grounded in God's own love, which has been revealed in Christ. This emphasis on God's love occurs throughout the Pauline Epistles. In Romans, Paul says that the justified will not be disappointed in their hope for final salvation because God's love has been poured into their hearts through the power of the Holy Spirit (5:5). Since God manifested this love in Christ who died for them when they were still sinners (v. 8), the justified can be confident that nothing will separate them from the love that God has shown them in Christ (8:35-39). In 2 Corinthians Paul writes that since he has come to the realization that Christ died for all, his life has been determined by the "love of Christ" (5:14), by which he means Christ's love for him, which leads to his love for Christ.[18] Paul makes a similar statement in Galatians where, in a moment of intimate self-revelation, he unabashedly proclaims that he lives "by faith in the Son of God, who loved me and gave himself for me" (2:20).

18. The genitives that occurs in Rom 5:5 (*hē agapē tou theou*); 8:35 (*tēs agapēs tou Christou*); and 2 Cor 5:14 (*hē agapē tou Christou*) can be construed in different ways: God's love for us or our love for God (Rom 5:5), Christ's love for us or our love for Christ (Rom 8:35; 2 Cor 5:14). I have interpreted them as subjective genitives: God's love for us and Christ's love for us.

In Ephesians, he grounds this love in God's eternal redemptive plan: "In love he destined us for adoption to himself through Jesus Christ" (1:4-5, NAB).[19] According to Ephesians, God is rich in mercy because of the great love with which he loved us (2:4). Believers have been "rooted and grounded in love" (3:17) so that they can know "the love of Christ" — Christ's love for them and their love for him — that surpasses all knowledge (3:19). Christ's own love for the church provides the paradigm for how husbands should love their wives (5:2, 25). This emphasis on the priority of God's love continues in the Pastorals. The appearance of God's "loving kindness" *(philanthrōpia)* is the result of God's mercy (Tit 3:4-5), and the grace and love that believers experience is the result of belonging to Christ (1 Tim 1:14; 2 Tim 1:13). The love that believers should extend to others, then, has its origin in God's love, which was manifested in Christ and dwells in their hearts. It is "the God of love and peace" (2 Cor 13:11) who empowers believers to love others, and it is the Spirit who pours this love into their hearts. Thus Paul can say that love is the fruit of the Spirit (Gal 5:22).

Second, having been loved by God, Paul lives his life in a way that accords with God's own love, which he experiences in Christ. Paul is not ashamed to express his love for his converts. In exhorting the Philippians he writes: "Therefore, my brothers and sisters, whom I love and long for, my joy and crown, stand firm in the Lord in this way, my beloved" (4:1). Although he has the authority to command Philemon to do what he commands, he says: "yet I would rather appeal to you on the basis of love" (v. 9). And when he reminds Timothy of how he conducted himself, he writes: "you have observed my teaching, my conduct, my aim in life, my faith, my patience, my love, my steadfastness" (2 Tim 3:10). The manner in which he insists upon his love for the Corinthians is especially telling. Despite the difficulties he encountered with them, he regularly assures them of his love for them. In 1 Corinthians, after exhorting them not to fall into factions, he asks if they would prefer that he came with a stick rather than "with love in

---

19. Eph 1:4-5 presents a translation problem since the last words of v. 4 ("in love") can be construed as the first words of a new sentence as in the NAB ("as he chose us in him, before the foundation of the world, to be holy and without blemish before him. *In love* he destined us for adoption to himself through Jesus Christ, in accord with the favor of his will") or as the last words of the previous sentence as in the NRSV ("he chose us in Christ before the foundation of the world to be holy and blameless before him *in love*. He destined us for adoption as his children through Jesus Christ, according to the good pleasure of his will"). Here I am following the NAB.

a spirit of gentleness" (4:21). He then concludes the letter: "My love be with all of you in Christ Jesus" (16:24), the sense being that his love for them is rooted in the communion they share with him in Christ. In 2 Corinthians, a letter in which he must deal with a severe challenge to his authority, he explains that he earlier wrote a harsh letter to let them know of the abundant love that he has for them (2:4).[20] In describing his conduct as God's servant, he points to his "genuine love" (6:6), and despite their mistrust of him, he regularly affirms his love for the Corinthians (8:7; 11:11; 12:15). Texts such as these indicate that Paul seeks to conduct his life in a way that corresponds to God's love, which he experienced in Christ.

Third, in light of God's own love and his love for his converts, Paul exhorts the recipients of his letters to love God and each other. In 1 Thessalonians, he praises his new converts for their "labor of love" (1:3), by which he means their loving service toward each other. He even affirms that there is no need for him to write to them on the topic of mutual charity *(philadelphias)* since they have been taught by God *(theodidaktoi)* to love one another (4:9). Aware of their love, he prays that they will abound in love for each other all the more, even as he loves them (3:12). And since they belong to "the day," he exhorts them to put on the "breastplate of faith and love" (5:8). In 2 Thessalonians he thanks God because their love for each other continues to grow (1:3), and he prays that the Lord will direct their hearts to the love of God, which can be construed as God's own love or their love for God (3:5). In Philippians he prays that the love of the Philippians will increase ever more (1:9), and he exhorts them to be of the same mind with the same love for each other (2:2). He commends the Colossians for their love (1:4), and he exhorts them to clothe themselves with love, which "binds everything together in perfect harmony" (3:14). In Ephesians he exhorts his auditors to bear with one another in love (4:2) and to speak the truth in love so that the body (the church) will be built up in love (vv. 15-16). In a word, just as Christ loved them and gave himself up for them, so they must conduct their lives in love (5:2). Paul's instruction on love plays an important role in 1 Corinthians since some of the Corinthians have not correctly understood the nature of their new freedom in Christ or the purpose of the spiritual gifts they have received. Accordingly

20. The harsh letter is a letter Paul wrote between the writing of 1 and 2 Corinthians in response to the painful visit he experienced at Corinth, when someone offended him (2 Cor 1:23–2:4). Like the letter alluded to in 1 Cor 5:9, this letter has been lost. Paul, however, refers to it in 2 Cor 2:4, 9; 7:8, 12.

Paul must remind them that whereas knowledge makes a person conceited, loves builds up the community (8:1), and that those who love God are known by God (v. 3). After an extensive description of love in ch. 13, he exhorts the Corinthians to pursue love (14:1). These themes continue in the Pastorals where Paul writes that the aim of his instruction is the love that comes from a pure heart, a good conscience, and sincere faith (1 Tim 1:5). Accordingly, Timothy is to pursue "righteousness, godliness, faith, love, endurance, gentleness" (6:11; see also 2 Tim 2:22). Titus is to tell older men to be sound in faith and in love (Tit 2:2) and to encourage young women to love their husbands and children (v. 4). This exhortation to love God and each other plays a central role in Pauline ethics because love mirrors God's love in Christ, and Paul's love for those who are in Christ.

Fourth, Paul describes love in concrete and specific ways. In Romans he says that love must be "genuine" (*anypokritos,* 12:9), by which he means that it must be sincere, not the occasion for pretense or hypocrisy. Believers are to be devoted to each other in mutual love (*philadelphia,* 12:10), aware that love does no wrong to the neighbor (13:10). In 1 Corinthians he writes: "Love is patient; love is kind; love is not envious or boastful or arrogant or rude. It does not insist on its own way; it is not irritable or resentful; it does not rejoice in wrongdoing, but rejoices in the truth. It bears all things, believes all things, hopes all things, endures all things" (13:4-7). Paul refers to the genuineness of his own love in 2 Cor 6:6, and in that same letter he calls on the Corinthians to show the genuineness of their love by completing the collection for Jerusalem, which they began a year earlier (8:8). The kind of love Paul has in view requires believers to serve each other in love (Gal 5:13), to bear with one another in humility, gentleness, and patience (Eph 4:2). Love, then, is more than an emotion or feeling since it involves the sacrifice of self that Paul exemplifies in his own life, which is patterned after the self-sacrificing love of Christ. Because love involves self-sacrifice on a daily basis, Paul speaks of the "labor of love" (1 Thess 1:3), thereby highlighting the effort and work that it entails.

Fifth, Paul views love as the fulfillment of the law. He says that those who are guided by the Spirit are no longer under the law (Gal 5:18) and that Christ is the end of the law (Rom 10:4). But he also insists that the justified fulfill the law through the love commandment. For example, in Galatians he exhorts his converts to serve each other in love because the whole law is "summed up" (*peplērōtai*) in a single commandment: "You shall love your neighbor as yourself" (Gal 5:14, quoting Lev 19:18). In Romans he expands on that statement: "Owe no one anything, except to love one another; for the one who loves another has fulfilled *(peplēroken)* the law. The command-ments, 'You shall not commit adultery; You shall not murder; You shall not steal; You shall not covet'; and any other commandment, are summed up in this word, 'Love your neighbor as yourself.' Love does no wrong to a neigh-bor; therefore, love is the fulfilling *(anakephalaioutai)* of the law" (13:8-10). Paul does not violate the Decalogue, nor does he encourage his converts to ignore it. But instead of urging them to do the individual commandments of the law, he exhorts them to fulfill the whole law through the love com-mandment, confident that those who love their neighbor will not contra-vene its commandments.[21]

In affirming that love is the fulfillment of the commandments, Paul has in view the kind of love that Christ exemplified throughout his life, and especially in his death. Thus he tells his Galatian converts that they will fulfill "the law of Christ" *(ton nomon tou Christou)* by bearing one an-other's burdens (Gal 6:2). The law of Christ, to which he refers, is not a new set of rules and regulations that Christ brought but the law as lived by Christ, who surrendered his life "for us," or as Paul says in Galatians, "for me" (2:20).[22] Accordingly, when describing his behavior, he insists that he is not outside or apart from God's law but in or within the law of Christ (1 Cor 9:21), by which he means that he lives his life according to Christ.[23] The law that guided Paul in his own life, and which ought to guide the jus-tified in their lives, is the law of Christ — the manner in which Christ ful-filled the law in his life and death through the love commandment.

In telling his converts that they are no longer under the law, Paul re-minds them that they have been transferred to the realm of the Spirit, which empowers them to live in a way pleasing to God. His purpose is not to contravene the law, or to criticize it, but to remind his converts that they have been transferred into the realm of Christ where it is possible to fulfill

21. Although this may seem to be a semantic difference, it reveals something about Paul's new understanding of the law. Whereas formerly he devoted himself to "doing" the individual prescriptions of the law, now he seeks to "fulfill" the deepest meaning of the law, which he finds in the love commandment. This approach has the possibility of giving more attention to the inner meaning of the law.

22. For a full discussion of what Paul means by "the law of Christ," see J. M. G. Barclay, *Obeying the Truth: A Study of Paul's Ethics in Galatians* (Edinburgh: T. and T. Clark, 1988), 125-45.

23. The Greek phrases that Paul uses here are *anomos theou* and *ennomos Christou*. The first has the sense of being lawless before God, the second has the sense of being within the boundaries of the law because one is in Christ.

the deepest meaning of the law through the love commandment as lived by Christ.

The law is and remains an authentic expression of God's will, but the justified should not approach it in terms of "doing" its individual precepts as if they could justify themselves before God but in terms of fulfilling its deepest requirement through the love commandment. Thus Paul tells the Galatians that those who do the law for the purpose of justifying themselves will separate themselves from Christ and fall from God's grace (5:4). What matters is not circumcision or the lack of it but "faith working through love" (5:6), by which Paul means a faith that expresses itself in love for others.[24] The love commandment is the fulfillment of the law because it is the perfect expression of how Christ lived.

An Eschatological Ethic

Convinced that the one whom God raised from the dead will return at the end of the ages to inaugurate the general resurrection of the dead, the final judgment, and the coming of God's kingdom in power, Paul encourages his converts to live their lives in light of the imminent return of their Lord. In doing so, he develops an eschatological ethic that views the present age as giving way to the coming age, which has already made its appearance in Christ's death and resurrection. How believers conduct themselves in the present is of the utmost importance because their salvation is nearer now than when first they believed (Rom 13:11). Since the night of the old age is far advanced and the day of the new age is fast approaching, believers must live in a way that corresponds to the new age that will be fully revealed at the parousia: they must put on the Lord Jesus Christ.

In his earliest correspondence, Paul reminds the Thessalonians that the day of the Lord will come like "a thief in the night" (1 Thess 5:2).[25] Therefore, since they are "children of light and children of the day," they must remain sober and aware, putting on the "breastplate of faith and love" and the helmet that is the "hope of salvation" (vv. 5, 8). Aware that his converts will stand in judgment before God, Paul prays that they will be

---

24. The Greek is *pistis di' agapēs energoumenē*. If the participle is taken as a passive, it could mean "faith made effective through love." If the participle is taken as a middle, it would could mean "faith expressing itself through love." The latter seems preferable. Faith expresses itself through love.

25. Jesus uses a similar expression in his eschatological discourse (Matt 24:43).

strengthened in holiness so that they can be "blameless" before God at the Lord's parousia (3:13; 5:23). Paul utters a similar prayer at the beginning of his letter to the Philippians, when he prays that the recipients' love will overflow with knowledge and insight so that they can determine what is best and be "pure and blameless" at Christ's coming (1:9-10). Although 1 Timothy may not have been written by Paul, it also highlights the need to be blameless on the day of the Lord. Addressing a solemn charge to Timothy, Paul writes: "In the presence of God, who gives life to all things, and of Christ Jesus, who in his testimony before Pontius Pilate made the good confession, I charge you to keep the commandment without spot or blame until the manifestation of our Lord Jesus Christ, which he will bring about at the right time" (6:13-15).

Paul exhorts his converts to remain blameless until the day of the Lord because he knows that the parousia will be a day of judgment. For example, in Romans he warns his auditors to refrain from judging each other, "for we will all stand before the judgment seat of God" (14:10). Altering the metaphor slightly, in 2 Corinthians he reminds the Corinthians that they must always seek to please the Lord because "all of us must appear before the judgment seat of Christ, so that each may receive recompense for what has been done in the body, whether good or evil" (5:10).[26] A similar theme occurs in 2 Timothy, where Paul solemnly urges Timothy "in the presence of God and of Christ Jesus, who is to judge the living and the dead, and in view of his appearing and his kingdom" to proclaim the message of the gospel, whether convenient or inconvenient (4:1-2). Having fought the good fight, finished the race, and kept the faith, the Paul of the Pastorals expresses his confidence that a "crown of righteousness" has been reserved for him, "which the Lord, the righteous judge, will give me on that day, and not only to me but also to all who have longed for his appearing" (v. 8).

In addition to inaugurating the general resurrection of the dead and the final judgment, the parousia will usher in the final stage of the kingdom of God. Employing this theme, which plays such a central role in the Synoptic Gospels, Paul reminds his converts that the unjust will not enter the kingdom of God (1 Cor 6:9-10). Eph 5:5 also echoes this theme: "Be sure of this, that no fornicator or impure person, or one who is greedy

---

26. Paul can speak of the judgment seat of God (Rom 14:10) as well as the judgment seat of Christ (2 Cor 5:10) just as he can speak of the Spirit of God and the Spirit of Christ (Rom 8:9). While judgment belongs to God, Christ will be the agent through whom God will judge the world.

(that is, an idolater), has any inheritance in the kingdom of Christ and of God." The common theme of these texts can be stated in this way: the manner in which believers conduct themselves in the present will play a decisive role in their fate at the end of the ages. Believers have already been justified and reconciled by God's grace on the basis of faith; they have not earned their justification. But even the justified and reconciled will be judged on the basis of what they have done or failed to do.

In addition to alerting believers to the final judgment that will accompany the parousia, Paul reminds them that they are living between the ages — the old age that is in the process of passing away and the new age that has made its appearance in Christ. For example in 1 Corinthians 7, a chapter that deals with marriage and virginity, Paul warns the Corinthians that "the appointed time has grown short; from now on, let even those who have wives be *as though* they had none, and those who mourn *as though* they were not mourning, and those who rejoice *as though* they were not rejoicing, and those who buy *as though* they had no possessions, and those who deal with the world *as though* they had no dealings with it. For the present form of this world is passing away" (vv. 29-31). The fivefold use of "as though" in this passage provides Paul's audience with a powerful "eschatological reservation" that can be explained in this way: Since the present age will be dissolved when the Lord appears, believers should not live in the present as if it were the final age. Rather, they ought to live with the knowledge that the present age in which they are living will soon give way to the new age that will supplant it. In addition to motivating believers to live a morally good life, then, hope in the parousia allows believers to view the present age in a new way: the world they experience is already giving way to the new age that ought to determine their conduct even now.

Coherence and Meaning in Pauline Ethics

In this chapter I have described Pauline ethics in terms of (1) God's saving work in Christ, which makes the moral imperative possible, (2) the Spirit that empowers believers to live a morally good life, (3) the sacraments, by which believers participate in Christ's life, (4) the love commandment by which believers pattern their lives after Christ's life, and (5) the eschatological hope, which provides believers with motivation and insight to live the moral life in the present. While each of these highlights a particular aspect of Pauline ethics, all of them converge on a single point: God's saving grace in Christ. The soteriological dimension of the moral life, the gift of the Spirit, the sacraments, the love commandment, and eschatological hope are the outcome of God's saving grace in Christ. What is "new" in Pauline ethics, then, is not the individual moral commandments of Paul's teaching (many of which are grounded in Israel's moral teaching and Hellenistic philosophy) but the manner in which he relates them to Christ. It is Christ who models and makes the moral life possible; it is Christ who is the origin and goal of the moral life Paul proposes.

The moral life that the Pauline letters propose is both an individual and communal ethic. On the one hand, it is the individual who must respond to the saving grace of Jesus Christ. It is the individual who must commit himself or herself to the new life that has been made possible through God's redemptive work. On the other, the individual lives this life in the context of a believing community. Apart from this believing community, which is the body of Christ, the moral life is impossible. Apart from this believing community, in which the Spirit dwells, the moral life is a fruitless effort. But in and with this community, which is the sanctified sphere of the church, all things are possible. A truly Pauline ethic, then, appreciates the proper balance between the individual and the community, the person and the church.

FOR FURTHER READING

Burridge, Richard A. *Imitating Jesus: An Inclusive Approach to New Testament Ethics.* Grand Rapids: Eerdmans, 2007. Pages 81-154.

Collange, Jean-François. *De Jésus à Paul, L'Éthique du Nouveau Testament.* Le Champ Éthique 3. Geneva: Labor et Fides, 1980.

Deidun, T. J. *New Covenant Morality in Paul.* AnBib 89. Rome: Biblical Institute Press, 1981.

Dunn, James D. G. *The Theology of Paul the Apostle.* Grand Rapids: Eerdmans, 1988. Pages 625-69.

Furnish, Victor Paul. *The Moral Teaching of Paul.* 3rd ed. Nashville: Abingdon, 2009.

————. *Theology and Ethics in Paul.* Nashville: Abingdon, 1968.

Hahn, Ferdinand. *Theologie des Neuen Testaments,* vol. 1: *Die Vielfalt des Neuen Testaments. Theologiegeschichte des Urchristentums.* Tübingen: Mohr Siebeck, 2002. Pages 268-95.

Harrington, Daniel J., and James F. Keenan. *Paul and Virtue Ethics: Building*

Bridges between New Testament Studies and Moral Theology. Lanham: Rowman and Littlefield, 2010.

Lovering, Eugene H., and Jerry L. Sumney. *Theology and Ethics in Paul and His Interpreters: Essays in Honor of Victor Paul Furnish.* Nashville: Abingdon, 1996.

Marxsen, Willi. *New Testament Foundations for Christian Ethics.* Minneapolis: Fortress, 1993. Pages 142-227.

Matera, Frank J. *New Testament Ethics: The Legacies of Jesus and Paul.* Louisville: Westminster John Knox, 1996. Pages 119-247.

O'Toole, Robert. *Who Is a Christian: A Study in Pauline Ethics.* Zacchaeus Studies: New Testament. Collegeville: Liturgical, 1990.

Pregeant, Russell. *Knowing Truth, Doing Good: Engaging New Testament Ethics.* Minneapolis: Fortress, 2008. Pages 216-82.

Ridderbos, Herman. *Paul: An Outline of His Theology.* Grand Rapids: Eerdmans, 1975. Pages 253-326.

Rosner, Brian S. *Paul, Scripture and Ethics: A Study of 1 Corinthians 5–7.* Biblical Studies Library. Grand Rapids: Baker, 1994.

Rosner, Brian S., ed. *Understanding Paul's Ethics: Twentieth Century Approaches.* Grand Rapids: Eerdmans, 1995.

Sampley, J. Paul. *Walking between the Times: Paul's Moral Reasoning.* Minneapolis: Fortress, 1991.

Schnackenburg, Rudolf. *Die sittliche Botschaft des Neuen Testaments,* vol. 2: *Die urchristlichen Verkündiger.* HTKNT Supplementband. Freiburg: Herder, 1988. Pages 13-109.

Schnelle, Udo. *Apostle Paul: His Life and Theology.* Grand Rapids: Baker, 2003. Pages 546-58.

Schrage, Wolfgang. *The Ethics of the New Testament.* Philadelphia: Fortress, 1998. Pages 163-78.

7. Waiting for the Final Appearance of God's Saving Grace

Introduction

For those who are in Christ, the present is determined by the future as well as by the past. On the one hand, the justified live in God's saving grace because of the eschatological deed that God has accomplished in his Son whereby God conquered the powers of sin and death that held sway over the old age. Consequently, the justified now live in the realm of God's Spirit. No longer under the law, they live under the power of God's grace (Rom 6:15). No longer determined by the power of the flesh, they live according to the power of God's Spirit (8:9). No longer in the old Adam, they live in the eschatological Adam — the new human being — in the community of the church. On the other hand, the justified live in anticipation of the final appearance of God's saving grace that will occur when their Lord returns, the dead are raised, the world is judged, the kingdom of God appears, and God will be all in all (1 Cor 15:23-28).

The justified live, then, between the ages, between what has already happened in Christ's death and resurrection and what will occur when he returns. What has already happened has irretrievably altered their lives. But how can the future, which has not happened, touch their lives? The answer to this question is the paradoxical nature of the new life the justified enjoy. For those who are "in Christ" the future has invaded the present. Through the saving grace of Jesus Christ and the gift of the Spirit, the justified already experience something of resurrection life, the fullness of which they will enjoy at the resurrection of the dead. The present life of the justified, then, is an "eschatological existence" because God's future has made its appearance in the life of the justified.[1] Inasmuch as Christ has put an end to the old age of sin and death and inaugurated the new age of grace and life, "the ends of the ages" have come upon the justified (1 Cor 10:11).[2] The eschatological existence of the justified, then, means that believers already experience something of the future, which is molding and defining their lives.

This eschatological existence by which the justified experience something of the future in the present is the starting point for any consideration of Pauline eschatology. This concept is also the key to understanding the hope that believers have for the parousia. For when eschatology is understood in light of the eschatological existence that believers enjoy, it becomes apparent that it is concerned with the present as well as with the future. Furthermore, it is this eschatological existence that gives birth to the hope that believers have for the future.

The justified wait in hope for the final appearance of God's saving grace because they already experience something of that grace, the fullness of which is yet to be revealed. They experience the Spirit as the "first installment" (2 Cor 1:22; 5:5), the "first fruits" of the salvation that awaits

---

1. Rudolf Bultmann (*The Theology of the New Testament* [New York: Charles Scribner's Sons, 1951], 1:187-352) develops this theme of eschatological existence throughout his section on the theology of Paul. By eschatological existence he means that believers are not merely waiting for eternal life; they already experience something of the resurrection life for which they long in their experience of the Spirit. "Rather, everything indicates that by the term 'Spirit' he [Paul] means the eschatological existence into which the believer is placed by having appropriated the salvation deed that occurred in Christ" (p. 335). "Life is already here; for Christ's resurrection is conceived not just as the first case of rising from the dead, but as the origin of the resurrection life of all believers, which necessarily proceeds from it and hence can be regarded as already present in its origin" (pp. 347-48). The point, then, is that in virtue of Christ's death and resurrection the future has broken into the present life of the justified through the power of God's Spirit. It is in and by this Spirit that the justified live in anticipation of final salvation. Udo Schnelle (*Apostle Paul: His Life and Theology* [Grand Rapids: Baker, 2003], 581) writes: "The new being of baptized believers can be described in both functional and temporal aspects as eschatological existence: they participate fully in the ultimate turn of the ages brought about by God's act in Jesus Christ, and know that they will live their lives in a present already determined by the future."

2. By the expression "the ends of the ages" *(ta telē tōn aiōnōn)*, Paul means that believers stand at that point in history where the old and the new ages meet. On the one hand, Christ's redemptive work has put an end to the old age. On the other hand, it has inaugurated the new age. Consequently believers stand at the very point where these two ages meet. While the old age continues to linger, the new age has already made its appearance in their lives.

them (Rom 8:23). In Christ believers see the "first fruits" of the general resurrection of the dead in which they will share (1 Cor 15:20, 23).[3] Since God
has already justified them, they are confident that their acquittal in Christ
is the verdict they will hear at the last judgment (Rom 8:31-39). Having experienced something of the righteousness, the peace, and the joy of the
Spirit that characterizes the kingdom of God (14:17), they believe that the
fullness of the kingdom is at hand. It is little wonder then that the Pauline
letters are filled with hope and anticipation of what is to come. For if the
Spirit of God dwells in them, God will raise their mortal bodies (8:11).[4] It is
this experience of the future in the present that provides the justified with
their vibrant hope for the Lord's return.

The Pauline letters are filled with language that anticipates the coming
of the Lord.[5] They employ a series of nouns that focus on the "coming"
(parousia), the "manifestation" *(epiphaneia)*, the "revelation" *(apokalyp-
sis)*, and "the day" *(hēmera)* of the Lord. They also use verbs that indicate
that the Lord will "come" *(erchomai)*, "appear" *(phaneroumai)*, and "be revealed" *(apokalyptomai)*. Still other verbs highlight that believers "wait
for" and "expect" *(prosdechomai, apekdechomai, ekdechomai, prosdokaō,
anamenō)* his return. Other verbs *(engizō)* indicate that the Lord is near.
The regularity with which this language occurs shows that there is an abid-
ing confidence within the Pauline letters that the Lord will return soon.
When he does, the dead will be raised, judgment will occur, God's kingdom will make its appearance, and God will be all in all.

But inasmuch as the future has not happened, it cannot be described
once and for all. Every attempt to speak about the future is an act of imagi-

---

3. The Greek terms that Paul uses are *arrabōn* (2 Cor 1:22; 5:5) and *aparchē* (Rom 8:23;
1 Cor 15:20, 23). The first is a commercial term that refers to a down payment on goods pur-
chased. The second is an agricultural term that refers to the first fruits of the coming harvest.
When applied to the Spirit, the first term identifies the Spirit as the down payment toward the
fullness of salvation that is to come. When applied to Christ, the second term views the risen
Lord as the first fruits of a harvest that will occur at the general resurrection of the dead.

4. In Colossians and Ephesians this experience is so vibrant that those letters speak of
believers as already raised up with Christ (Eph 2:6; Col 3:1), by which they mean that inasmuch as believers are "in Christ," they participate in his resurrection life. Such an understanding of being raised up with Christ does not exclude the general resurrection of the
dead. Rather, it implies it all the more.

5. Osvaldo D. Vena (*The Parousia and Its Rereadings: The Development of the Eschatological Consciousness in the Writings of the New Testament* [Studies in Biblical Literature 27;
New York: Peter Lang, 2001], 112-13) provides a helpful chart of the vocabulary the NT employs to describe the parousia. In this section, I am summarizing that chart.

nation. This is why the Pauline letters make abundant use of Jewish and Hellenistic imagery to describe the events of the end time.[6] Moreover, even though I have spoken of the parousia, the general resurrection of the dead, the judgment, and the kingdom of God, the Pauline letters do not describe the events of the end time in a uniform way. Paul addresses the issues surrounding the Lord's return *as occasion requires.* For example, whereas in 1 Thessalonians he must assure the Thessalonians that the dead will not be disqualified from the salvation Christ will bring at his parousia, in 1 Corinthians he must persuade the Corinthians that the dead will be raised and transformed when the Lord returns. Paul supposes that those who read his letters already know something about Christ's return. Thus there is no need for him to explain statements such as the fervent prayer that concludes 1 Corinthians, "Our Lord, Come!" (16:22). Paul assumes that this is the ardent prayer of all who believe in Christ.

In what follows I have adopted an approach that proceeds somewhat chronologically, bringing together letters that manifest similar themes: Waiting for the Parousia, Waiting for the Resurrection of the Dead, Waiting for God's Final Victory in Christ, Waiting for a Heavenly Inheritance, and Waiting for the Final Appearance of Christ. After I have examined these themes, I will provide a brief theological reflection on Pauline eschatology.

Waiting for the Parousia

Written from Corinth about A.D. 50, 1 Thessalonians is the earliest Pauline letter we possess that contains an extended discussion about the parousia.[7] It is also the letter in which the Apostle most frequently employs *parousia* to refer to the Lord's "coming" (2:19; 3:13; 4:15; 5:23).[8] Accordingly, it is a good starting point to begin our investigation.

6. For a summary of the OT, Apocalyptic, and Hellenistic background that informs the NT understanding of the parousia, see A. L. Moore, *The Parousia in the New Testament* (NovTSup 13; Leiden: Brill, 1966), 7-34; Joseph Plevnik, *Paul and the Parousia: An Exegetical and Theological Investigation* (Peabody: Hendrickson, 1997), 3-44; Vena, *The Parousia and Its Rereadings*, 9-104.

7. For the dating of the letter, see Abraham J. Malherbe, *The Letters to the Thessalonians* (AB; New York: Doubleday, 2000), 71-74.

8. The only other uses of this term in the Pauline letters are found in 2 Thess 2:1, 8 and 1 Cor 15:23. The Greek word *parousia* means "presence." Consequently, it is not always used as a technical term for the Lord's return. For example, in 2 Cor 10:10 Paul employs it to refer

The first three chapters of 1 Thessalonians are, for all practical purposes, an extended thanksgiving in which Paul expresses his joy and gratitude that the Thessalonians have persevered in their faith despite persecution and affliction.[9] In the midst of this thanksgiving, Paul recalls how they turned from idols to serve the living and true God in order to wait for his Son who will come from heaven to rescue them from the coming wrath, by which Paul means God's judgment (1:9-10).[10] As most commentators note, these verses probably echo Paul's earliest preaching to the Thessalonians, in which he called on them to turn from the worship of idols to the one true God, the God of Israel, who is about to judge the world through his Son. In the face of this imminent judgment, Paul summoned the Thessalonians to believe in God's Son, whom God raised from the dead and who will soon return to carry out God's judgment.[11] This text suggests that preaching about the parousia played an important role in Paul's initial evangelization at Thessalonica. The death of certain members of the community, however, occasioned questions and concerns among the Thessalonians that Paul addresses in 4:13–5:11.

Having believed Paul's gospel that God's Son was about to return and rescue them from the coming wrath, the Thessalonians were distraught about the fate of believers who had already died. Did their death mean they would not be gathered with the Lord at the parousia? Did their death mean their faith had been in vain? Although this issue appears strange to contemporary believers who find it difficult to believe that the Lord will return in their lifetime, the death of those who died before the parousia presented a serious problem for Paul's converts at Thessalonica who concluded that believers who had died would not enjoy the benefits of Christ's parousia.[12]

---

to his physical presence. In Matt 24:3, 27, 37, 39; Jas 5:7-8; 1 John 2:28; and 2 Pet 1:16; 3:4, 12, however, it refers to the Lord's return.

9. Note the two explicit thanksgiving sections in the first chapters of 1 Thessalonians: 1:2-10 and 2:13-14.

10. The concept of "wrath," which occurs rather frequently in the Pauline letters, should not be confused with an emotion of God, as though God becomes angry. In the Pauline letters it refers to God's just reaction in the face of sin. In most instances, it is best interpreted in terms of God's just judgment against sin.

11. Luke's account of Paul's speech at Athens follows a similar pattern (Acts 17:22-31). Note how the speech ends: "because he has fixed a day on which he will have the world judged in righteousness by a man whom he has appointed, and of this he has given assurance to all by raising him from the dead" (17:31).

12. Since Paul had been preaching for nearly twenty years before he wrote 1 Thessalonians, we can suppose that this was not a new issue. It was an issue for the Thessalonians,

Paul responds to the Thessalonians in two ways. First, he addresses their concern about the fate of those who have died by explaining the implications of their faith in Christ's resurrection: when Christ returns, God will bring forth those who have believed, risen and alive, with Christ (4:13-18). Drawing on a "word of the Lord" that he received (4:15), Paul outlines the events that will take place:[13] (a) the Day of the Lord will begin with a heavenly command, the voice of an archangel, and a trumpet blast that no one will be able to mistake; (b) the Lord will descend from heaven, and the dead who have believed in him will be raised; (c) those who are alive at the Lord's coming will be taken up into the clouds with those who have been raised to be with the Lord.[14] This description of the parousia is limited in scope because Paul's purpose is to address the immediate concern of the Thessalonians rather than provide them an extended teaching on the Lord's return.[15] Accordingly, he merely assures the Thessalonians that believers who die before the Lord's coming will be raised from the dead when he returns, but he does not discuss *how* the dead will be raised, nor does he say anything about the judgment that will accompany the parousia. Paul's principal concern is to remind the Thessalonians of something they should have known from his foundational preaching but did not comprehend: faith in Christ's resurrection is the ground for their own resurrection.

---

however, who had only recently been converted to faith in Christ and who had not previously experienced the death of one of their members. This suggests that even though the parousia was an integral part of the gospel that Paul preached to the Thessalonians, he did not anticipate all the ramifications of this teaching for their lives.

13. James D. G. Dunn (*The Theology of Paul the Apostle* [Grand Rapids: Eerdmans, 1998], 303) writes about the word of the Lord: "It is more likely, then, that the 'word of the Lord' was an inspired utterance or prophecy given to Paul (privately or in the Christian assembly, perhaps drawing on earlier Jesus tradition) as he mediated prayerfully on the Thessalonian distress." Whatever its precise origin, it appears to have been some sort of prophetic word rather than a word of the earthly Jesus.

14. For a discussion of the background to the imagery that Paul employs here, see Plevnik, *Paul and the Parousia*, 57-63. "The images of the cry of command, the archangel's call, and the trumpet of God in 1 Thess 4:16-18 depict the Lord's coming from heaven, while the image of the cloud depicts the taking up of the faithful . . . the first three are used in the OT and in Jewish apocalyptic literature in depictions or theophanies or the day of the Lord" (p. 63). Plevnik notes that the "cry of command" is given by God, or by the Lord himself, whereas the trumpet signals the powerful event that is about to take place when the Lord comes (p. 64).

15. It is not unreasonable to assume that Paul had already spoken to the Thessalonians at length about the parousia when he evangelized them, even though they do not appear to have fully understood him.

Second, after assuring the Thessalonians that those who have died believing in Christ will participate in the parousia, Paul reminds them how they should live in view of the coming parousia.[16] Since the Lord will return suddenly and unexpectedly, it is imperative for them to conduct themselves with vigilance and sobriety as those who belong to the light rather than the darkness (5:1-11).[17] The sudden appearance of the Lord will only surprise those who belong to the night, whereas those who believe in Christ will not be caught off guard. By employing the metaphors of light and darkness, night and day, Paul indicates that the Thessalonians, who belong to the new age, are engaged in a cosmic struggle that requires the breastplate of faith and love and the helmet of their hope for the salvation Christ will bring (5:8).

To summarize, in 1 Thessalonians hope for the Lord's return plays a central role in the life of those who believe in Christ. Believers live in hope of the imminent return of their Lord who will rescue them from the coming wrath. Aware that Christ's parousia will be sudden and unexpected, they conduct themselves as people about to experience God's final victory.

Although the parousia plays a central role in 2 Thessalonians, many exegetes argue that it was written by someone other than Paul, though in his name, at a later date.[18] It is not surprising, then, that those interested in establishing the theology of the historical Paul rarely consider this letter. Given the nature of my Pauline theology, however, with its focus on the theology in the entire collection of Paul's letters, I treat 2 Thessalonians at this point because of its literary and theological relationship to 1 Thessalonians.[19]

As was the case with 1 Thessalonians, the occasion of 2 Thessalonians

16. This point is made by Vena (The Parousia and Its Rereadings, 122).

17. Plevnik (Paul and the Parousia, 111) notes that vigilance and sobriety are "modes of eschatological existence."

18. In more recent years, a number of scholars, with whom I would align myself, are more open to the Pauline authorship of 2 Thessalonians. For example, Robert Jewett (The Thessalonian Correspondence: Pauline Rhetoric and Millenarian Piety [Foundations and Facets; Philadelphia: Fortress, 1986], 17-18) writes: "Thus the dilemma of 2 Thessalonians could be summed up as follows: While the likelihood of definitively proving Pauline authorship of 2 Thessalonians remains at a modest level, the improbability of forgery is extremely high." In his recent commentary, Malherbe (Letters to the Thessalonians, 349-75) defends the Pauline authorship of 2 Thessalonians.

19. 2 Thessalonians echoes major themes of 1 Thessalonians such as the gospel, the election and sanctification of the Thessalonians, and the need to imitate Paul. In addition to these themes, it echoes the language found in 1 Thessalonians. Thus it presents itself as a letter related to 1 Thessalonians.

determines what Paul writes about the parousia. That occasion can be summarized as follows. The afflictions the Thessalonians are presently enduring on account of their faith have become more intense (1:5-12). As a result of these afflictions some have prophesied that the Day of the Lord has come (2:1-2).[20] Believing that the day has arrived, some of the Thessalonians are no longer working for their livelihood but relying on others to support them, thereby living in a way that Paul characterizes as "disorderly" (3:6-15).

Paul's response to the situation is twofold. First, he assures the Thessalonians that the afflictions are for the sake of the kingdom of God. Therefore, God will punish those who are afflicting them when Jesus is revealed with his angels (1:5-10). Although the description of the Lord's coming echoes what Paul wrote in 1 Thessalonians, 2 Thessalonians introduces a new element in order to assure the Thessalonians that they will be avenged: Jesus will return with his mighty angels to inflict punishment on those who are afflicting them. The purpose of the text, then, is not to give a new description of the parousia but to assure the Thessalonians that their afflictions will be repaid when the Lord is revealed.

Second, in 2:1-12 Paul addresses the claim that the Day of the Lord is present. Here, he reminds the Thessalonians of what he has already told them (v. 5). The Lord's parousia will not take place until the great "rebellion" *(apostasia)* comes and "the lawless one" *(ho hyios tēs apōleias)* is revealed (v. 3). At the present time, something/someone is restraining this lawless figure (vv. 6-7), but when the lawless one is revealed, the Lord will destroy him at "the manifestation of his coming" (v. 8).[21] In effect, just as Jesus told his disciples what must occur before he returns (Matt 24:3-28), so Paul reminds the Thessalonians what must happen before the parousia occurs.

20. Malherbe (*Letters to the Thessalonians,* 417) says that the perfect of the Greek should be translated "has come" or "is present." It does not mean that it is coming or is near. Exactly what is meant by this, however, is not clear. The fact that Paul says that certain events must take place before the Lord's arrival suggests that some may have thought that this event had, in some sense, already occurred.

21. While Paul seems to presuppose that the Thessalonians know what he means by the restrainer and the lawless one, his meaning is no longer apparent to contemporary readers. The lawless one, however, appears to be a human figure completely opposed to God's will, in complete contrast to Christ, who does God's will. Thus 2 Thessalonians refers to the parousia of the lawless one (2:9) and the parousia of Christ (v. 8). The restrainer has been associated with Paul, his preaching, the Roman Empire, Christ, and God. Knowledge of the precise identification of the restrainer, however, is not necessary for the interpretation of the text.

For many interpreters, the apocalyptic timetable here stands in tension with 1 Thess 5:1-3, where Paul warns the Thessalonians that the parousia will come unexpectedly. In their view, this tension indicates that 2 Thessalonians is a pseudonymous writing. The theological value of what 1 and 2 Thessalonians affirm about the parousia, however, is dependent not on the question of Pauline authorship but on the manner in which they present the parousia as an integral part of God's salvific work in Christ. In both letters, the parousia is central to the gospel Paul preaches inasmuch as it signifies God's final victory in Christ (1) over the power of death, as witnessed by the resurrection of the dead, (2) over the power of injustice, as seen in God's judgment on those who afflict the elect, and (3) over the power of all that is evil and rebellious against God, as seen in the destruction of the lawless one. Paul presents this theme of God's victory over sin and death again in the material to which we now turn: 1 and 2 Corinthians and Philippians.

Waiting for the Resurrection of the Dead

Eschatological hope, by which I mean hope for the fullness of salvation that Christ will bring at his parousia, plays an important role in Paul's Corinthian correspondence as well as in his letter to the Philippians. In 1 Corinthians, Paul thanks God that his converts have been so richly endowed with the gifts of the Spirit and are presently waiting for the revelation of their Lord. He is confident that God will strengthen them so that they will be blameless on the day of Christ's parousia (1:7-8). He tells the Corinthians that since the time before the Lord's return is short, they should live as people who understand that the world as they know it is passing away (7:29-31). He reminds them that every time they celebrate the Eucharist they are proclaiming the Lord's death until he comes (11:26). Finally, he concludes with a liturgical prayer in Aramaic that expresses the community's hope for the parousia: *marana tha,* "Our Lord, come!" (16:22). Although there are not as many explicit references to the parousia in 2 Corinthians and Philippians, Paul continues to anticipate the salvation that is about to come. He says that "on the day of the Lord Jesus" he will boast in the Corinthians and they in him (2 Cor 1:14). They have already received the Spirit as the "first installment" of their salvation (1:22). They are being transformed into the image of the risen Christ from one state of glory to another (3:18), and God, who raised Jesus from the dead, will raise them as well (4:14). In Philippians, Paul expresses his confidence that God, who began a good work in the Philippians, will bring that work to completion "on the day of Jesus Christ" (1:6), and he prays that they will be filled with knowledge and insight to determine what is best in order to be pure and blameless on the "day of Christ" (vv. 9-10). If they remain blameless and innocent, Paul will be able to boast on "the day of Christ" that he did not labor in vain (2:15-16). Their citizenship is in heaven, and it is from there that their Savior will come (3:20).

Whereas it was necessary for Paul to respond to questions about the parousia in his Thessalonian correspondence, this is no longer so in his Corinthian and Philippian correspondence. In these letters, he refers to the parousia and the eschatological hope of his converts as something taken for granted: the Lord will return, and when he does those who believe in him will be saved. The new element in these letters is *the transformation of the believer* that will occur at the resurrection of the dead. To be sure, the resurrection of the dead plays an important role in the argument of 1 Thessalonians, where Paul assures his audience that at the parousia God will raise the dead who have believed in Christ. But Paul did not discuss what it means to be raised from the dead since this was not the issue at Thessalonica. What was not an issue at Thessalonica, however, becomes a serious problem at Corinth: what does Paul mean by the resurrection of the dead?

He addresses this question in 1 Corinthians 15, where he must persuade his Corinthian converts that the general resurrection of the dead is non-negotiable. In 2 Corinthians 4–5 he addresses the topic a second time in a more personal manner, in light of his own hope for resurrection and transformation. Then in Philippians 3 he professes his hope that his body will be conformed to the glorious body of the risen Christ. The new element of eschatological hope in these letters, then, is *the transformation of the believer* that will occur at the resurrection of the dead, which will occur when Christ returns.

Paul's most important statement about the parousia and resurrection of the dead comes in 1 Corinthians 15, where he must answer two questions: Will there be a resurrection from the dead (v. 12)? And with what kind of body will the dead be raised (v. 35)? He proceeds in the following way. First he reminds the Corinthians that Christ's resurrection is central to the gospel that he and all of the apostles preach (vv. 1-11). Second, he shows the intimate relationship between the resurrection of Christ and the resurrection of those who believe in him (vv. 12-34). If there is no general resurrection of the dead, then Christ has not been raised from the dead, and if Christ has not been raised from the dead, then the faith of those who have believed in the gospel is in vain. But if Christ has been raised from the dead, as the gospel proclaims, then there will be a general resurrection of the dead. Christ's resurrection, then, is not an isolated event but the beginning of the general resurrection of the dead. Third, Paul argues that resurrection is a process of transformation rather than of resuscitation from the dead (vv. 35-58). The body of the believer is changed and transformed by the power of God's Spirit; it is no longer an earthly body but a spiritual body.

The central text in which Paul describes the eschatological hope of believers is 15:20-28. Having reminded the Corinthians of the centrality of Christ's resurrection, he envisions the following scenario. First, he recalls what has already happened: Christ, who is the "first fruits" of the general resurrection, has been raised from the dead. Second, at the present time the risen Lord is ruling and subjecting every enemy to himself. Third, when Christ returns, the general resurrection of the dead will occur. Fourth, when the dead are raised, the last and greatest enemy, death, will be destroyed. Fifth, when death is destroyed at the general resurrection of the dead, Christ will hand over the kingdom to his Father and be subject to God as a son is subject to his father. Thus God will be all in all. Having established that there will be a general resurrection of the dead, in vv. 42-55 Paul describes the resurrection that believes will enjoy in terms of transformation. The natural body that believers possess will be transformed into a spiritual body no longer subject to corruption. Rather, it will be transformed by the power of God's Spirit, and believers will enjoy the resurrection experience of their risen Lord.

Paul returns to the topic of resurrection in 2 Corinthians from another vantage point. Whereas in 1 Corinthians he discussed it within the context of the parousia and God's cosmic victory over death, in 2 Corinthians he considers it within the context of his apostolic sufferings. The result is a more personal statement about the resurrection that has led some to argue that Paul altered his thinking about the resurrection of the dead.[22]

22. While some believe that Paul has significantly altered his thinking about the parousia and the general resurrection of the dead between the writing of 1 and 2 Corinthians, this is unlikely. First, the two letters were probably written within a year or two of each other, even if 2 Corinthians is a composite letter. Second, if Paul had changed his mind on this issue, that would have undermined the defense of his apostleship that he undertakes in 2 Corinthians. The more likely solution is that Paul is approaching the topic of the resurrection from a more personal stance in 2 Corinthians 5.

Paul begins by describing his apostolic sufferings (4:7-12). Although he is afflicted in every way, the sufferings he endures have not crushed him because he knows that he is being given up to death so that the life of Jesus may be manifested in his mortal flesh. Consequently, he carries "the death of Jesus" in his body (v. 10), by which he means the sufferings he has endured for Christ on behalf of the gospel. Having described his apostolic sufferings, Paul expresses his hope in the resurrection of the dead (vv. 13-18). Like the speaker of the psalm who says, "I believed and so I spoke," Paul proclaims the gospel despite his sufferings because he believes "that the one who raised the Lord Jesus will raise us also with Jesus, and will bring us with you into his presence" (v. 14).[23] It is precisely his hope in the resurrection, then, that enables Paul to preach the gospel despite the suffering and affliction his ministry entails. Even though his outer self is wasting away, he does not despair because his inner self is already being renewed day by day (v. 16).[24]

Having explained how hope for the resurrection sustains him in the midst of his apostolic afflictions, in 2 Cor 5:1-10 Paul expresses his longing to be clothed with the resurrection body that God has already prepared for him. He knows that the body he presently inhabits is a fragile tent that can be destroyed at any moment, but he is confident that God has already prepared a "building" for him, "a house not made with hands, eternal in the heavens" (v. 1). While he inhabits the tent that is his mortal body, Paul groans because he longs to be clothed with his heavenly dwelling, his resurrection body (v. 2). Indeed, he is confident that once he puts on this heavenly dwelling he will not be "naked," that is, without a body (v. 3). And so in his tent-like mortal body he groans that he will not be found "unclothed" at death but clothed with a heavenly body "so that what is mortal may be swallowed up by life" (v. 4).[25]

---

23. The text comes from Ps 116:10 (LXX 115:1). Here, Paul may be reading the text christologically, as Thomas D. Stegman (*Second Corinthians* [Catholic Commentary on Sacred Scripture; Grand Rapids: Baker, 2009], 113) notes: "Paul evokes the story of Ps 116 because *it resembles the story of Jesus*. Thus it is Jesus whom Paul has in mind in quoting the psalm. . . . These words are the testimony of Jesus, now raised from the dead (v. 14), to his own faithfulness, which was grounded in his trust in God to vindicate him."

24. The outer self and the inner self are not body and soul but the person viewed from two different aspects. The outer self is what is seen and so passing away; the inner self is what cannot be seen and so endures. In both instances, Paul has the whole person in view.

25. What Paul writes here about the mortal being *swallowed up* by life is an echo of what he writes in 1 Cor 15:54: "When this perishable body puts on imperishability, and this

Although the language and imagery of 2 Corinthians 5 differ from that of 1 Corinthians 15, and although Paul appears to be reckoning with the possibility of his death before the parousia, the eschatological hope of both texts is the same: the final salvation that will occur when the earthly body is transformed into a heavenly, spiritual body. As he writes 2 Corinthians 5, Paul has not forgotten what he wrote in 1 Corinthians. He is as confident as ever that there will be a parousia, although perhaps less confident that he will experience it.[26] But whereas in 1 Corinthians his purpose was to persuade the Corinthians that there will be a resurrection of the dead, in 2 Corinthians his purpose is to provide a *personal testimony* of his faith in the resurrection despite the afflictions he endures. The "new" element in 2 Corinthians is Paul's conviction that something of the transformation he will experience at the resurrection of the dead has *already* begun in and through his apostolic sufferings.

The theme of transformation plays an important role in Paul's letter to the Philippians as well. Toward the end of an autobiographical statement (3:2-11) in which he compares the righteousness that he attained under the law with the righteousness that comes from God, Paul expresses his desire to know Christ "and the power of his resurrection and the sharing of his sufferings by becoming like him in his death, if somehow I may attain the resurrection from the dead" (vv. 10-11). As he did in 2 Corinthians, Paul draws a relationship between present suffering and future resurrection. Seeking to share in the resurrection of the dead, he strives to know the power of Christ's resurrection, which is inseparable from participation in Christ's sufferings. For just as Christ suffered and was raised from the dead, so those who conform themselves to his sufferings will attain to the resurrection of the dead. Not having attained the resurrection yet, Paul seeks to lay hold of the goal for which Christ took hold of him — resurrection from the dead (v. 12).[27] Accordingly, he strives for "the prize of the

---

mortal body puts on immortality, then the saying that is written will be fulfilled: 'Death has been *swallowed up* in victory.'" This is a clear indication that Paul has not forgotten what he wrote earlier.

26. Indeed, Paul alludes to the parousia in 2 Cor 4:14 when he writes that believers will be brought into the Lord's presence: "because we know that the one who raised the Lord Jesus will raise us also with Jesus, *and will bring us with you into his presence*." However, given the near escape from death that he experienced in Asia (1:8-11), it is possible that Paul is now reckoning with the possibility of his death before the parousia.

27. The NET Bible catches the play on words in the Greek when it translates this text: "I strive *to lay hold of* that for which Christ Jesus also *laid hold of* me."

heavenly call of God in Christ Jesus" (v. 14), by which he means resurrection from the dead.

Paul concludes his discussion with a bold call for the Philippians to imitate him. Contrasting his behavior with the conduct of those whose "minds are set on earthly things" (3:19), he reminds them that "our citizenship is in heaven, and it is from there that we are expecting a Savior, the Lord Jesus Christ. He will transform the body of our humiliation that it may be conformed to the body of his glory, by the power that also enables him to make all things subject to himself" (vv. 20-21). With this statement the apostle, who has already reckoned with the possibility of dying before the parousia (1:23), affirms the connection between parousia and resurrection. The eschatological salvation of those who believe in Christ will be fulfilled at the parousia when their Savior will conform their earthly bodies to his resurrection body, a process that begins when one conforms oneself to the Lord's suffering. The manner in which Paul presents eschatological hope in his Philippian and his Corinthian correspondence can be summarized in terms of transformation: those who have conformed themselves to Christ's sufferings will be transformed by his resurrection.[28]

Waiting for God's Final Victory in Christ

In Romans, Paul's discussion of eschatological hope introduces new elements while remaining in continuity with what he has already said. For example, he insists that the salvation for which believers hope is near (13:11-12). Likewise, he frequently refers to the coming judgment of God. On the one hand, the wicked are already experiencing God's wrath/judgment because God has abandoned them to their own devices (1:18-32). On the other, there will be a final judgment "on the day of wrath, when God's righteous judgment will be revealed" (2:5). On that day God will judge "the secret thoughts of all" (v. 16) and will "judge the world" (3:6). Accordingly, all will stand before "the judgment seat of God" (14:10). The most distinctive aspects of Paul's eschatology in Romans, however, are found (1) in 5:1-11 and 8:18-39, where he describes the eschatological hope of the justified, and (2) in 11:25-32, where he reveals the mystery of Israel's destiny in light of the parousia.

---

28. Vena (*The Parousia and Its Rereadings*, 159) correctly notes that if one were to summarize Pauline eschatology in one concept, that concept would be "transformation."

Paul's discussion of the eschatological hope of the justified introduces and concludes his discussion in chs. 5–8 of the new existence the justified enjoy in Christ. His train of thought in these chapters can be summarized as follows:

5:1-11   The hope the justified have for salvation is trustworthy.
5:12–8:17 The justified enjoy a new existence in Christ.
8:18-39   The hope of the justified is cosmic in scope.

Paul begins his discussion of hope by reminding his audience of their new situation: justified, they are at peace with God and can boast in their "hope of sharing the glory of God" (5:1-2). Despite their present afflictions, they will not be disappointed by this hope because God's love has been poured into their hearts through the Holy Spirit, which has been given to them (v. 5). Drawing a contrast between the past and present of the justified, Paul explains the grounds for their hope. If Christ died for them when they were sinners, then they can be all the more confident — now that God has justified them — that they *will be saved* from the coming wrath (vv. 8-9). And if they were reconciled to God through Christ when they were God's enemies, they can be all the more confident — now that God has reconciled them to himself — that they *will be saved* by "his life" (v. 10), by which Paul means the life of the risen Lord. This tension between what has *already* happened (justification and reconciliation) and what has *not yet* occurred (final salvation) is crucial for understanding Paul's eschatology. Believers *already* live an eschatological existence because God has justified and reconciled them to himself, but they are *not yet* saved. Final salvation will only occur at the general resurrection of the dead when the last and greatest enemy — death — is destroyed. At the present time, then, believers live in the firm hope of final salvation: they have been saved in hope (8:24).

Paul sets aside the theme of eschatological hope that he introduced in 5:1-11 to explain how the eschatological Adam has freed the justified from the power of sin that frustrated their ability to fulfill the law so that they now live by the power of God's Spirit (5:12–8:17). The indwelling of the Spirit, Paul affirms, is the assurance of future resurrection (8:11). The Spirit already empowers the justified to address God as "Father," thereby revealing they are children of God and fellow heirs with Christ. As fellow heirs with Christ they can be confident that just as God glorified Christ by raising him from the dead, so God will glorify them by raising them from the dead, provided they suffer with Christ (vv. 15-17). Paul's train of thought can be summarized in this way:

> The Spirit makes the justified sons and daughters of God.
>> The justified are joint heirs with Christ.
>>> Christ has *already* received the inheritance of resurrection life.
>>> The justified *will* receive this inheritance if they suffer with Christ.

In 8:18-39 Paul returns to the theme of eschatological hope that he introduced in 5:1-11. But whereas earlier he spoke of the hope that the justified have for salvation, now he specifies salvation as resurrection from the dead and expands its horizon to include the whole of creation. Personifying inanimate creation as if it were a living being, Paul imagines creation eagerly waiting for the revelation of God's children (8:19), by which he means the glorification they will enjoy at the resurrection of the dead when they will be conformed to Christ's resurrection. The implication of Paul's statement is that creation has been frustrated from achieving its God-given goal because of Adam's sin. If creation is to attain its destiny, humanity must fulfill its destiny by being conformed to the risen Christ. The "groans" of creation, then, are the birth pangs of the new age (v. 22). The justified, who have received the "first fruits of the Spirit," also groan as they wait for "the redemption" of their bodies (v. 23), which will occur at the general resurrection of the dead. Then their mortal bodies will be glorified and transformed by the power of God's Spirit. When humanity fulfills its destiny at the resurrection of the dead, creation will be set free from the futility to which it was subjected by God because of human sinfulness and so fulfill its destiny.

Paul is confident of God's eschatological victory on behalf of the justified because he understands the full plan of God, a theme that Colossians and Ephesians will develop when they speak of the mystery that has been revealed to Paul. Everything works for the good of the justified because God knew, predestined, and conformed them to the image of his Son so that the Son might be the firstborn of a large family. In calling the Son the firstborn, Paul has in view the resurrection of the dead.[29] The purpose of God's redemptive work in Christ, then, finds its goal in the resurrection of

---

29. In the Colossians hymn Paul uses the same term to refer to Christ, the firstborn from the dead: the beginning of the resurrection of the dead.

the dead, which is the climax of a plan Paul summarizes in this way: God predestined, God called, God justified, God glorified (Rom 8:30).

Paul concludes his discussion with a rhetorical flourish. Employing a series of questions whose answer is obvious, he asks who can stand against the justified if God is on their side (8:31-39). With these questions Paul returns to the theme of judgment that occurs throughout this letter: "*Who will bring any charge against God's elect?* It is God who justifies. *Who is to condemn?* It is Christ Jesus, who died, yes, who was raised, who is at the right hand of God, who indeed intercedes for us" (vv. 33-34). The justified will stand before God's tribunal, but they need not fear; for God has already pronounced the verdict of acquittal.

In 11:25-32 Paul broaches the topic of eschatological hope once more. This unit comes toward the end of chs. 9–11, a section in which Paul must deal with the most difficult question that confronts his gospel: Do the refusal of the majority of Israel to believe in Christ and the influx of Gentiles who have embraced the gospel mean that God has rejected Israel in favor of the Gentiles (11:1)? While Israel has stumbled over the stumbling stone of the crucified Messiah, Paul maintains that its failure has played a crucial role in the acceptance of the gospel by the Gentiles. Confident that Israel's rejection is not final, Paul exclaims, "if their stumbling means riches for the world, and if their defeat means riches for Gentiles, how much more will their full inclusion mean!" (v. 12). Repeating this in a slightly different way he writes: "if their rejection is the reconciliation of the world, what will their acceptance be but *life from the dead!*" (v. 15).[30] Although life from the dead could be taken metaphorically, the central role that the resurrection of the dead plays in ch. 8 suggests that Paul has something more in view: Israel's acceptance of the gospel will usher in the resurrection of the dead!

When Paul finally comes to the close of Romans 11, he reveals what he calls "this mystery" (v. 25). At the present time a hardening has come upon a part of Israel until the full number of Gentiles enters the eschatological people of God. When that number is complete, "all Israel will be saved" (v. 26). To explain how this will come about, Paul draws on Isa 59:20-21: "Out of Zion will come the Deliverer; he will banish ungodliness from Jacob. And this is my covenant with them, when I take away their sins" (vv.

---

30. The Greek text here is difficult. I take "their rejection" as referring to Israel's rejection of the gospel rather than to God's rejection of Israel since Paul has already affirmed that God has not rejected his people (11:1).

26-27). But, whereas in the Greek and Hebrew texts of Isaiah it is God who *comes to* deliver Jerusalem, in Paul's christological reading of this text it is Christ: the Deliver (Christ) will *come out of* Zion (the heavenly Jerusalem) to remove ungodliness from Jacob/Israel, thereby saving Israel.[31]

The eschatological hope that Paul presents in Romans is intimately related to the present eschatological existence of the justified who already experience something of resurrection life through the gift of the Spirit, even as they "groan" for the redemption of their bodies, which will occur at the resurrection of the dead. But whereas in the letters we have examined thus far the focus was on the human subject, in Romans the horizon of Paul's eschatological vision includes the liberation of creation and the restoration of Israel. In the language of Christiaan Beker, Paul anticipates the coming triumph of God.[32]

Waiting for a Heavenly Inheritance

Pauline eschatology takes a new turn in Colossians and Ephesians. The temporal imagery of an imminent parousia gives way to the spatial imagery of hope for a heavenly inheritance, and the tension between what has already happened and what has not yet occurred begins to collapse into an eschatology that gives greater attention to the experience of salvation here and now.[33] Believers have been transferred into the kingdom of the beloved Son (Col 1:13), saved by God's grace (Eph 2:5, 8), and raised up with Christ (Col 3:1; Eph 2:6). In a word, Colossians and Ephesians exhibit the characteristics of a realized eschatology, an eschatology that focuses on the present benefits of God's redemptive work in Christ. This is not to say that

---

31. Several authors note the importance Paul gives to his mission of bringing in the full number of the Gentiles in order to usher in the end and the restoration of Israel. Dunn (*The Theology of Paul the Apostle,* 312) writes: "The end of history was only a mission away." Vena (*The Parousia and Its Rereadings,* 154) remarks: "At the time of the writing of the letter to the Romans Paul believes his mission to be unique. . . . he thinks he is somehow called to play the role of the precursor in Jewish apocalyptic."

32. This expression echoes the title of Beker's book, *Paul the Apostle: The Triumph of God in Life and Thought* (Philadelphia: Fortress, 1980).

33. Joseph Burgess ("The Letter to the Colossians," in *Ephesians, Colossians, 2 Thessalonians, The Pastoral Epistles* [Proclamation Commentaries; Philadelphia: Fortress, 1978], 55, 56) writes: "In the letter to the Colossians there is no question but that there are two levels, the world above and the world below. . . . Salvation is a fact; what happens now and in the future is that it is made known and made manifest."

these letters have completely shifted the emphasis from the future to the present. As we shall see, hope for a heavenly inheritance plays a significant role in these letters. But whereas the eschatological hope of the letters studied above involves an imminent parousia that will usher in the resurrection of the dead, the eschatological hope in Colossians and Ephesians is one that waits for the revelation of what is above, in the heavenly places, thereby obviating the problem of a delayed parousia.[34]

Written in response to a teaching that was giving as much, or more, authority to "the elemental spirits of the universe" (2:8, 20) than it was to Christ, Colossians affirms that God conquered these hostile cosmic powers once and for all through the triumph of the cross (vv. 13-15).[35] In a hymn-like passage that highlights Christ's unique role in the order of creation and redemption (1:15-20), Paul maintains that the fullness of God dwells in Christ (v. 19). If this is so, then the Colossians need not fear the hostile cosmic powers, which they are tempted to appease through ascetic practices (2:16-23). The role of Paul's eschatology in Colossians, then, is to remind his audience of what God has *already* done for them in Christ. They have been rescued from the power of darkness and transferred into the kingdom of his beloved Son (1:13). In their baptism they were raised as well as buried with Christ (2:12). Having been raised with Christ, they should seek the things that are above, where he is seated at God's right (3:1). In effect, Paul employs a realized eschatology to respond to the crisis that he (or the one writing in his name) must address at Colossae.

Elements of an eschatology orientated to the future as well as to the present, however, continue to play an important role in Colossians. For example, Paul speaks of the hope that is laid up for the Colossians in heaven (1:5), "the inheritance of the saints in the light" (v. 12), the "hope promised by the gospel" (v. 23), and their "hope of glory" (v. 27). Moreover, Colossians employs phrases that recall the language Paul employs in 1 Thessalonians where he says that he hopes to present the Thessalonians "blameless" on the day of the parousia (1 Thess 3:13; 5:23). For example, he tells the Colossians that Christ has reconciled them in order to present

---

34. I am not implying that the delay of the parousia led to a new way of presenting the eschatological hope of those who believe in Christ. Whether that problem influenced the writing of these letters — and I am inclined to think that it did not — the result is that these letters present eschatological hope in a way that bypasses, and to some extent resolves, the problem of a delayed parousia.

35. The elemental powers are the cosmic powers that God overcame through Christ's death on the cross.

them "holy and blameless and irreproachable" (1:22), and Paul writes that he teaches everyone "in all wisdom" so that he may "present everyone mature in Christ" (v. 28). Although Colossians employs the notion of being presented at the parousia in a new way (it is now *Christ* who presents believers to himself rather than Paul [v. 22], and Paul presents everyone as *mature* in Christ [v. 28]), it echoes the language the Apostle employs in 1 Thessalonians when speaking of the parousia.

In three other texts Colossians betrays elements of a more traditional eschatology. First, in calling Christ "the firstborn from the dead" (1:18), Colossians implies that believers will also be born from the dead after the pattern of Christ.[36] Second, Colossians complements its teaching that believers have already been raised with Christ by reminding its audience that their resurrection life is presently "hidden with God," and will only be revealed when Christ is revealed (3:3-4), presumably at the parousia. Finally, Colossians continues to employ the traditional Pauline notion of the wrath of God coming upon the disobedient (v. 6).

Colossians presents us with an example of Pauline eschatology in transition. On the one hand, it alludes to traditional eschatological themes such as the parousia, the general resurrection of the dead, and the coming judgment. On the other hand, something new has begun to emerge. Hope is stored like a treasure in heaven above.[37] Believers have already been raised up with Christ in baptism so that their life, like their hope, is hidden with Christ in heaven above. Thus the temporal imagery of the present and future is giving way to the spatial imagery of what is below and what is above. While this shift of perspective avoids the problems caused by the temporal imagery of the parousia, it begins to diminish the tension between the "already" and "not yet" that has resulted in Paul's powerful eschatological reservation about the present world (1 Cor 7:29-31). The emphasis is not so much on the present form of the world that is fading away as it is on the heavenly realm that is above.

The eschatology of Ephesians continues the movement begun in

36. See Rom 8:29, where Paul speaks of the risen Christ as the firstborn of a large family. He is the firstborn because he is the first to have been raised from the dead.

37. Margaret Y. MacDonald (*Colossians and Ephesians* [SP 17; Collegeville: Liturgical, 2000], 37) explains the distinctive notion of hope in Colossians in this way: "Hope here has a specialized significance. It is less an attitude to foster than an object to be seized. In essence the term functions as a synonym for eternal life. Where to locate salvation is a central concern of Colossians. The notion of a heavenly store of eternal life fits with the cosmological interests of the letter and probably reflects the nature of the conflict at Colossae. . . ."

Colossians toward a more realized eschatology. For example, whereas 1 Corinthians says that Christ must reign "until he has put all his enemies under his feet" (15:25), Ephesians affirms that God has already "put all things under [Christ's] feet and has made him the head over all things for the church" (1:22). And, whereas Galatians states that a person is "justified by faith" (Gal 2:16), Ephesians affirms that believers have been "saved" by faith (2:5, 8-9). Finally, Ephesians draws a striking parallel between the resurrection and enthronement of Christ and those who believe in him: just as God exercised his power by raising Christ from the dead and seating him "at his right hand in the heavenly places" (1:20), so God has raised believers with Christ and seated them with him "in the heavenly places in Christ Jesus" (2:6).

To be sure, Ephesians still manifests elements of a future-oriented eschatology. It speaks of the "promised Holy Spirit" as "the pledge of our inheritance toward redemption as God's own people" (1:13-14) and of the Spirit with which believers were marked "with a seal for the day of redemption" (4:30).[38] It reminds believers of the "hope" to which they were called and their "inheritance" among the saints (1:18; see 2:12; 4:4; and 5:5, where the language of "hope" and "inheritance" also appears). Moreover, it is aware that the present days are evil (5:16), that believers are at war with cosmic powers (6:12), that there will be a judgment (v. 8), and that "in the ages to come" God will show "the immeasurable riches of his grace and kindness toward us in Christ Jesus" (2:7). Ephesians, then, presents its audience with hope for the future rather than an imminent parousia.

The new dimension in the eschatology of Ephesians can be attributed, at least in part, to its understanding of the divine economy. Writing to a new generation of Gentile believers, the Paul of Ephesians reminds his audience of the mystery of Christ that was made known to him and that he now communicates to them: they are "fellow heirs, members of the same body, and sharers in the promise in Christ Jesus through the gospel" (3:6). It is this mystery, which is at the heart of God's economy of salvation, that provides Ephesians with the impetus to develop its distinctive eschatology.

Paul refers to the divine economy of God's salvation at the outset of the letter where he speaks of God's "plan for the fullness of time, to gather up all things in him [Christ], things in heaven and things on earth" (1:10).[39]

---

38. Similar language occurs in Rom 8:23; 2 Cor 1:22; 5:5.

39. The Greek verb that Ephesians employs here is *anakephalaiōsasthai*. Paul uses the

The eschatological goal of God's redemptive plan, then, is to bring everything into perfect unity in Christ. God has already seated the risen Christ at his right hand, above every cosmic power, putting all things under his authority, and making him the head of the church, which is his body (vv. 20-23). God's plan to sum up all things in Christ, then, is being fulfilled as this body grows into Christ, who is its head.

Paul expresses the growth of the body toward its eschatological goal on several occasions. He notes that in Christ, "the whole structure is joined together and grows into a holy temple in the Lord; in whom you also are built together spiritually into a dwelling place of God" (2:21-22). He speaks of the gifts that the risen Lord gives to the church "until all of us come to the unity of the faith and of the knowledge of the Son of God, to maturity, to the measure of the full stature of Christ" (4:13). And he exhorts his audience to "grow up in every way into him who is the head, into Christ" (v. 15). It is through these metaphors of growth, then, that Ephesians develops its eschatology.[40] The Christian life is not merely a matter of waiting for something to happen: it is a dynamic movement and growth into the one who is the goal of the divine economy.

Whereas the eschatology of Colossians looks to the world above, the eschatology of Ephesians anticipates the recapitulation of all things in Christ. Both letters are aware of traditional themes such as hope, inheritance, and judgment. The new situations they address, however, require them to present eschatological hope in a way that goes beyond hope for an imminent parousia.

Waiting for the Final Appearance of Christ

Although the Pastoral Epistles may have been composed toward the end of the first century by someone writing in Paul's name, they manifest a remarkably vibrant eschatology that is seemingly unfazed by the "delay" of

---

same word in Rom 13:9, where he says that the commandments "are *summed up* in this word, 'Love your neighbor as yourself.'" The use of this word in Ephesians is at the origin of the teaching of Irenaeus about the recapitulation that occurred in Christ: "The ground lost in the Fall was regained, and a new order of spiritual progress initiated." John Lawson, *The Biblical Theology of Irenaeus* (London: Epworth, 1948), 145.

40. Andrew Lincoln (*The Theology of the Later Pauline Letters* [NTT; Cambridge: Cambridge University Press, 1993], 116-17) highlights the role that "growth" plays in the eschatology of Ephesians.

the parousia.[41] Pointing to the hope that believers have for eternal life and warning them of the coming judgment, these letters remind believers that they are living in the last times prior to "that day" when the Lord will return.[42] But whereas the Pauline letters we have examined thus far tend to speak of the "parousia" and the "Day of the Lord," the Pastorals employ the term *epiphaneia* ("appearance," "manifestation," "epiphany") to describe the first as well as the second coming of Christ.[43] By doing so, they develop a distinctive eschatology defined by two appearances: (1) the appearance of the one who appeared in the flesh to bring life and salvation to all and (2) the appearance of the Savior who will appear at God's chosen time to judge the living and the dead. The church lives in the period between these two appearances, a time the Pastorals characterize as the "last days."[44]

Each of the three Pastoral Epistles refers to these two appearances, thereby suggesting that their hope for the Lord's final appearance is grounded in the salvation that Christ brought at his first appearance. For example 1 Tim 3:16 summarizes the "mystery of our religion" in this way: He was *revealed* in flesh, vindicated in spirit, seen by angels, proclaimed among Gentiles, believed in throughout the world, taken up in glory." Thus, the "mystery" is expressed in terms of the initial appearance of Christ (what later theology would call the incarnation), his resurrection,

---

41. Philip H. Towner (*The Goal of Our Instruction: The Structure of Theology and Ethics in the Pastoral Epistles* [JSNTSup 34; Sheffield: JSOT, 1989], 74) notes this when he writes: "Thus the widespread view that the Pastorals depict a dramatically reduced sense of expectancy caused by the disappointment over the delay of the parousia must be judged inadequate."

42. For example, the following texts speak of the hope that believers have: 1 Tim 1:1 ("Christ Jesus *our hope*"); 4:10 ("because we have *our hope* set on the living God"); Tit 3:7 ("according to *the hope of eternal life*"). Other texts give the distinct impression that the Pastorals envision their recipients as living in the last days or that the last days are at hand: 1 Tim 4:1 ("Now the Spirit expressly says that *in the later times* some will renounce the faith . . ."); 2 Tim 3:1 ("You must understand this, that *in the last days* distressing times will come"); 4:3 ("For *the time is coming* when people will not put up with sound doctrine . . ."). Still other texts speak of the coming judgment: 1 Tim 5:24 ("The sins of some people are conspicuous and precede them to *judgment*"); 2 Tim 4:1 ("In the presence of God and of Christ Jesus, who is *to judge* the living and the dead"); v. 8 ("which the Lord, the *righteous judge,* will give to me on that day"). Finally, there are frequent references to "life" and "eternal life" that also point to the future (1 Tim 1:16; 6:12, 19; 2 Tim 1:1; Tit 1:2; 3:7).

43. In 2 Tim 1:10 the noun is used of the first appearance of the Lord. In 1 Tim 6:14; 2 Tim 4:1, 8; and Tit 2:13 it refers to his second appearance. The verb *epiphainō* occurs twice (Tit 2:11; 3:4), as does *phaneroō* (1 Tim 3:16; 2 Tim 1:10). Both are used of the first appearance.

44. This point is made by Towner in his chapter on eschatology (*The Goal of Our Instruction,* 61-74).

his presentation to the angelic court, the proclamation of the gospel, and his ascension. The one who is presently in heaven is the one who appeared in the flesh. Toward the end of this letter, in a final charge to Timothy, Paul reminds his delegate of the Lord's final appearance: "In the presence of God, who gives life to all things, and of Christ Jesus, who in his testimony before Pontius Pilate made the good confession, I charge you to keep the commandment without spot or blame until the *manifestation* of our Lord Jesus Christ, which he [God] will bring about at the right time" (6:13-15). In 1 Timothy, then, the one who has already appeared "in the flesh" will appear again at God's appointed time, perhaps even in Timothy's lifetime.

In 2 Timothy, a letter Paul writes as he comes to the end of his apostolic ministry (4:6-8), the great Apostle makes several references to the first and second appearances of the Lord. At the outset of the letter, he encourages Timothy to "rekindle the gift of God" that Timothy received when he laid his hands on him and to join him in "suffering for the gospel, relying on the power of God" (1:6, 8). Next, Paul recalls how God exercised this power in Christ's first appearance. God saved and called them according to his own purpose and grace, which he granted to them in Christ Jesus before time began (v. 9). Hidden until now, this grace has been revealed "through the appearing of our Savior Christ Jesus, who abolished death and brought life and immortality to light through the gospel" (v. 10). This is the gospel, Paul says, that he was appointed to preach and for which he now suffers. He is not ashamed of the gospel because he knows that the Lord will guard what he has entrusted to Paul "until that day," namely, the day of the Lord's second appearance (vv. 11-12).

According to this rich passage, the first appearance of Christ Jesus revealed the purpose of God, which had been established in eternity before the ages began. Thus the first appearance resulted in the destruction of death and the revelation of life, which is presently being preached through the gospel. While this passage affirms that believers already enjoy salvation and life in virtue of Christ's first appearance, there are other texts in this letter that indicate that believers are not yet finally saved. In a hymn-like passage, for example, Paul affirms: "If we have died with him, *we will also live with him;* if we endure, *we will also reign with him;* if we deny him, *he will also deny us*" (2:11-12). In another passage, he warns Timothy about Hymenaeus and Philetus, who are claiming "that the resurrection has *already* taken place" (v. 18), thereby rejecting a realized eschatology. In yet another place, he solemnly charges Timothy "in the presence of God and of Christ Jesus, who is to judge the living and the dead, *and in view of his appearing* and his kingdom," to preach the gospel (4:1). Finally, Paul reminds Timothy how he has kept the faith: "From now on there is reserved for me the crown of righteousness, which the Lord, the righteous judge, *will give me on that day,* and not only to me but also to all who have longed for his *appearing*" (v. 8). According to 2 Timothy, then, Christ Jesus brought salvation and life at his first appearance and will judge the living and the dead at his second appearance. Given what Paul has said about the error of those who think that the resurrection of believers has already occurred, it is apparent that the resurrection of the dead will accompany this appearance.

The letter to Titus also refers to both the first and second appearances of Christ. Having exhorted Titus to train people in conduct that is consistent with sound teaching, in 2:11-14 Paul explains why Titus must do this: The grace of God has already appeared bringing salvation to all. This salvation trains those who have been saved to renounce impiety and live upright lives as they "wait for the blessed hope and the *manifestation* of the glory of our great God and Savior, Jesus Christ," who gave his life in order to "purify for himself a people of his own who are zealous for good deeds."[45] In this theologically rich statement, Paul speaks of the first and second appearances to undergird the morally good life that salvation makes possible. The purpose of the first appearance was to empower believers to live upright lives so that they will be a purified people who belong to God. Consequently, those who have received this salvation live upright lives as they wait for their "blessed hope" and "the manifestation of the glory" of their great God and Savior. The second appearance then is grounded in the first. It is precisely because they have been trained by the salvation they received at the first appearance to live upright lives that the saved wait for the second appearance.

Toward the end of this letter, Paul refers to the appearance of "the goodness and loving kindness of God our Savior" (3:4), which made its appearance in Jesus Christ. He thus supports his teaching on justification, noting that God "saved us, not because of any works of righteousness that we had done, but according to his mercy, through the water of rebirth and renewal by the Holy Spirit" (v. 5). He also notes that God poured out this

---

45. This text can be construed in two ways. Either it refers to our great God *and* to our Savior Jesus Christ, or it refers to our great God, who is our Savior Jesus Christ. I interpret it as referring to Jesus, whom the letter thus identifies as our great God and Savior, because one article governs both "God" and "Savior" and because the letter envisions a single second appearance: the appearance of Christ, which is the appearance of God.

Spirit "through Jesus Christ our Savior, so that, having been justified by his grace, we might become heirs according to the *hope of eternal life*" (vv. 6-7). Thus the justification believers experience as a result of the first appearance becomes the ground for their hope of eternal life that will attend the second appearance.

The Pastoral Epistles provide us with an interesting example of an eschatology that highlights the present and future aspects of eschatology. In light of the appearance of the Lord that has already occurred, they affirm that believers presently enjoy salvation and life. In light of the appearance for which believers long, they remind their recipients that the final act in the drama of salvation has not taken place. Consequently, even though these letters employ the language of salvation in a way the non-disputed Pauline letters do not, they understand the fundamental distinction between what has already happened and what has not yet occurred. Moreover, like the non-disputed Pauline letters they draw a close relationship between what has already happened and what is to take place, thereby grounding the hope for salvation in what God has already done in Christ. Put another way, it is precisely because God has already appeared in Christ to bring salvation and life to all that believers trust that God will appear again in Christ to complete the salvation that has appeared in Christ. The first appearance, then, is the ground of hope for the second, and the second appearance the completion of the salvation revealed at the first.

Coherence and Meaning in Pauline Eschatology

The manner in which I have organized this chapter highlights the different ways in which the Pauline letters express the hope believers have for final salvation: believers are waiting for the parousia, they are waiting for the resurrection of the dead, they are waiting for God's final victory in Christ, they are hoping for a heavenly inheritance, and they are waiting for the final appearance of Christ. While it is tempting to provide a synthesis that integrates these, such a synthesis would be misguided given the occasional nature of the Pauline letters, not all of which may have been written by Paul. A more fruitful approach is to make some statements that highlight the coherence and meaning of Pauline eschatology.

First, the resurrection of Christ is the ground for hope in the parousia. If the resurrection of Christ were merely an isolated event, something that happened to him, there would be no reason to hope for Christ's return.

Paul, however, insists that Christ's resurrection is the first fruits of the general resurrection of dead, which began in Jesus the Messiah. It is Christ's resurrection, then, that undergirds the hope believers have for their own resurrection, which will occur at the parousia.

Second, because the resurrection of the believer is grounded in the resurrection of Christ, the parousia will always be imminent. From the perspective of Pauline theology, the resurrection is the decisive event in human history. It is the event that brings an end to the old age and ushers in the new age. Before the resurrection, humankind lived in the old age dominated by the powers of sin and death. As long as it lived in that age, the end was always in some indeterminate future. But now that the resurrection of the dead has begun in Christ, his parousia is always imminent for those who believe in him. Put another way, whereas formerly the parousia could not have happened because Christ had not been raised from the dead, now it can happen at any moment because God has raised him from the dead.

Third, the transcendent nature of the parousia requires believers to employ religious imagery to express their hope in Christ's return. Although the parousia will occur in history, it will not be like any other event of history. Inasmuch as the parousia will be the revelation of God's power in the risen Christ, it is a transcendent event that can never be adequately described in human language. Those who try to express something of the transcendent dimension of this event, then, must use religious imagery, which will always be inadequate. To say that Christ will come down from heaven and that believers will be caught up with him in the clouds, for example, cannot express the transcendent reality of the parousia, although it has undoubtedly helped generations of believers comprehend something of that reality. Those who speak of the parousia, therefore, must not confuse imagery with reality.

Fourth, the present eschatological existence of the believer is an integral part of Pauline eschatology. Although the parousia points to a future transcendent event, believers already experience something of that event in their present eschatological existence. The experience of the Spirit and the experience of salvation that believers already enjoy is a proleptic experience of the parousia. Indeed, it is precisely because believers already experience something of the future in the present that they can be confident that their Lord will return. The salvation that results from the appearance of the Lord assures them of his second appearance, just as his resurrection from the dead gives them confidence for their own resurrection.

Fifth, the parousia is an act of God rather than the culmination of a his-

torical process. Although 2 Thessalonians speaks of certain events that must occur before the parousia, the parousia is not the outcome or culmination of historical events. It is not the result of humanity's growth and progress. It is not so much a matter of humanity coming to God as it is a matter of God coming to humanity. The epiphany language of the Pastorals is especially helpful in this regard since it highlights the unexpected nature of this transcendent event. The transcendent appearance of God will be the gracious and unexpected epiphany of God that rescues humanity from its own devices.[46]

Sixth, the parousia proclaims the ultimate victory of God. Inasmuch as the parousia will usher in the resurrection of the dead and the final judgment, it proclaims the final victory of God over the powers of sin and death. Death will no longer be victorious because the dead will have been raised, and sin will be defeated because God will have pronounced the last and final judgment, the only judgment that will endure. Faith in the parousia, then, is faith in God, the confident assurance that God will be victorious, that creation will achieve its purpose, and that God will be all in all.

Seventh, the parousia proclaims that Christ will play the decisive role in God's final victory over sin and death. Just as the parousia is a statement about God, so it is an affirmation about Christ in relationship to God. For in addition to proclaiming the ultimate victory of God, the parousia announces that Christ will be the one by whom God will be victorious. As God once effected salvation by the appearance of Christ, so God will effect final salvation by the second appearance of Christ. In a way known only to God, God will be victorious in Christ.

FOR FURTHER READING

Barth, Karl. *The Resurrection of the Dead.* New York: Arno, 1977.
Beker, J. Christiaan. *Paul the Apostle: The Triumph of God in Life and Thought.* Philadelphia: Fortress, 1980. Pages 135-81.

46. Joseph Ratzinger (*Eschatology: Death and Eternal Life* [2nd ed.; Washington: Catholic University Press, 1988], 213) puts it well when he writes: "Faith in Christ's return is, therefore, in the first place, the rejection of an intra-historical perfectibility of the world. . . . And so, over and above this preliminary statement, we must add that faith in Christ's return is also the certitude that the world will, indeed, come to its perfection, not through rational planning but through the indestructible love which triumphed in the risen Christ."

Bultmann, Rudolf. "Man between the Times according to the New Testament." Pages 248-66 in *Existence and Faith: Shorter Writings of Rudolf Bultmann.* Cleveland and New York: World, 1960.

Cerfaux, Lucien. *Christ in the Theology of St. Paul.* New York: Herder and Herder, 1959. Pages 31-106.

Dunn, James D. G. *The Theology of Paul the Apostle.* Grand Rapids: Eerdmans, 1998. Pages 294-315.

Hahn, Ferdinand. *Theologie des Neuen Testaments,* vol. 1: *Die Vielfahlt des Neuen Testaments. Theologiegeschichte des Urchristentums.* Tübingen: Mohr Siebeck, 2002. Pages 307-22.

Kreitzer, L. J. "Eschatology." Pages 253-69 in *Dictionary of Paul and His Letters,* ed. Gerald F. Hawthorne, Ralph P. Martin, and Daniel G. Reid. Downers Grove: InterVaristy, 1993.

Ladd, George Eldon. *A Theology of the New Testament.* Grand Rapids: Eerdmans, 1974. Pages 550-68.

Moore, A. L. *The Parousia in the New Testament.* NovTSup 13. Leiden: Brill, 1966.

Plevnik, Joseph. *Paul and the Parousia: An Exegetical and Theological Investigation.* Peabody: Hendrickson, 1997.

Räisänen, Heikki. *The Rise of Christian Beliefs: The Thought World of the Early Christians.* Minneapolis: Fortress, 2012. Pages 79-113.

Ratzinger, Joseph. *Eschatology: Death and Eternal Life.* 2nd ed. Washington: Catholic University of America Press, 1988.

Ridderbos, Herman. *Paul: An Outline of His Theology.* Grand Rapids: Eerdmans, 1975. Pages 487-562.

Schnelle, Udo. *Apostle Paul: His Life and Theology.* Grand Rapids: Baker, 2003. Pages 577-97.

Schreiner, Thomas R. *Paul, Apostle of God's Glory in Christ: A Pauline Theology.* Downers Grove: InterVarsity, 2001. Pages 453-84.

Vena, Osvaldo D. *The Parousia and Its Rereadings: The Development of the Eschatological Consciousness in the Writings of the New Testament.* Studies in Biblical Literature 27. New York: Peter Lang, 2001.

Vos, Geerhardus. *The Pauline Eschatology.* Grand Rapids: Baker, 1979.

Vouga, François. *Une Théologie du Nouveau Testament.* MdB 43. Geneva: Labor et Fides, 2001. Pages 391-437.

Witherington, Ben, III. *Jesus, Paul and the End of the World: A Comparative Study of New Testament Eschatology.* Downers Grove: InterVarsity, 1992.

―――. *Paul's Narrative Thought World: The Tapestry of Tragedy and Triumph.* Louisville: Westminster/John Knox, 1994. Pages 186-204.

8. The God Revealed through the Saving Grace of Jesus Christ

Introduction

Pauline theology begins and ends with God. It begins with the God who revealed his Son to Paul, and it ends with the God who will be all in all when the Son will subject himself to the One who subjected everything to him (1 Cor 15:28). It is appropriate, then, to conclude this Pauline theology with a consideration of the God who is revealed in the saving grace manifested in Jesus Christ.[1] Before proceeding to this task, however, some preliminary remarks are in order.

First, we can assume that the pre-Christian Paul understood God in terms of his rich Jewish heritage and Pharisaic traditions. As a Jew, Paul would have confessed: "Hear, O Israel: The LORD is our God, the LORD alone" (Deut 6:4). He believed that the God of Israel created the world, chose the Jewish people from all the nations of the world to be his special people, revealed his will in Torah, and will judge the world on the last day.

---

1. J. Christiaan Beker (*The Triumph of God: The Essence of Paul's Thought* [Minneapolis: Fortress, 1990], 115) highlights the centrality of God in Paul's thought when he writes: "Paul's theology is marked by its *theocentric* character. Contrary to common consensus that posits a christological scheme of promise and fulfillment, Paul refuses to spiritualize the promises of the Old Testament. . . . The focal point of Paul's thought is therefore theocentric because it longs for the public manifestation of God's reign and triumph." Thomas Schreiner (*Paul: Apostle of God's Glory in Christ* [Downers Grove: InterVarsity, 2001], 35) makes a similar statement when he writes: "The passion of Paul's life, the foundation and capstone of his vision, and the animating motive of his mission was the supremacy of God in and through the Lord Jesus Christ."

Finally, as a Pharisee, Paul believed in and hoped for the resurrection of the dead (Acts 23:6).[2]

Second, we can assume that Paul's core beliefs about God remained in place. His faith in Christ did not annul or distort his faith in the God of Israel. For example, in his defense before the Roman governor Felix, Paul says: "But this I admit to you, that according to the Way, which they call a sect, I worship the God of our ancestors, believing everything laid down according to the laws or written in the prophets, I have a hope in God — a hope that they themselves also accept — that there will be a resurrection of both the righteous and the unrighteous" (Acts 24:14-15). Although the words belong to Luke, I suspect that Paul would have embraced them. The difference between Paul and his compatriots is not that he has ceased to believe in the law and the prophets but that he believes that the resurrection of the dead has begun in the Messiah.[3]

Third, the new element in Paul's understanding of God comes from his encounter with the risen Christ: his Damascus road experience. At that moment he understood that the crucified Jesus is the risen Lord, an insight that eventually led him to identify Jesus as the Son of God, the very image of God's glory (2 Cor 4:4). The crucified Jesus was risen and alive because the God of Abraham, Isaac, and Jacob raised him from the dead. If this is so, then the resurrection of the dead has begun in the Messiah, the eschatological Adam, who has become the progenitor of a new humanity that will share in his resurrection.

---

2. James D. G. Dunn (*The Theology of Paul the Apostle* [Grand Rapids: Eerdmans, 1998], 29) insists on the continuity of Paul's thought about God: "As will quickly become evident, these shared beliefs [about God] were Jewish through and through. . . . Thus in Romans his language again and again falls into the rhythm of traditional Jewish affirmations about God. . . . In other words, Paul's conversion had not changed his belief in and about God. It was the Creator God of Genesis who had also enlightened him (2 Cor. 4.6, echoing Gen. 1.3). It was the God who had called Jeremiah who had also chosen him (Gal. 1.15, echoing Jer. 1:5). It was the grace of this God which had made him what he was (1 Cor. 15:10). In short, his most fundamental taken-for-granted remained intact." Udo Schnelle (*Apostle Paul: His Life and Theology* [Grand Rapids: Baker, 2003], 392-93) is more guarded: "Paul's *theology* per se is in direct continuity with the fundamental Jewish affirmation: God is one, the Creator, the Lord who will bring his creative purpose to completion. At the same time, Christology effects a basic change in Paul's *theology*, for Paul proclaims christological monotheism."

3. Schnelle (*Apostle Paul,* 395) notes: "*The* distinguishing characteristic of the God proclaimed by Paul is that God raised Jesus from the dead (cf. 1 Thess 1:10; 4:14; 1 Cor 15:12-19), God is the source of all *charis* (Rom 1:7; 3:24; 1 Cor 15:10) and the goal of redemptive history (1 Cor 15:20-28)."

Paul's understanding of God is both old and new. On the one hand it is old inasmuch as it remains in continuity with Israel's faith and understanding of God — at least from Paul's perspective. On the other hand, it is new inasmuch as Paul now understands who God is and what God is doing in light of the saving grace manifested in Jesus Christ. Thus we might say that whereas Paul's understanding of Christ is theological, his understanding of God is christological.[4]

In explaining his own understanding of Paul's theology, Rudolf Bultmann once noted that Paul's theology is not a speculative system: "It deals with God not as He is in Himself but only with God as He is significant for man, for man's responsibility and man's salvation." Bultmann then went on to make this well-known statement, which defines his approach to Paul's theology: "Every assertion about God is simultaneously an assertion about man and vice versa. For this reason and in this sense Paul's theology is, at the same time, anthropology."[5] While I agree that Paul's theology is not a speculative system, I would amend Bultmann's statement to read: every assertion about God is simultaneously an assertion about *Christ,* and vice versa. For this reason and in this sense Paul's theology is, at the same time, *Christology.*

Given these presuppositions, how should we proceed? First, it is important to remember that what Paul says about God is determined, in large measure, by the occasional nature of his correspondence. For example, election plays an important role in the manner that he portrays God in his Thessalonian correspondence because Paul must remind his Gentile converts that the only God, the God of Israel, has called them to belong to the eschatological people of God. Similarly, the economy of God's redemptive plan plays a central role in Ephesians because Paul (or someone writing in his name) must remind the recipients of that letter of the mystery of God that has been revealed in Christ, namely, that Gentiles and Jewish believers form a new humanity in Christ.

Second, although "God" *(theos)* is one of the most frequent words in the Pauline letters, the task of uncovering what these letters affirm about

4. Francis Watson ("The Triune Divine Identity: Reflection on Pauline God Language, in Disagreement with J. D. G. Dunn," *JSNT* 80 [2000]: 91-124, here 117) makes this point when he writes: "If, however, God is — finally and ultimately, not just provisionally and in passing — the God who raised Jesus our Lord from the dead, the God and Father of our Lord Jesus Christ, then God's own identity is determined by the relation to Jesus just as Jesus' identity is determined by the relation to God."

5. Rudolf Bultmann, *Theology of the New Testament* (New York: Charles Scribner's Sons, 1951), 1:190-91.

God should not be reduced to a concordance study.[6] To comprehend what the Pauline letters say about God it is important to seek the inner logic of what Paul writes about God. For example, Paul speaks differently in 1 Thessalonians about the way in which God deals with the Jewish people than he does in Romans because he is responding to different situations. In 1 Thessalonians he affirms that the wrath of God has come upon the Jews for persecuting him and preventing others from speaking to the Gentiles so that they might be saved (1 Thess 2:15-16). But in Romans 9–11 Paul affirms the faithfulness of God to Israel because he must confront Gentile arrogance toward Israel (Rom 11:1-2, 29). Thus what appears to be a contradiction in Paul's understanding of how God is acting is, in part, the outcome of the occasional nature of his correspondence.

Third, given the occasional nature of the Pauline correspondence, it will be more helpful to look for the coherence and meaning of what Paul says about God rather than synthesize his thought. Every synthesis of Pauline theology is, of its very nature, limited and artificial. Therefore, rather than synthesize what the Pauline letters say about God, I will focus on the dominant themes of the different writings in light of the epistolary situations that occasioned them. In doing so, I hope to show that there is a coherence and logic to the theology of the Pauline letters, which is grounded in Paul's understanding of Christ as the one in whom God works and reveals himself. The principal themes I will investigate are (1) God who calls and elects, (2) God revealed in weakness and suffering, (3) God who justifies, (4) God who is faithful, (5) God who shares his name, (6) God revealed in Christ, (7) God revealed in the economy of salvation, and (8) God who is Savior.

God Who Calls and Elects

Although Paul did not write 1 and 2 Thessalonians to provide his converts with a theology of God, both letters presuppose an understanding of God that is rooted in Israel's traditional faith in God as well as in Paul's understanding of God as revealed in Jesus Christ. For example, when Paul ex-

---

6. "God" *(theos)* occurs 1317 times in the New Testament, 548 of which are in the Pauline letters: Romans (153), 1 Corinthians (106), 2 Corinthians (79), Galatians (31), Ephesians (31), Philippians (23), Colossians (21), 1 Thessalonians (36), 2 Thessalonians (18), 1 Timothy (22), 2 Timothy (13), Titus (13), and Philemon (2). These statistics do not include the times that God is the unexpressed subject of a verb or when a pronoun refers to God.

horts his Gentile converts at Thessalonica to live in holiness and honor rather than "with lustful passion, like the Gentiles who do not know God" (1 Thess 4:5), he implies that even though Gentiles worship many gods, they are ignorant of God because they do not know the God of Israel. Paul's Gentile converts at Thessalonica, however, are no longer in this situation because they have "turned to God from idols, to serve a living and true God," the God of Israel who raised Jesus from the dead (1:9). The new faith of Paul's Gentile converts, then, begins with a profound conversion from idols to the living God of Israel.

In light of his Damascus road experience, Paul identifies the God of Israel as "God the Father" or "God our Father" (1 Thess 1:1; 3:11; 2 Thess 1:1; 2:16). The designation of God as "Father" was not unfamiliar to Paul. As a pious Jew, he already knew that God was the Father of Israel (Exod 4:22-23; Deut 14:1; 32:6; Hos 11:1-3) and that Israel addressed God as its Father (Isa 63:16; 64:8). But with the appearance of God's Son, the designation of God as Father finds its deepest meaning in Christ, the perfect Son of God, whom God raised from the dead and designated as the one who would rescue believers from the coming judgment (1 Thess 1:10). It is because Jesus is the unique Son of God, then, that Paul identifies God as "the Father" or "our Father."

Paul's use of "gospel" in his Thessalonian correspondence highlights the centrality of God in his thought. The gospel that Paul preaches is "the gospel of God" (1 Thess 2:2, 8, 9) because it is God's own good news about his Son. It is God's gospel, God's own good news with which Paul has been entrusted (v. 4). Because the Thessalonians understood that the gospel Paul proclaimed originated with God, they received it as God's word rather than as a merely human word (v. 13). Through the gospel they embraced, they were taught by God to love one another (4:9). Furthermore, because the gospel originated with God, those who believe in it belong to "the churches of God" (2:14; 2 Thess 1:4).

The most distinctive aspect of Paul's theology of God in his Thessalonian correspondence is the manner in which he reminds his Gentile converts that the God of Israel has called, elected, loved, and sanctified them in his Son. Drawing on Israel's distinctive understanding of God as the one who elected and chose Israel from all the nations of the earth, Paul applies this election theology to the very Gentiles from whom Israel was called to separate itself. The application of this election theology, which would have disturbed many of Paul's contemporaries, provides an insight to the "newness" of his understanding of God in Jesus Christ; for it proclaims that the God who elected Israel is now calling and electing Gentiles who believe in his Son.

At the outset of 1 Thessalonians, Paul calls his converts "beloved by God" since God has chosen them (1:4). He exhorts them to lead a life worthy of God who calls them into his own kingdom and glory (2:12). Encouraging them not to be discouraged by their persecutions, he tells them that they were destined for this by God (3:3). In the great moral exhortation of ch. 4, Paul reminds the Thessalonians that God did not call them to impurity but to holiness (4:7). Then in ch. 5, he says that God did not destine them for wrath but for salvation (5:9). Finally, he concludes this letter, as he began it, with a statement of their election: "The one who calls you is faithful, and he will do this" (v. 24). This theme of God who calls and elects continues in 2 Thessalonians where Paul tells the Thessalonians that God chose them "as the first fruits for salvation through sanctification by the Spirit and through belief in the truth" (2:13). The upshot of this election theology is twofold. First, it reminds the Thessalonians that they belong to the eschatological people of God. Although Gentiles by birth, they have received a new identity as God's people. Second, the language of election identifies God as the God of Israel who chooses, elects, and sanctifies in Jesus Christ.

At the end of 1 Thessalonians, Paul identifies God as "the God of peace" (5:23), a phrase that also occurs in Rom 15:33; 16:20; 2 Cor 13:11; Phil 4:9; and Heb 13:20.[7] Although there is no comparable phrase in Israel's Scriptures, the recognition of God as the origin and author of peace occurs in several OT texts.[8] The sense of this phrase, which echoes the greeting of peace at the beginning of the letter, identifies God as the one who gives the fullness of peace through the salvation he has brought about in Jesus Christ.

Although it is not the purpose of Paul's Thessalonian correspondence to provide a comprehensive understanding of God, the manner in which it presents God is significant. Through the proclamation of the gospel, God is presently calling Gentiles as well as Jews into the eschatological people of God. God's will is their sanctification — their total dedication to God —

---

7. A similar phrase occurs in 2 Thess 3:16: "Now may the Lord of peace himself give you peace at all times in all ways." Here "the Lord of peace" may refer to Christ rather than to God.

8. C. E. B. Cranfield (*The Epistle to the Romans* [ICC; Edinburgh: T. & T. Clark, 1975], 2:779) lists the following texts as OT background: Lev 26:6; Num 6:26; Judg 6:24; Ps 29:11; Isa 26:12; Jer 16:5.

so that they will be blameless in holiness when Christ returns (1 Thess 3:13; 5:23) to rescue them from the coming wrath and bring them to the fullness of salvation that only the God of peace can bring about.

God Revealed in Weakness and Suffering

Given the complexity of the problems Paul encountered with the Corinthian community, it is not surprising that 1 and 2 Corinthians provide us with new insights into his understanding of God. As in his Thessalonian correspondence, his understanding of God is determined by how the God of his ancestors — the God of Israel — has revealed himself in Jesus Christ and is now at work in the community of the church through the power of the Spirit. However, since Paul must defend himself in 2 Corinthians from a series of criticisms about the nature and style of his apostleship, he tends to speak there about God in more personal terms than in 1 Corinthians.[9] Accordingly, whereas in 1 Corinthians he speaks of God in light of the numerous communal issues that he addresses, in 2 Corinthians he speaks of God in light of the personal criticism leveled against himself. In both letters he highlights the paradoxical way in which the God of power and wisdom is revealed in the weakness and folly of the cross and how the God who comforts and consoles is revealed in suffering and rejection.

First Corinthians

As in the Thessalonians correspondence, Paul describes God in 1 Corinthians as the one who calls and elects. Before turning to this theme, however, it will be helpful to summarize how Paul speaks about God and Christ, God and the Spirit, and God and those who proclaim the gospel.

In light of his Damascus road experience, it is no longer possible for Paul to think of God apart from Christ. Having seen the risen Lord (9:1; 15:8), he proclaims that God is the Father of Jesus Christ, the God who raised Jesus from the dead. At the outset of this letter, for example, he writes: "God is faithful; by him you were called into the fellowship of his

---

9. Although there are indications in 1 Corinthians that Paul is already defending himself from criticism (see 1 Cor 4:6-21; 9:1-2), this criticism has not yet resulted in the crisis that occasioned 2 Corinthians.

Son, Jesus Christ our Lord" (1:9). In ch. 15, where he argues for the resurrection of the dead, Paul grounds the resurrection of believers in the fact that "Christ has been raised from the dead" (15:20). Throughout the chapter the unexpressed subject of "raise" is God. The newness of Paul's understanding of God, then, can be summarized in two core beliefs: God is the one who raised Jesus from the dead, and God is the Father of Jesus the Christ.

In 8:6, at the beginning of a lengthy discussion of whether believers should participate in the cult of idols and eat food that has been sacrificed to idols, Paul summarizes his understanding of the relationship between God and Christ:

> yet for us there is *one God, the Father,*
> > from whom are all things
> > and for whom we exist,
> and *one Lord, Jesus Christ,*
> > through whom are all things
> > and through whom we exist.

As nearly all commentators note, this creed-like statement echoes Israel's own creed (Deut 6:4-5):

> Hear, O Israel: The LORD is our God, the LORD alone.
> You shall love the LORD your God
> > with all your heart,
> > and with all your soul,
> > and with all your might.

In accordance with his Israelite faith, Paul affirms that there is only one God, whom he identifies as the Father: the origin and goal of all that exists. The new element in Paul's confession is the introduction of Jesus Christ as the one Lord, whom Paul identifies as the mediator of God's creative work.[10] There is no confusion in Paul's thinking about the relationship between God and Christ: there is only one God, the Father. Thus while there

10. In the Septuagint text of Deuteronomy "Lord" replaces the divine name (Yhwh). In saying that "the LORD is our God, the LORD alone," Deuteronomy is affirming that "Yhwh is our God, Yhwh alone." Paul, however, applies "Lord" to the risen Christ, the name that was bestowed on Christ at his exaltation (Phil 2:9). In light of Jesus' sonship, Paul then identifies God as "Father."

are instances when Paul calls Christ "God" (Rom 9:5; Tit 2:13), there are no instances when he identifies Christ as "the Father." For Paul, Jesus is the Son of God, the one who shares God's name "Lord" (Phil 2:11).[11]

Paul affirms the centrality of God in the drama of salvation in three texts that speaks of the filial submission of Christ to the Father (1 Cor 3:21-23; 11:3; 15:28). In reading these texts, it is important to remember that Paul is not making a series of speculative statements about God and Christ but attending to practical issues and problems in the Corinthian community. For example, after a lengthy discussion of apostolic ministry, he affirms, "So let no one boast about human leaders. For all things are yours, whether Paul or Apollos or Cephas or the world or life or death or the present or the future — all belong to you, and you belong to Christ, *and Christ belongs to God*" (3:21-23). In his discussion of women prophets, he begins, "I want you to understand that Christ is the head of every man, and the husband is the head of his wife, *and God is the head of Christ*" (11:3). Finally, when he summarizes what will happen at the parousia, he writes: "When all things are subjected to him, then *the Son himself will also be subjected to the one who put all things in subjection under him, so that God may be all in all*" (15:28). In every instance, the purpose of these texts is to highlight the obedience of the Son to the Father.[12]

To summarize, Paul affirms that there is only one God, the Father of Jesus Christ, the God of Israel. The one God, however, is revealed in Jesus Christ, his unique Son, the exalted Lord, the mediator of God's creative and redemptive work.

In addition to what he says about God and Christ, Paul makes a number of remarks about God and the Spirit and about God and those who proclaim the gospel. In the context of a discussion about spiritual gifts in chs. 12–14, for example, his remarks anticipate later trinitarian theology:

11. My purpose in writing this is to reflect as accurately as I can what Paul, writing only a few years after Jesus' death, affirms about Christ. It is not to question what later creeds affirm about the Son being the second person of the Blessed Trinity.

12. Although these texts subordinate Christ to God, it is not their purpose to develop a doctrine of subordinationism, a teaching that tries to preserve monotheism by subordinating the Son and/or the Spirit to the Father. This teaching was condemned by the Council of Constantinople (381). It is important to recall that in addition to such texts that subordinate Christ to God, others highlight the equality of Christ and God (Phil 2:6). Neil Richardson (*Paul's Language about God* [JSNTSup 99; Sheffield: Sheffield Academic, 1994], 305) notes this: "Alongside the strongly subordinationist relationship of Christ to God, reflected in many of the linguistic patterns, a quasi-equal relationship is discernable, especially in the opening salutations."

> Now there are varieties of gifts,
>   but *the same Spirit;*
> and there are varieties of services,
>   but *the same Lord;*
> and there are varieties of activities,
>   but it is *the same God*
> who activates all of them in everyone. (12:4-6)

Although it is not Paul's purpose to develop a trinitarian theology in this text, the manner in which he relates the Spirit, the Lord, and God to each other is striking. A similar trinitarian text is found in 2 Cor 13:13.

> The grace of *the Lord Jesus Christ,*
> the love of *God,*
> and the communion of *the Holy Spirit* be with all of you.

From texts such as these, it is apparent that Paul's experience of God in Christ and the Spirit has broadened his understanding of God. God is one, but Paul now thinks of, and experiences, God in relationship to Christ and the Spirit.[13]

Finally, there are a number of texts in 1 Corinthians in which Paul speaks of God in relationship to the church and those who minister to it. For example, the community is "the church of God" (1:2), "God's field," "God's building" (3:9), "God's temple" (v. 16), whereas apostles are "God's servants" (v. 9) and "stewards of God's mysteries" (4:1). One plants, another waters, but only God gives the growth (3:6). Although these statements do not provide a speculative knowledge of God, they witness to the intimate relationship between the transcendent God who calls and elects and those who believe in him.[14]

---

13. Addressing the question of whether Paul was a trinitarian, Ron C. Fay ("Was Paul a Trinitarian: A Look at Romans 8," in *Paul and His Theology* [Pauline Studies 3, ed. Stanley E. Porter; Leiden: Brill, 2006], 327-45, here 343) writes: "Paul in Romans 8 hints at a Trinitarian doctrine, but was he really a trinitarian? In one sense, the answer must be no. Paul did not use the explicit terminology that would later characterize the historic conflict within the early Church. In a less formal sense, however, Paul was a trinitarian." Andrew K. Gabriel ("Pauline Pneumatology and the Question of Trinitarian Presuppositions," in *Paul and His Theology,* 347-62, here 362) comes to a similar conclusion: "Along with the remainder of Scripture, Pauline literature does not contain an articulation of a doctrine of the Trinity. Nevertheless, Paul's letters do exhibit Trinitarian presuppositions."

14. Victor Furnish (*The Theology of the First Letter to the Corinthians* [NTT; Cambridge:

As in his Thessalonian correspondence, Paul reminds the Corinthians that God chose and elected them. Sanctified in Christ, they have been called by the God of Israel to be holy with all who call on the name of the Lord Jesus Christ (1:2). The new aspect of Paul's theology of God in 1 Corinthians, however, is the manner in which he relates this election theology to his theology of the cross in order to highlight the paradoxical nature of God's power and wisdom.[15]

In response to a threat of factions and divisions within their congregation, Paul reminds the Corinthians of their election and the gospel he preached to them. In doing so, he provides them with an insight into the paradoxical nature of God's power and wisdom, which is disclosed through weakness and folly. First he insists that the message of the cross — the proclamation of the crucified Messiah — is foolishness to those who are perishing, but to those who are being saved it is the power of God (1:18). Jews demand signs and Greeks seek wisdom, but the gospel of the crucified Christ that Paul preaches is a stumbling block to Jews and foolishness to Gentiles. However, to those whom God has called, Jews and Gentiles alike, Christ is the wisdom and power of God; for God's foolishness (the crucified Christ) is wiser than human wisdom, and God's weakness (the crucified Christ) is stronger than human strength (vv. 22-25).[16]

Second, having reminded the Corinthians of the paradoxical nature of the message of the cross, Paul recalls the paradoxical nature of their own election (1:26-31). In electing them, God chose the foolish to shame the wise, the weak to shame the strong, the low and the despised to reduce to nothing those things that are something. Thus the very election of the Corinthians testifies to the paradoxical way in which God works through the cross.

Third, Paul reminds the Corinthians of his ministry among them when he proclaimed the gospel — the mystery of God (2:1-5). He did not preach

---

Cambridge University Press, 199], 28-48) provides a helpful overview of how Paul speaks of God in relation to the church and its ministers.

15. Pheme Perkins ("God's Power in Human Weakness: Paul Teaches the Corinthians about God," in *The Forgotten God: Perspectives in Biblical Theology: Essays in Honor of Paul J. Achtemeier,* ed. A. Andrew Das and Frank J. Matera [Louisville: Westminster John Knox, 2002] 145-62, here 156) develops this point in her essay. She writes: "For Paul, God's power in the world remains configured according to the pattern established by the cross. The Corinthians are denying the centrality of the cross and resurrection for bringing this age to its end."

16. For a detailed discussion of the power of God in 1 Corinthians, see Petrus J. Gräbe, *The Power of God in Paul's Letters* (2nd ed.; WUNT 123; Tübingen: Mohr Siebeck, 2008), 43-85.

in lofty words of wisdom lest their faith rest on his rhetoric rather than on what God had done in Christ. Instead, he came with the message of the crucified Christ so that their faith would be established on the power of God rather than on human wisdom.

Finally, Paul affirms that there is a wisdom in the gospel he preaches, but it is not the wisdom of this age (2:6-16). The wisdom he preaches is mysterious, hidden, predetermined by God. It is the proclamation of the crucified Christ, which is only accessible to the mature and spiritual, those who have been taught by God's Spirit.

The upshot of this remarkable passage (1:18–2:16) is a paradoxical theology that foreshadows the dialectical theology of Karl Barth and others: every human statement about God is negated in light of the gospel. In the face of the gospel all human power and wisdom are weakness and foolishness since the wisdom and power of God are revealed in the scandal of the cross. To understand who God is and how God acts one must embrace the scandal of the crucified Christ. For in the weakness and folly of the cross, the power and wisdom of God are found.

Paul's theology of God in 1 Corinthians can be summarized in terms of what it affirms about Christ, the Spirit, and the church. In Christ's death and resurrection, the power and wisdom of God are revealed in a startling way. Through the Spirit, this power and wisdom are made available to the members of the church whose election mirrors the paradoxical message of God's wisdom and power.

Second Corinthians

Paul's speech about God is more personal in 2 Corinthians. Other preachers, whom Paul views as false apostles, had come to Corinth, and in light of their ministry the Corinthians called into question the manner in which Paul exercised his ministry. Whereas these intruding apostles accepted the support of the Corinthians and enjoyed a glorious ministry, Paul endured suffering and affliction and, to the dismay of the Corinthians, refused their patronage. Rather than denying his afflictions, however, Paul embraced them, arguing that they legitimized him as an apostle of Christ.[17] As he de-

---

17. For a careful study of how "persecution" is used in the NT to legitimize apostolic power, see James A. Kelhoffer, *Persecution, Persuasion and Power: Readiness to Withstand Hardship as a Corroboration of Legitimacy in the New Testament* (WUNT 270; Tübingen:

fends his apostolic ministry, therefore, he speaks more personally of God in terms of the comfort and consolation God provided him in the midst of his afflictions on behalf of the gospel.

Paul's new way of speaking about God appears at the outset of 2 Corinthians, where he begins with an extended benediction rather than with a prayer of thanksgiving (1:3-7). In this benediction, he extols the God and Father of Jesus Christ as "the Father of mercies and the God of all consolation." It is God who has consoled Paul in all his afflictions so that he will be able to console those who are afflicted with the consolation he has received from God. Paul's afflictions, then, are not something to be ashamed of, nor do they call into question his apostleship. Rather, they are meant to console others and bring them to salvation. Through his sufferings and afflictions, then, Paul experiences God in a new way: the Father of Jesus Christ is the God of all consolation, the one who gives meaning to suffering and affliction.

In 1:8-11 Paul recalls an episode in his life that resulted in a more profound understanding of God. Alluding to a severe affliction he suffered in the Roman province of Asia (possibly an imprisonment at Ephesus), he writes that he despaired of life. Consequently, he resigned himself to a sentence of death, lest he rely on himself rather than on "God who raises the dead." God, however, rescued him from death. Whatever the precise circumstances of this affliction, it taught Paul that God who raises the dead rescues and comforts the afflicted.

In 4:7–5:10 Paul speaks of his sufferings and afflictions in light of his faith in the resurrection. First, he acknowledges that he holds the treasure of his apostolic ministry in "clay jars," by which he means his mortal and corruptible body. Thus it should be clear to all that the power of the ministry Paul exercises comes from God rather than from himself (4:7). Second, he affirms his faith in the resurrection when he writes: "the one [God, the Father] who raised the Lord Jesus will raise us also with Jesus, and will bring us with you into his presence" (v. 14). Third, after describing the sufferings he endures, he expresses his ardent hope for the resurrection body, a building from God, a house not made with hands, eternal in the heavens" (5:1), that God has prepared for him (v. 5). It is precisely through his sufferings and afflictions, then, that Paul knows God as the God of all consolation, God who raises the dead.

Mohr Siebeck, 2010). In the second chapter of his study he argues that Paul views withstanding persecution as a confirmation of one's identity among God's faithful people and that Paul points to his own persecutions to corroborate his apostleship.

The manner in which Paul speaks of his call and ministry in 2 Corinthians is instructive for understanding his theology of God. At the outset of a long section in which he describes his new covenant ministry, Paul portrays God as a conquering general who has taken him captive for the sake of the gospel and now leads him in a triumphant procession (2:14-17). Although the captives in such processions were humiliated, Paul willingly marches as God's prisoner. For in capturing him, God called and qualified Paul to be the minister of a new covenant empowered by God's own Spirit (3:5-6). Alluding to his call, Paul recalls how God brought him to the knowledge "of the glory of God in the face of Jesus Christ" (4:6), who is "the image of God" (v. 4). Looking back, Paul now understands how God was at work in his call/conversion. At that moment of Paul's humiliation and defeat, God revealed himself in Christ. He captured Paul so that he could be the minister of a new covenant empowered by God's own Spirit.

In his discussion of his new covenant ministry, Paul makes an important statement about God and Christ. Noting that those who are in Christ belong to a new creation, Paul affirms that "all this is from God, who reconciled us to himself through Christ, and has given us the ministry of reconciliation; that is, in Christ God was reconciling the world to himself, not counting their trespasses against them, and entrusting the message of reconciliation to us" (5:18-19). God is the central actor in this great drama of reconciliation. Taking the initiative, God reconciled humanity to himself by making Christ "to be sin" so that humanity might become "the righteousness of God" (v. 21). The God who reconciles humanity to himself, then, is the one who works in and through Christ, who is the image of God. Apart from Christ there is no new creation, there is no reconciliation; for it is in and through Christ that God has chosen to reveal himself.

The contribution of 2 Corinthians to the Pauline understanding of God can be summarized in this way. Because God is revealed in the crucified Christ who is the image and righteousness of God, God is revealed in the sufferings and afflictions of those who associate themselves with the crucified one. For just as Christ was crucified in weakness but now lives by the power of God (13:4), so those who share in his weakness will experience God's power. Paul's knowledge of this paradox was experiential rather than speculative. Having conformed himself to the crucified Christ, in whom God reconciled the world to himself, Paul experienced the God of all consolation in his sufferings and afflictions on behalf of the gospel; he experienced the God who raises the dead.

God Who Justifies

Like Paul's Thessalonian and Corinthian correspondence, his letter to the Galatians employs an election theology when speaking of God.[18] At the outset of the letter, for example, Paul rebukes his Gentile converts because they are "so quickly deserting the one [God] who called you in the grace of Christ and are turning to a different gospel" (1:6). Formerly they did not know God because they were enslaved to beings that were not gods (4:8). But "when the fullness of time had come, God sent his Son" (v. 4). Having embraced the gospel and received God's own Spirit, the Galatians now address God as "Abba, Father" (v. 6). They have come to know God, or to put it more accurately, they have come "to be known by God" (v. 9). Given their new relation to God, which presupposes their faith in the gospel of the crucified Christ (3:1), Paul is utterly astounded that the Galatians are tempted to submit themselves to circumcision and adopt the prescriptions of the Mosaic Law since God has already justified them by calling and electing them in Christ.

Paul views his relationship to God in terms of this election theology when he speaks of his call and conversion. God set him apart before he was born and called him through his grace in order to reveal his Son to him so that he might proclaim Christ among the Gentiles (1:15-16). The one who called Paul was the God of Israel, whom Paul so zealously served (so he thought) when he persecuted the church of God (1:13). But in light of his Damascus road experience, Paul has come to an understanding of God that is both traditional and innovative.

On the one hand, it is traditional because Paul is firmly convinced that God's plan has not changed. Reading Israel's Scriptures in light of Christ, he now realizes that God had already proclaimed the gospel to Abraham when God promised the patriarch that all the nations of the earth would be blessed in him (3:8). What God promised Abraham was fulfilled in Christ (v. 16), through whom the Gentiles have received "the promise of the Spirit through faith" (v. 14). According to Paul's reading of Israel's

---

18. Richard Hays ("The God of Mercy Who Rescues Us from the Present Evil Age: Romans and Galatians," in *The Forgotten God*, 123-44) approaches his discussion of "God" in Galatians in terms of the narrative about God that the letter presupposes. He summarizes that narrative under the following headings: God made promises to Abraham. God gave the Law. God sent his Son. God raised Jesus from the dead. God justifies the Gentiles through the faithfulness of Jesus Christ. God calls us into participation in the new covenant community. God supplies the Spirit. God will judge. God is the ultimate recipient of glory.

Scriptures, then, the promise God made to Abraham, not the Mosaic Law, is the key to understanding God's plan of salvation. Whereas the law excludes the Gentiles, the promise embraces them. What happened in Christ, then, was not a midcourse correction in God's plan but its fulfillment as already announced to Abraham. Reading Israel's Scriptures in light of Christ, Paul affirms that God's plan is faithful to the promises made to Abraham.

On the other hand, there is something innovative in Paul's understanding of God, although Paul would have insisted it was there from the beginning: namely, God's purpose includes Gentiles as well as Jews. As a zealous Pharisaic Jew, Paul understood his relation to God in terms of legal observance. He believed that God would justify him and all who faithfully observe the prescriptions of the law.[19] Thus those under the law were in a more advantageous position than the Gentiles, who did not know God's law. But in light of his Damascus road experience, Paul understood that God did not give the law to bring about righteousness or life; for if the law could have made people righteous and given life there would have been no need for Christ to die in order to rescue humanity from this present evil age (1:4; 2:21; 3:21).[20]

The new element in Paul's understanding of God as found in Galatians, then, is intimately related to Paul's teaching of justification by faith. In light of this teaching, Paul has come to a deeper appreciation of what it means to say that God is one. Whereas formerly he knew and confessed the one God of Israel, now he understands that the promises of Israel's God include the Gentiles as well as the Jewish people; for God does not acquit people on the basis of what they do but on the basis of what he has done in Christ.

Paul's experience of God is not merely doctrinal; it is intensely personal, mediated by Christ and the Spirit. In a statement about his relationship to Christ, for example, Paul writes: "For through the law I died to the law, so that I might live to God. I have been crucified with Christ; and it is no longer I who live, but it is Christ who lives in me. And the life I now live

19. It is important to note that not even the pre-Christian Paul thought he could justify himself before God. Rather, whereas he formerly believed that God would justify those who were faithful to the law, now he believes that God will justify those who believe in Christ. Thus, justification depends on faith in Christ rather than upon doing the works of the law.

20. From Paul's new perspective in Christ, God gave the law as a temporary measure to deal with transgressions in the period before the appearance of Abraham's descendant, the Christ.

in the flesh I live by faith in the Son of God, who loved me and gave himself for me" (2:19-20). Here Paul affirms that before he could "live for God" he had to die to his former way of relating to God, which was based on legal observance. He then notes that the new source of his inner self is Christ, the Son of God, who loved him and gave himself for him. There are two things to note here. First, Paul lives for God because Christ lives in him. Second, instead of saying that Christ loved *us* and died *for us,* as he usually does, Paul personalizes God's redemptive act in terms of what the Son of God has done *for him.* Paul's experience of God, then, is both personal and christocentric. He lives for God because Christ lives in him.

Paul, and all who believe the gospel, also experience God through the Spirit that dwells in them. The gift of the Spirit is the fulfillment of God's promise to Abraham (3:14). God has sent the Spirit of his Son into the hearts of the justified, and it is this Spirit that cries out "Abba, Father," thereby indicating that the justified are God's children (4:6). It is the same Spirit that empowers the justified to live in a way pleasing to God. The Spirit who cries out "Abba, Father" and leads, guides, and empowers the justified is the way in which the justified experience God.[21]

To summarize, Galatians introduces a new element in the Pauline understanding of God that Paul will develop further in Romans. The justified know God as the one who has justified them on the basis of what God has done rather than on the basis of who they are and what they have done. The plan of the one God, revealed in Christ and experienced through the Spirit, embraces Gentiles as well as Jews.

God Who Is Faithful

From beginning to end, Romans is about God.[22] The reason for this is simple. Although Romans is not a theological treatise, Paul appears to have written it, at least in part, to present the Romans with an exposition of "the

---

21. I am not implying there are two different experiences of God, one christocentric and the other pneumatic. Those who are in Christ experience the Spirit, and those who experience the Spirit are in Christ.

22. J. A. Fitzmyer (*Romans: A New Translation with Introduction and Commentary* [AB 33; New York: Doubleday, 1993], 104) notes that "God" is the word that occurs most frequently in Romans apart from articles, prepositions, and pronouns. It occurs more often in Romans (153 times) than in any other NT writing apart from the Acts of the Apostles (168 times). Acts, however, is ten chapters longer than Romans.

gospel of God (1:1), the "gospel concerning his Son" — the Davidic Messiah who was enthroned in power as the Son of God at his resurrection from the dead. The gospel that Paul preaches, then, is God's own good news about his Son, in whom God manifested his saving righteousness. Paul is eager to preach this gospel to the Romans because the gospel is the power of God that brings salvation to Gentiles as well as to Jews. Moreover, when the gospel is proclaimed, the righteousness of God, by which Paul means God's saving justice, is revealed (1:16-17). The gospel that Paul preaches in Romans is, then, about God. Since anything short of a full-fledged commentary is inadequate to describe what Paul says about God in Romans, I will focus on the most prominent ways in which he presents his understanding of God: (1) the righteousness of God, (2) the wrath of God, (3) the impartiality of God, (4) God who raises the dead, (5) the love of God, (6) the Spirit of God, (7) God who predestines and calls, and (8) God who is incomprehensible.[23]

The Righteousness of God

The theme of Romans is the righteousness of God (*dikaiosynē theou*). Taken as a subjective genitive, this expression refers to a quality of God.[24] Whereas there is a judicial aspect to God's righteousness in Romans (see 3:5), Paul tends to use this expression in a manner that highlights God's salvific work in Christ, whereby God justifies sinful humanity. Understood in this way, God's righteousness takes on a dynamic quality that manifests his saving justice and covenant loyalty in the death and resurrection of Je-

---

23. As with Galatians (n. 18 above), Hays ("The God of Mercy") approaches his study of "God" in Romans in terms of the narrative about God that the letter presupposes. He summarizes this narrative under the following headings: The one God is the creator of the world. The world is alienated from God. God made promises to Abraham. God's saving will is expressed through election. God gave the law. God sent his Son. God raised Jesus from the dead. God calls and justifies Gentiles. God hardens Israel. God will save Israel in the end. God is at work in the church through the Holy Spirit. God hears prayer. God calls us to obedient service. God wills and works in the church. God will judge the world. God receives eschatological glory. Hays notes that while Galatians and Romans tell essentially the same story, Romans has some distinctive features and explores "the mysterious subplot" (139) regarding the hardening and salvation of Israel.

24. The opening chapters of Romans mention several other qualities of God: eternal power, divine nature (1:20), immortality (v. 23), kindness, forbearance, patience (2:4), impartiality (v. 11), but righteousness is clearly the dominant trait of God in Romans.

sus Christ.[25] As Romans unfolds, it becomes apparent that Paul employs God's righteousness to highlight the gracious and unexpected manner in which God justifies the ungodly and manifests his covenant loyalty, even when the covenant has been breached. God's righteousness is another way of speaking of God's integrity, God's faithfulness to the divine self.

Although Paul announces the righteousness of God at the outset of Romans (1:17), he explores the wrath of God before developing the theme of God's righteousness in 3:21-26. In this dense text, Paul explains that the righteousness of God has been manifested in Christ "whom God put forth as a sacrifice of atonement *(hilastērion)* by his blood" (v. 25) to demonstrate his own righteousness (vv. 25-26). The new aspect of God's righteousness, as revealed by the gospel, is the manner in which God has manifested it: in the crucified Messiah whom God raised from the dead. Paul's contemporaries would have been familiar with the powerful act of God's saving righteousness that Isaiah announced when Israel was in exile: "I will bring near my deliverance *(dikaiosynē)*, my salvation *(sōtērion)* has gone out and my arms will rule the peoples" (Isa 51:5). But none could have imagined that God would manifest such saving righteousness in a crucified Messiah. Accordingly, when Paul asks why the Gentiles who were not seeking righteousness found it whereas Israel, which pursued a law of righteousness, did not attain the goal of that law (9:30-31), he explains that Israel, ignorant of God's own righteousness revealed in Christ, sought to establish its own righteousness. It doing so, it did not submit to the righteousness of God (10:3).

The final manifestation of God's righteousness, according to Paul, has been revealed in Christ. To understand what it means to say that God is righteousness, one must embrace the scandal of the cross.

The Wrath of God

What Paul says about the righteousness of God is intimately related to what he writes about the wrath of God *(orgē theou)*, which Paul introduces immediately after his first announcement of the righteousness of God:

25. Fitzmyer (*Romans*, 106) notes that whereas in the early books of the OT God's righteousness "is a quality of God manifested in judicial activity; God 'judges' with 'uprightness,'" in the postexilic period God's righteousness takes on an added nuance whereby it is viewed as "the quality whereby God acquits his people, manifesting toward them a gracious, salvific power in a just judgment."

"For the wrath of God is revealed from heaven against all ungodliness and wickedness of those who by their wickedness suppress the truth" (1:18). The wrath of God, however, is not an emotion of God, as if God becomes angry. Rather, it is the just judgment of God that God manifests in the face of human sinfulness.[26] For example, Paul poses the following objection to his gospel: "But if our injustice serves to confirm the justice of God, what should we say? That God is unjust to inflict wrath on us?" (3:5). He replies: "By no means! For then how could God judge the world?" (v. 6). Here, the wrath of God refers to God's just judgment. Further confirmation for this is found in the warning that Paul gives to an imaginary interlocutor who refuses to repent: "But by your hard and impenitent heart you are storing up wrath for yourself on the day of wrath, when God's righteous judgment will be revealed" (2:5). The day of wrath will be the day of God's righteous judgment.

The Gentile world, which refused to acknowledge God, even though it knew something of God, experienced God's wrath inasmuch as God gave the Gentiles over to their own sinfulness (1:24, 26, 28). God's wrath, understood as God's judgment, has come upon the Jewish world because it has not done the law (4:15). Accordingly all, even the justified, will stand before the judgment seat of God (14:10). Those who have been justified by the blood of Christ, however, will be saved from God's wrath — God's just judgment against sin — on that day (5:9). However, whereas the wicked experience the righteousness of God as God's wrath, the righteous experience the wrath of God as God's righteousness. Thus the righteousness of God and the wrath of God are like two sides of a coin. Both refer to the same quality of God, but, depending on their relation to God, people experience this quality differently.

Just as Paul introduces a surprisingly new notion of God's righteousness, which is manifested in the crucified Messiah, so he introduces a new aspect of God's wrath: for those who have been justified, the wrath of God is the saving justice of God.

---

26. J. A. Fitzmyer (in *Paul and His Theology: A Brief Sketch*, 2nd ed. [Englewood Cliffs: Prentice Hall, 1989], 42) writes about the wrath of God: "It is the OT way of expressing God's steadfast reaction as a judge to Israel's breach of the covenant relation (Ezek 5:13; 2 Chr 36:16) or to the nations' oppression of his people (Isa 10:5-11; Jer 50[LXX 28]:11-17. Related to 'the Day of Yahweh' (Zeph 1:14-18), wrath was often conceived of as God's eschatological retribution. For Paul it is either already 'manifested' (Rom 1:18) or still awaited (Rom 2:6-8)."

The Impartiality of God

The manner in which Paul understands God's righteousness and wrath is intimately related to his understanding of God's impartiality. Paul affirms the salvation-historical priority of Israel when he writes that the gospel offers salvation to everyone who believes, "to the Jew first and also to the Greek" (1:16). But he also writes: "there will be anguish and distress for everyone who does evil, the Jew first and also the Greek, but glory and honor and peace for everyone who does good: the Jew first and also the Greek. God shows no partiality" (2:9-11). Because God is impartial, God will judge people on the basis of what they do rather than on the basis of who they are.

Paul was not the first to affirm God's impartiality. Israel also testified to the divine impartiality (Deut 10:17-18; Sir 35:12-16; Wis 6:7). But whereas Israel tended to affirm God's impartiality toward those within the covenant community, Paul employs his understanding of God's righteousness to highlight God's impartiality toward Gentiles and Jew. For example, there is no distinction between Gentiles and Jews in God's sight because all have sinned. Consequently, all are freely justified by God's grace (3:22-24). Affirming that God belongs to the Gentiles as well as to the Jews, Paul concludes: "God is one; and he will justify the circumcised on the ground of faith and the uncircumcised through that same faith" (v. 30).

Paul's understanding of God's righteousness and wrath leads to a more profound understanding of God's impartiality. For if all find themselves liable to God's wrath, and if God has freely manifested his saving righteousness to all, no matter who they are, then God is utterly impartial.

God Who Raises the Dead

At the core of Paul's understanding of God is the conviction that God raised Jesus from the dead. Paul does not simply believe in God, he believes in the God who raised Jesus from the dead. Like his understanding of God's wrath and impartiality, Paul's understanding of God as the one who raises the dead is related to the righteousness of God. In his discussion of Abraham, for example, Paul employs Gen 15:6 to show that Abraham was justified on the basis of his trusting faith in God's promise. Focusing on the quality of Abraham's faith, Paul notes that Abraham believed in God "who gives life to the dead and calls into existence the things that do not exist" (Rom 4:17). Despite his advanced age and the dead womb of Sarah, Abraham was "fully convinced that God was able to do what he had promised" (v. 21). At the end of this discussion, Paul writes that God reckoned Abraham's faith as an act of righteousness: "Now the words, 'it was reckoned to him,' were written not for his sake alone, but for ours also. It will be reckoned to us who believe in him who raised Jesus our Lord from the dead" (vv. 23-24). With these words, Paul establishes a nexus between his teaching on justification by faith and his understanding of God who raises the dead.

In Romans 10 Paul draws another connection between God's righteousness and faith in God who raises the dead. After describing the nearness and accessibility of God's righteousness (10:6-8), Paul concludes: "if you confess with your lips that Jesus is Lord and believe in your heart that God raised him from the dead, you will be saved" (v. 9). Those who believe that God raised Jesus from the dead will be saved because there is an intimate connection between what God has done for Jesus and what God will do for those who believe in him. The justified have died to the law so that they may belong to God who raised Jesus from the dead (7:4). They can be confident that if the Spirit of God dwells in them, then God will raise them from the dead just as he raised Jesus from the dead (8:11).

The pre-Christian Pharisaic Paul also believed in God who raises the dead, but he would never have said God "justifies the ungodly" (4:5). It is only in light of the cross that he can make such a bold assertion (5:6). The new element in the way that Paul understands God and the resurrection of the dead is his conviction that the resurrection of the dead has already begun, thereby revealing a strikingly new aspect of God's righteousness in the crucified Messiah. The God in whom Paul believes is the God who raises the dead, the God who raises the one who died an ungodly death for the ungodly.

The Love of God

Paul speaks of God's love for the first time in Romans 5, after he has explained how God's saving righteousness has rectified sinful humanity. Having shown that believers have been justified by faith and are at peace with God, Paul turns his attention to the eschatological hope of the justified (5:1-2). He assures his audience that they can have full confidence in this hope "because God's love has been poured into our hearts through the

Holy Spirit that has been given to us" (v. 5). While it is possible to construe "the love of God" as our love for God, the immediate context suggests that Paul has in view God's love for us, which we experience through God's Spirit. This interpretation is confirmed in the verses that follow (vv. 6-8). Employing words that have similar sounds, Paul notes that when we were helpless *(asthenōn)*, at just the right time, Christ died for the ungodly *(asebōn)*. Noting how extraordinary it is for someone to die for another, Paul concludes: "But God proves his love for us in that while we still were sinners Christ died for us" (v. 8). Later, at the end of ch. 8, he asks a series of questions that echo what he has said in 5:1-8: "If God is for us, who is against us?" (8:31); "Who will separate us from the love of Christ?" (v. 35).

Several points need to be made here. First, Paul's understanding of God's love is rooted in God's righteousness, which God manifested in the death of his Son. Second, Paul speaks of God's love in terms of Christ and the Spirit. Third, although Paul is not developing a teaching on the Trinity, the manner in which he speaks of God's love being poured into the believer's heart and verified by the death of God's Son indicates that Paul is beginning to think of God in a new way.

The Spirit of God

The new way in which Paul thinks about God includes his understanding of the Spirit, which believers experience because of the righteousness of God revealed in Christ. Through the death and resurrection of Christ, the power of God's Spirit is at work in all who entrust themselves to God's saving justice.

In Romans 8 Paul speaks of the Spirit in several ways. First, the Spirit of God is presently at work in the lives of the justified so that they can live in a way pleasing to God (8:4-10). Second, possession of the Spirit assures the justified that as God raised Jesus from the dead, so God will raise their mortal bodies at the general resurrection of the dead (vv. 11-13). Third, the gift of the Spirit identifies the justified as sons and daughters of God, enabling them to cry out, "Abba, Father" (vv. 14-17). Fourth, the Spirit intercedes with God on behalf of the justified with "sighs too deep for words," words that only God understands (vv. 26-27). Since the Spirit of God has been given in virtue of God's saving justice in Christ, Paul identifies the Spirit of God as the Spirit of Christ (v. 9). Furthermore, he affirms the intimate relationship between God and the Spirit when he writes: "God, who searches the heart, knows what is the mind of the Spirit, because the Spirit intercedes for the saints according to the will of God" (v. 27).

While the Spirit of God was not a foreign notion to the pre-Christian Paul or his contemporaries, the new element in Paul's thinking about God and the Spirit is twofold. First, the experience of the Spirit is intimately related to God's redemptive work in Christ. The justified experience the Spirit — and so God — through the risen Lord. Second, whereas in Israel's Scriptures the powerful experience of the Spirit was reserved for a few, now this experience is available to all the justified. This experience of God in Christ through the power of the Spirit will develop in later theology into a trinitarian understanding of God.

God Who Predestines and Calls

A constant in Paul's understanding of God has been the theme of election. God is the one who calls and elects people in Jesus Christ. It is not surprising, then, that this theme also occurs in Romans. At the outset of the letter, for example, Paul identifies the Romans as those who are "called to belong to Jesus Christ" (1:6). In Romans 8–11, however, this theme takes on greater prominence.

In 8:28-30 Paul summarizes the plan of God in five movements: God foreknew, God predestined, God called, God justified, and God glorified. While the first three movements (foreknew, predestined, called) refer to the past and the fifth (glorified) to what is yet to be, the fourth (justified) concerns the present, and it is on the basis of this present justification that Paul understands God's plan. Because God has already justified those who believe in Christ, Paul concludes that God must have called them, predestined them, and known them in advance. And because they have been justified, Paul is confident they will be glorified at the general resurrection of the dead.[27]

27. What Paul says about predestination, in my view, is not to be equated with the Augustinian and Calvinist teaching on double predestination. While Paul affirms that God has predestined the justified, he never explicitly says that God predestines others for wrath and judgment. For example, in the difficult text of Rom 9:22 ("What if God, desiring to show his wrath and to make known his power, has endured with much patience the objects of wrath that are made for destruction?"), Paul applies the example of a potter to God to highlight the sovereign freedom of God to do as God wishes. He does not employ it to develop a doctrine of double predestination, nor does he *explicitly* affirm that God has destined certain

In chs. 9–11 Paul employs his election theology in his discussion of Israel. First, he shows God's elective purpose in calling Israel into existence (9:6-18). Next, he explains that God's elective purpose is at work at the present time in the eschatological people of God whom God is calling not only from among the Jews but from among the Gentiles as well (v. 24). Finally, he insists that God "has not rejected his people whom he foreknew" (11:2) because "the gifts and the calling of God are irrevocable" (v. 29).

Several points need to be made here. First, God always works on the principle of election, which is another way of speaking of God's grace and mercy (9:16). Second, God's purpose in electing Israel was to prepare for the eschatological people of God that would include Gentiles as well as Jews. Third, because the gift and call of God are irrevocable, even the disobedience of Israel plays a role in God's elective plan. For once the full number of Gentiles enters the eschatological people of God, all Israel will be saved (11:26).

God Who Is Incomprehensible

At the end of Romans 11 Paul discerns something of the plan of God: At one time the Gentiles were disobedient but now they have received mercy because of Israel's disobedience. But in virtue of the mercy shown the Gentiles, Israel will also receive mercy. Thus Paul concludes that God "imprisoned all in disobedience so that he may be merciful to all" (11:32). Reflecting on the wonder of God's plan revealed in Christ, Paul marvels at the "depth of the riches and wisdom and knowledge of God" (v. 33). While Paul has been able to pierce something of the mystery of God in Christ, God's ways remain incomprehensible.

To summarize, what Paul says about God in Romans is grounded in his experience of the righteousness of God revealed in Christ. In light of God's righteousness Paul understands the wrath of God, the impartiality of God, the power of God to raise the dead, the love of God, the Spirit of God, God's

---

people for destruction. Schnelle (*Apostle Paul,* 401), however, maintains that "Paul clearly advocates a double predestination. God calls whom he wills, and rejects whom he wills." While I disagree with Schnelle on the point of double predestination, I agree with his explanation of the theological meaning of predestination (403). He writes: "The exclusive doctrine of justification and the statements about predestination are thus both in the service of preserving God's freedom and the gift nature of salvation, which is not at human disposal" (402-3).

elective purpose, and the incomprehensibility of God. It is an understanding of God that is christological, pneumatological, and experiential.

God Who Shares His Name

Paul's speech about God in Philippians echoes themes with which we are already familiar. God is "our Father" (1:2; 4:20), the "God of peace" (4:9), the one who calls believers in Christ Jesus (3:14). Moreover, as he does in other letters, Paul speaks about God with an intimacy and familiarity that the Philippians also enjoy. For example, he gives thanks to God whenever he remembers the Philippians, and God is his "witness" how he longs for them (1:3, 8). God is the One who is at work within the Philippians enabling them "both to will and to work for his good pleasure" (2:13). They are to be "blameless and innocent, children of God without blemish" (v. 15); they worship "God in the Spirit" (3:3). Therefore, they are not to worry but to let their requests be made known to God (4:6), for God will satisfy their every need in Christ (v. 19). What Paul writes about God in Philippians reveals an intimate familiarity with the transcendent God because he and the Philippians enjoy the righteousness that comes from God, the righteousness based on faith (3:9), "through Jesus Christ for the glory and praise of God" (1:11).[28]

The most distinctive aspect of Paul's understanding of God in Philippians, however, is found in the hymn-like passage in which he celebrates Christ's self-abasement and exaltation by God (2:6-11). Although I have already examined this hymn in terms of its Christology, it will be helpful to see what it reveals about God.

The hymn begins by affirming that prior to his self-abasement, Christ enjoyed the same status as God.[29] He was in "the form of God," which the hymn equates with "equality with God" (2:6). The one who shared the status of God, therefore, took the form of a slave, was born in human likeness and found in human form (v. 7).[30] Having described how the preexistent

28. Whereas in Romans Paul speaks of God's own righteousness, here he speaks of the gift of righteousness that God grants in Christ.

29. Although the hymn begins with a relative pronoun ("who") rather than with an explicit identification of the subject of the hymn, it is clear from 2:5 that Paul has "Christ Jesus" in view. Thus the preexistent one is the Christ who became incarnate in Jesus.

30. The use of the same Greek word *(morphē)* in vv. 6 and 7 ("in the form of God," "in the form of a slave") indicates that "form" points to the inner reality of what is being spoken

one abased himself to the point of death on a cross (v. 8), the passage explains how God exalted him by bestowing upon him "the name that is above every other name" (v. 9) so that at Jesus' name every tongue should confess that Jesus is *kyrios* to the glory of God the Father (v. 11).[31]

The name that God gives the exalted Christ, then, is God's name, *kyrios* ("Lord"), which the Septuagint supplies for the divine name (Yhwh). Although the significance of "Lord" can easily be overlooked since Paul uses it with such regularity in speaking of Christ, this passage highlights the deepest meaning of this appellation.[32] By calling Christ "Lord," Paul indicates that Christ bears God's own name, which God granted him. Although Paul does not speculate about the preexistence of Christ, what he says in this passage has implications for a theology of God, namely, the preexistent one enjoys a new status in virtue of his self-abasement and exaltation, for God has granted him his own name. To confess Christ as "Lord," then, is to address him with the name that belongs to God. Expressed in Johannine language, to see and hear the Lord Jesus Christ is to hear and see the Father.

God Revealed in Christ

Like Philippians, Colossians establishes an intimate relationship between God and Christ: the mystery of God *is* Christ. Therefore, to know Christ is to know God.[33]

---

about. It is not that Christ was like God or like a slave. Rather, he truly participated in the divine being just as he truly participated in human existence.

31. Here the hymn echoes Isa 45:23-24, in which the prophet says that all will acknowledge Yhwh because of the righteousness Yhwh will manifest on Israel's behalf when Yhwh rescues Israel from exile: "By myself I have sworn, from my mouth has gone forth in righteousness a word that shall not return: 'To me every knee shall bow, every tongue shall swear.' Only in the LORD, it shall be said of me, are righteousness and strength; all who were incensed against him shall come to him and be ashamed."

32. Apart from those instances in which "Lord" is used in scriptural quotations, where it usually (but not always) refers to God, nearly all other uses of "Lord" refer to Christ.

33. David M. Hay ("All the Fullness of God: Concepts of Deity in Colossians and Ephesians" in *The Forgotten God*, 163-79, here 163) provides a comprehensive overview of "God" in Colossians and Ephesians. He writes: "God is not simply one subject among many in these writings — rather, God permeates all subjects and assertions. Time and again discrete references to God seem intended to remind readers or hearers of the letters that everything they say is backed by infinite and irresistible authority."

Paul thanks God that the gospel has borne abundant fruit among the Colossians. From the first day they heard it, they "truly comprehended the grace of God" (1:6). Accordingly, Paul prays that they will be filled with the knowledge of God's will as they grow in their knowledge of God (vv. 9-10). This knowledge is experiential rather than purely intellectual since the Colossians have experienced God through Christ as the one who rescued them from the power of darkness and brought them into the kingdom of his own Son (v. 13). God is the one who raised them up with Christ in faith through his own power (2:12). God is the one who made them alive with Christ by disarming and triumphing over the cosmic powers that formerly enslaved them (vv. 13, 15). Consequently, their lives are now "hidden with Christ in God" (3:3).

Although it was Epaphras who taught the gospel to the Colossians (1:7), Paul presents himself as the one whom God commissioned to make the word of God fully known: "the mystery that has been hidden throughout the ages and generations but has now been revealed to his saints" (v. 26). The mystery of God that Paul reveals through the gospel is the presence of Christ in them: "the one in whom are hidden all the treasures of wisdom and knowledge" (v. 27; 2:3).

As in Philippians Paul employs a hymn-like passage to explain the relationship between God and Christ (1:15-20). The hymn proclaims that Christ is "the image of the invisible God" (v. 15). In him "the fullness of God was pleased to dwell" (v. 19), and through him God reconciled everything to himself (v. 20). Consequently, to know Christ is to know God. Echoing this passage later in the letter, Paul writes: "in him the whole fullness of deity dwells bodily" (2:9), so that the reality is Christ (v. 17). This christological knowledge of God defines the distinctive manner in which the Colossians know God. However, whereas Philippians emphasizes the way in which God is revealed in the self-abasement and exaltation of Christ, Colossians highlights the mystery of God revealed in Christ, a topic that Ephesians develops in greater detail.

God Revealed in the Economy of Salvation

Whereas Colossians speaks of the mystery of God, which is Christ, Ephesians speaks of the mystery of Christ (3:4): "that is, the Gentiles have become fellow heirs, members of the same body, and sharers in the promise in Christ Jesus through the gospel" (v. 6). This change of vocabulary does not mean that Colossians and Ephesians are referring to different mysteries since Colossians also speaks of "the mystery of Christ" (4:3). Ephesians, however, is more specific in the way that it defines the mystery: the mystery of God which is revealed in Christ is visible in the church. Alluding to his call, Paul writes that he became a servant *(diakonos)* according to the gift of God's grace to preach to the Gentiles "and to make everyone see what is the plan of the mystery hidden for ages in God who created all things; so that *through the church* the wisdom of God in its rich variety might now be made known to the rulers and authorities in the heavenly places" (3:9-10). The dominant way in which Paul speaks of God in Ephesians, then, is in terms of the mystery of Christ, which is the revelation of God's plan, which until now has been hidden for ages past.

The centrality of God's plan in Paul's thinking about God is apparent from the opening benediction, in which he summarizes what God has done and is doing in Christ (1:1-14). The God and Father of Jesus Christ has *blessed* believers in every way and *chosen* them in Christ before the foundation of the world. Through Christ, God *destined* them for *adoption* as his own children. Through Christ, God has effected *redemption* and made known the mystery of his will, a *plan* to gather up all things in Christ so that believers, who have been sealed with the Spirit, which is the assurance of their heavenly *inheritance,* might live for the praise of *God's glory.* In this benediction, Paul presents the full sweep of God's plan, much as he does in Rom 8:28-30. But whereas in Romans he sketches the divine plan in bold strokes, here he presents it in detail in terms of election, redemption, inheritance, the recapitulation of all things in Christ, and God's final glory. The mystery of Christ, as outlined by Paul, reveals a divine economy that God has carefully planned and carried out in his Beloved.

To carry out this plan, God exercised his great power when he raised Christ from the dead and seated him at his right hand, above every cosmic power in this age and in the age to come. God's power has already put all things under Christ's authority, making him the head of the church, which is his body (1:20-23).

God has also displayed his power in those whom he has called. Rich in mercy, God has given the elect new life with Christ by raising and seating them with him in the heavenly places. God has shown the riches of his grace by the kindness he has extended toward those whom he called, saving them by grace. Indeed, God created the elect in Christ for the good works that he prepared beforehand.

The manner in which Paul speaks of God's power and work in Ephesians is striking when compared to what he writes in 1 Corinthians and Romans. In 1 Corinthians the power of God is manifested in the weakness and folly of the cross (1:22-25), and Christ's enemies are presently being subdued (15:24). In Romans, the justified have died with Christ (6:3) and the presence of the Spirit assures them of their resurrection with Christ (8:11). In Ephesians, however, the power of God is displayed in the resurrection and exaltation of Christ, whom God has already exalted over the cosmic powers, and believers are already the beneficiaries of this display of God's power inasmuch as they have been raised and seated with Christ in the heavenly places. Given the way in which Ephesians speaks about what God has done in Christ, it is not surprising that some judge it to be deutero-Pauline. But even if it was written by another, something else is at work at here. Whereas in 1 Corinthians and Romans the cross tends to play a more prominent role in Paul's understanding of God, in Ephesians the resurrection and enthronement of Christ play the more prominent role. This is not to say that Ephesians neglects the cross or that 1 Corinthians and Romans neglect the resurrection. Rather, the way in which these letters present God varies to the extent that they begin with one or the other.

To summarize, Ephesians presents a Pauline theology for a new generation of Gentile believers. At the heart of this letter is a theology of God that explains the economy of God revealed in Christ: God's plan to unite Gentiles and Jews in the body of Christ, the church.

God Who Is Savior

1 Timothy describes God in several ways. It speaks of "the blessed God" (1:11), "the King of the ages, immortal, invisible, the only God" (v. 17), "the living God" (3:15; 4:10), "God, who gives life to all things" (6:13), and God who is the "only Sovereign, the King of kings and Lord of lords" (v. 15).[34] Furthermore, because of the particular problems that it must address, 1 Timothy affirms the goodness of creation. It notes that God created mar-

---

34. Fitzmyer ("The Savior God: The Pastoral Epistles" in *The Forgotten God*, 181-96, here 182) explains this emphasis on the one God in this way: "Part of the reason why the Pastorals were composed was to offset influence of contemporary folk religion in the Greco-Roman world of the eastern Mediterranean area. Polytheism or some form of henotheism prevailed there, and emperor worship was widespread. Consequently, the teaching in the Pastorals about the one God is a forthright rebuttal of such claims and a reaffirmation of the Christian monotheism based on its Jewish heritage."

riage and food "to be received with thanksgiving" (4:4), and that God "richly provides us with everything for our enjoyment" (6:17). In addition to the goodness of creation, 1 Timothy highlights the universal scope of God's salvation. The Savior God "desires everyone to be saved and to come to the knowledge of the truth" (2:4), a theme that Titus echoes when it says that "the grace of God has appeared, bringing salvation to all" (Tit 2:11). In contrast to the rich descriptions of God in 1 Timothy, 2 Timothy simply speaks of "God" or "God the Father." Titus adds the description "God, who never lies" (1:2).

The most distinctive way in which 1 Timothy and Titus speak of God is as "Savior," a title that the other Pauline letters, including 2 Timothy, do not apply to God, even though they regularly refer to salvation and to believers being saved.[35] In 1 Timothy, for example, Paul writes that he is an apostle by the command of "God our Savior and of Christ Jesus our hope" (1:1). Praying for rulers is "acceptable in the sight of God our Savior" (2:3). God is the "Savior of all people, especially of those who believe" (4:10). In his letter to Titus, Paul says that he was entrusted with the word of God by the command "of God our Savior" (1:3). Slaves are to show fidelity so that they will be "an ornament to the doctrine of God our Savior" (2:10). Finally, he notes that "the goodness and kindness of God our Savior has appeared" (3:4).[36]

Second Timothy and Titus also identify Christ as "Savior." For example in 2 Tim 1:9-10 Paul begins: God "saved and called us with a holy calling, not according to our works but according to his own purpose and grace." He continues: "This grace was given to us in Christ Jesus before the ages began, but it has now been revealed through the appearing of our Savior Christ Jesus, who abolished death and brought life and immortality to light through the gospel." By noting that God saved us and then saying that this was revealed by the appearance of the Savior, Christ Jesus, 2 Timothy

---

35. Although Paul uses the verb "save" and the noun "salvation," he rarely makes God the explicit subject of the verb. In most instances, the unexpressed subject of the verb or the implied actor who brings about salvation is God. Two examples will suffice. First, in Rom 10:9-10, Paul writes, "because if you confess with your lips that Jesus is Lord and believe in your heart that God raised him from the dead, *you will be saved.* For one believes with the heart and so is justified, and one confesses with the mouth *and so is saved.*" The one who will bring about this salvation is God. Second, in Rom 1:16, Paul writes: "For I am not ashamed of the gospel; it is the power of God for *salvation* to everyone who has faith, to the Jew first and also to the Greek." The source of this salvation is God. In 1 Thess 5:9 and 2 Thess 2:13 God is explicitly named as the subject who destines or chooses believers for salvation.

36. The only other places in the NT where God is called "Savior" are Luke 1:47 and Jude 25.

indicates that it was through Christ that God manifested his salvation. A similar point is made in Titus: "But when the goodness and loving kindness of God our Savior appeared, he saved us, not because of any works of righteousness that we had done, but according to his mercy, through the water of rebirth and renewal by the Holy Spirit." It then concludes: "This Spirit he poured out on us richly through Jesus Christ our Savior, so that, having been justified by his grace, we might become heirs according to the hope of eternal life" (3:4-7). Here Titus equates the appearance of the goodness and loving kindness of the Savior God with Jesus Christ through whom the Spirit was poured out.

By calling God as well as Christ "Savior," the Pastorals establish an intimate relationship between God and Christ that can be summarized in this way: The Savior God accomplishes the work of salvation in the Savior Christ Jesus. To know Christ Jesus, then, is to know the Savior God. Since Titus draws such a close link between God and Christ, it can even predicate "God" of Christ by saying, "we wait for the blessed hope and the manifestation of the glory of our great God and Savior, Jesus Christ" (2:13).[37]

Coherence and Meaning in Pauline Theology

The different ways that the Pauline letters speak of God is due to their occasional nature and to the possibility that some of them may have been written by others in Paul's name. Consequently, it is not possible to bring what these letters affirm about God into a perfect synthesis. Nonetheless, since all of them — even those that Paul may not have written — are grounded in Paul's experience of God's saving grace on the Damascus road, there is a certain coherence to what they affirm about God, which I summarize in the following statements.

First, Pauline theology identifies the God and Father of Jesus Christ with the God of Israel. The God of whom Paul speaks throughout his letters is the God of Abraham, Isaac, and Jacob, the God who revealed himself to Moses and spoke through the prophets. Although some of Paul's Jewish contemporaries may have accused him of abandoning his ancestral faith,

---

37. Fitzmyer ("The Savior God," 188) notes that this verse can be construed in three ways: (1) the glory of our great God *and* our Savior Jesus; (2) the glory of our great God and Savior, *which glory is* Jesus Christ; (3) the glory of our great and God Savior Jesus Christ. I have taken it in the third sense, in which "God" is predicated of Jesus Christ.

Paul insists that the God who appeared to him in Christ and whom he proclaims in Jesus Christ is the God of Israel. The new creation in Jesus Christ does not do away with Paul's ancestral faith in God.

Second, the Pauline letters describe God in a variety of ways. God is the one who calls and elects, the God of hope, the God of love, the God who raises the dead, the God who is faithful, the God who justifies the ungodly, the God who judges, the God who comforts and consoles, and the Savior God. The most consistent way in which the letters identify God, however, is as "God our Father" or "the God and Father of Jesus Christ." This, of course, is not a gender statement, as if God were male as opposed to female. Rather, it is a relational statement, clarifying the relationship between God and Jesus and enabling Paul to identify God through his experience of the Son. Thus it would be a mistake to abandon speaking of God as "Father," even though it can give the mistaken impression of gender. It would be an even greater mistake to interpret "Father" in terms of sexual gender.[38]

Third, God is mysterious and near, transcendent and immanent. God is transcendent and remains unknowable unless God first reveals himself. This is why the Pauline letters speak of the mystery hidden for ages until it was revealed in Jesus Christ. But God is also near and immanent because he has been revealed through his Son and experienced through the Spirit. It is this Spirit that enables the justified to call the transcendent God "Abba" in the way the Son does. It is because God is so near and immanent that Paul can speak of him with confidence and intimacy.

Fourth, God works on the basis of election, calling people to salvation on the basis of grace rather than on the basis of works. This is the most difficult aspect of the Pauline notion of God to comprehend since it appears utterly unfair. Why does God call and elect some and not others? Why are some among the elect, while others are not? From a purely human perspective there is no answer to these questions since God remains mysterious. God is, after all, utterly transcendent and free. But from the perspective of the divine economy of salvation, which Paul knows in Christ, the election and call of some does not exclude the salvation of the many.

Fifth, Pauline theology celebrates the divine economy, which God foreordained from the beginning. What happened in Christ was not a mid-

---

38. Watson ("The Triune Divine Identity," 114-15) notes: "If Jesus is Son of God, then God is the God and Father of our Lord Jesus Christ: the purpose of the father/son language is to indicate that God and Jesus are identified by their relation to each other, and have no existence apart from that relation."

course correction, as if the original plan of God had failed. God's plan of salvation remains the same. It always had Christ is view. This is why Paul writes that the singular heir of God's promise to Abraham is Christ (Gal 3:16) and why he affirms that Christ is the end of the law (Rom 10:4). If it did not appear that way from the beginning, it is because the hidden mystery of God's plan has only now been revealed in Christ. Once the mystery of God's redemptive plan has been revealed, however, it is clear that there has always been one plan, which is revealed in Christ.

Sixth, Pauline theology is christological. Paul knows and understands God in terms of Christ. Although he once knew God apart from Christ, he no longer knows God except in Christ. Every statement Paul makes about Christ, then, is a statement about God, and whatever he says about God is a statement about Christ. Paul sees God's work in the death and resurrection of Christ, for Christ has become the locus of God's revelation. God has revealed something of the divine self in nature, but the fullness of who God is has been revealed in Christ, the image of the invisible God.

Seventh, Pauline theology is pneumatological, and so implicitly trinitarian. If God is revealed in Christ, God is experienced in the Spirit of God, which is the Spirit of Christ. It is the Spirit that makes God known and knowable. The Spirit gives life and is the promise of resurrection life. To experience the Spirit is to know the risen Lord; it is to know God. Although Paul does not develop a doctrine of the Trinity — three persons in one God — what he says about Christ and the Spirit opens the way to thinking about the one God as a Trinity of persons.

Paul's most enduring legacy to our understanding of God is the manner in which he compels us to rethink our notion of God by reminding us that God, who manifests power in the weakness and folly of the cross as well as in the power and strength of the resurrection, cannot and will not be confined to human categories.

FOR FURTHER READING

Becker, Jürgen. *Paul: Apostle to the Gentiles.* Louisville: Westminster John Knox, 1993. Pages 57-81.

Beker, J. Christiaan. *Paul the Apostle: The Triumph of God in Life and Thought.* Philadelphia: Fortress, 1980. Pages 379-86.

Bultmann, Rudolf. *Theology of the New Testament.* Vol 1. New York: Charles Scribner's Sons, 1951. Pages 65-92.

Dunn, James D. G. *The Theology of Paul the Apostle.* Grand Rapids: Eerdmans, 1998. Pages 25-50.

Fay, Ron C. "Was Paul a Trinitarian: A Look at Romans 8." Pages 327-45 in *Paul and His Theology.* Pauline Studies 3, ed. Stanley E. Porter. Leiden: Brill, 2006.

Fitzmyer, Joseph A. "The Savior God: The Pastoral Epistles." Pages 181-96 in *The Forgotten God: Perspectives in Biblical Theology: Essays in Honor of Paul J. Achtemeier on the Occasion of His Seventy-fifth Birthday,* ed. A. Andrew Das and Frank J. Matera. Louisville: Westminster John Knox, 2002.

Furnish, Victor Paul. *The Theology of the First Letter to the Corinthians.* NTT. Cambridge: Cambridge University Press, 1999. Pages 28-48.

Gabriel, Andrew K. "Pauline Pneumatology and the Question of Trinitarian Presuppositions." Pages 347-62 in *Paul and His Theology.* Pauline Studies 3, ed. Stanley E. Porter. Leiden: Brill, 2006.

Gräbe, Peter J. *The Power of God in Paul's Letters.* 2nd ed. WUNT 123. Tübingen: Mohr Siebeck, 2008.

Hay, David M. "All the Fullness of God: Concepts of Deity in Colossians and Ephesians." Pages 163-79 in *The Forgotten God: Perspectives in Biblical Theology: Essays in Honor of Paul J. Achtemeier on the Occasion of His Seventy-fifth Birthday,* ed. A. Andrew Das and Frank J. Matera. Louisville: Westminster John Knox, 2002.

Hays, Richard. "The God of Mercy Who Rescues Us from the Present Evil Age: Romans and Galatians." Pages 123-44 in *The Forgotten God: Perspectives in Biblical Theology: Essays in Honor of Paul J. Achtemeier on the Occasion of His Seventy-fifth Birthday,* ed. A. Andrew Das and Frank J. Matera. Louisville: Westminster John Knox, 2002.

Perkins, Pheme. "God's Power in Human Weakness: Paul Teaches the Corinthians about God." Pages 145-62 in *The Forgotten God: Perspectives in Biblical Theology: Essays in Honor of Paul J. Achtemeier on the Occasion of His Seventy-fifth Birthday,* ed. A. Andrew Das and Frank J. Matera. Louisville: Westminster John Knox, 2002.

Richardson, Neil. *Paul's Language about God.* JSNTSup 99. Sheffield: Sheffield Academic, 1994.

Schnelle, Udo. *Apostle Paul: His Life and Theology.* Grand Rapids: Baker, 2003. Pages 392-409.

Schreiner, Thomas R. *Paul: Apostle of God's Glory in Christ.* Downers Grove: InterVarsity, 2001. Pages 15-35.

Watson, Francis. "The Triune Divine Identity: Reflections on Pauline God Language, in Disagreement with J. D. G. Dunn." *JSNT* 80 (2000): 99-124.

Index of Subjects

Index of Authors

Index of Scripture Citations